BLACK WOMEN IN
UNITED STATES HISTORY

Editor

DARLENE CLARK HINE

Associate Editors

ELSA BARKLEY BROWN

TIFFANY R. L. PATTERSON

LILLIAN S. WILLIAMS

Research Assistant

EARNESTINE JENKINS

A CARLSON PUBLISHING SERIES

See the end of this volume for a comprehensive
guide to this sixteen-volume series.

Daughters of Sorrow

ATTITUDES TOWARD BLACK WOMEN, 1880-1920

Beverly Guy-Sheftall

CARLSON
Publishing Inc

BROOKLYN, NEW YORK, 1990

See the end of this volume for a comprehensive guide to the sixteen-volume series of which this is Volume Eleven.

Library of Congress Cataloging-in-Publication Data

Guy-Sheftall, Beverly.
    Daughters of sorrow : attitudes toward Black women, 1880-1920 /
Beverly Guy-Sheftall.
        p.   cm. — (Black women in United States history ; v. 11)
    Includes bibliographical references.
    ISBN 0-926019-17-1
    1. Afro-American women—Public opinion—History. 2. Public
opinion—United States—History. 3. United States—Race relations.
I. Title. II. Series.
E185.86.B543 vol. 11
973'.0496073 s—dc20
[973'.0496073]   90-1398

Typographic design: Julian Waters

Typeface: Bitstream ITC Galliard

The index to this book was created using NL Cindex, a scholarly indexing program from the Newberry Library.

Printed on acid-free, 250-year-life paper.

Manufactured in the United States of America.

This book was originally written as a Ph.D. dissertation at Emory University in 1984. It has been edited for publication here.

Contents

For my mother, Ernestine
who would have been proud

my father, Walter
my sisters, Carmella and Francine

and

for all those Black women and men
who have kept the faith.

List of Illustrations

All illustrations are used courtesy of the Moorland-Spingarn Research Center, Howard University, unless otherwise indicated.

ONE

Introduction: The Case for the Study

Clearly, women have been the victims of scholarly neglect. Black women, possessing a double minority status, have received even less scholarly attention.

Bettye Collier Thomas, 1980

When it came to the black woman, scholars found it exceedingly difficult to separate her from the oppressed black subgroup and to treat her as a distinct entity, possessing a history and culture of her own. Before the study of black women can take off, the larger society must be educated to see black women as distinct historical beings.

Darlene Clark Hine, 1982

While scholars have maintained an interest in analyzing the "race-thinking" that emerged during the nineteenth century as a central current in Western thought[1] and in exploring attitudes toward blacks during various points in American history,[2] it is difficult to find in this literature an assessment of differences in attitudes toward black males and females. Almost without exception, both sexes are lumped together in studies of the development of racist theories. Moreover, these studies deal only with how blacks are perceived by whites. This tendency to see blacks as an undifferentiated mass and to overlook black women in matters pertaining to "the woman question" because of the relative unimportance of their gender was recognized by black women in particular during this period.

In studying the status of Afro-American women . . . it ought to be borne in mind that such social differentiations as "women's interests, children's interests" that are so finely worked out in the social development of the more favored

1

races are but recent recognitions in the progressive life of the Negro race. Such specializing had no economic value in slavery days. . . . If within thirty-five years they [black women] have become sufficiently important to be studied apart from the general race problem and have come to be recognized as an integral part of the general womanhood of American civilization that fact is a gratifying evidence of real progress.[3]

This study will explore, in part because other works have failed to do so, attitudes between 1880 and 1920 that have been frequently expressed about black women by whites, male and female, and by black males. The perceptions that black women had about themselves as a group will also be analyzed. The period from 1880-1920, sometimes referred to as the Progressive era, was chosen for a variety of reasons. Though numerous attempts have been made to ascertain societal attitudes on a variety of issues during a time when the "progressive" generation came of age in a new scientific, industrialized world, the intellectual history of the period remains elusive. Though much time and energy have been spent trying to understand and synthesize the varied intellectual currents flowing through this transitional stage in American history and though much has been written about the "progressive" mind on a variety of issues, relatively little scholarly work has been done on the intersection of race and gender during this period. Such an examination is important. First, this period witnessed the awakening of women to the possibility of full equality with men and an outpouring of popular and scientific material on "the woman question," much of which focused on woman's nature. Since 1880-1920 was a high point in women's history, a time during which the notion of an emancipated womanhood was beginning to be taken seriously, an examination of attitudes toward black women was imperative, especially since this was, paradoxically, the period during which blacks were at their lowest point. Ironically, however, the cult of True Womanhood, or domesticity, was still an integral part of the ideological fabric, despite the push for equality, and it resulted in a complex set of ideas about the values and code of behavior that women should adopt. An examination of attitudes toward black women sheds light on the class nature of the cult of True Womanhood since only a certain segment of the female population was able to act out its tenets. An analysis of the impact of the cult of domesticity (despite its limited applicability) on nineteenth-century ideas about women is crucial if one is to understand the particular situation of black women during one of the most important periods in their history.

Unlike other studies that focus on attitudes toward a particular racial group, this study deals not only with how members of the majority group view a particular segment of the black population but also with how dominant members within that racial group view another segment of their own community. It also provides insights into how this same group saw themselves. Since black and white males share the same gender identity, it is instructive to explore their attitudes toward black women and to note the points at which these attitudes intersect and diverge. Similarly, since black and white women share the same gender identity it is important to explore whether "common bonds of womanhood"[4] cause them to share similar attitudes about the "woman question" as it relates to black women. And finally, since white men and women, as well as black men and women, share the same racial identity, an analysis of the extent to which race is more significant than gender in the formulation of attitudes about a particular group, in this case black women, can provide some explanation, perhaps, for the difficulty that black and white women have had historically creating a viable sisterhood in various reform movements, even women's right struggles, on the basis of their common gender identity.

A review of the secondary sources reveals an almost total absence of critical material relating specifically to male attitudes, especially black, toward black women. A recent issue of *Phylon* contains an article on present attitudes of middle-class black men toward black women and women's issues in general, in which Noel Cazenave asserts:

> Unfortunately, while a great deal of research has been done on the attitudes of whites toward blacks . . . little data are available on the view of black men on the gender related issues affecting black (and other women) in America. To the extent that black men are "significant others" and are intimately involved with black women . . . the attitudes of these males should have an important impact on how these women see their world and their place within it. Black men can either support the social advancement of the woman, or adopt the role of their most immediate and most pervasive oppressors.[5]

While the list of works on the racial attitudes of whites is extensive (as illustrated in Note two), it includes only occasional references to black women as distinct from black men. Similarly, while in recent years a few studies on the history of American women or American attitudes toward women have emerged,[6] they generally ignore black women, or what is worse, make generalizations about attitudes toward women that do not apply to them. Other sources of information on attitudes toward black

3

women—studies that focus on black sexuality, interracial marriage, or the sexual attitudes of Americans and their connection with racism—usually neither focus on a particular historical period nor include adequate discussion of black male attitudes toward black women.[7] Rather, the emphasis is on the attitudes of black males toward white women.

While secondary sources on race-thinking are replete with details on the racial attitudes of white males, the scholarship on black male attitudes toward black women is woefully inadequate, especially for the period between 1880 and 1920. The two exceptions are Lawrence Friedman's *The White Savage, Racial Fantasies in the Post-Bellum South*, published in 1970, and a recently published article on black male perspectives concerning the nineteenth-century woman. The former contains a too brief discussion of black male attitudes toward black women in the post-bellum South, and the main argument is that black activists, in their attempt to cultivate a sense of black dignity and promote racial integrity and purity, exalted black women and sought to protect them from white male sexual aggression. Though his explanation for their motives is suspect—to maintain exclusive use of their women's bodies—Friedman is unique among those who explored racial attitudes because he at least paid some attention to black men. His argument is especially significant because he saw a similarity in the views of black and white men toward women since they both tended to idolize their own women to the point of dehumanization.

> Clearly, white Southern racists and black activists looked at women in similar terms. Both viewed the female as a second sex with distinctly limited privileges. But the parallel ran even closer. Since antebellum days, Southern planters had idolized the white woman as a jewel of the universe, adorning her in finery and speaking of her as a near goddess. . . . By the turn of the century, as articulate Negro activists busied themselves on the racial front, many thought in the same terms. Like whites of the "Brownlow tradition," they paid homage to the shrine of womanhood. But though they exalted and demanded protection for black women threatened by white assault and though the white male exalted a white woman who black males rarely endangered, men of both races considered "their" women in the same light. Both claimed guardianship over "their" women; both elevated the female above the state of mortals. Southern males, white and black, were therefore participating in the dehumanization of women. . . . Hence, the effort to fortify racial pride through exaltation of pure womanhood was likely as disastrous for the black race as for the white.[8]

A diametrically opposed view is expressed by Rosalyn Terborg-Penn in the only study I have been able to discover that deals exclusively with black male attitudes toward black women in a particular time period. Her primary purpose is to explore the several perspectives of black men on the "woman question." By analyzing their proposed strategies, speeches, and articles, she hoped to reveal their attitudes toward women and to compare them with those of white men. Her main points are that black male leaders were more sympathetic to women's rights than their white male counterparts, perceived women to be equal to men, and felt that they should unite in defense of black women; moreover, they felt that black women were especially vulnerable to sexual attacks by white men, should have the same educational and political rights as men, and should share in correcting societal ills, especially racial ones.[9] Her argument that in general most prominent black men by the turn of the century expressed an egalitarian view of the relationship between black men and women is the exact opposite of Friedman's argument and indicates that, at least in the scanty literature on the subject, the issue surrounding the nature of black male attitudes toward black women is far from settled.

The situation with respect to the availability of critical material dealing with white female attitudes toward black women is even more dismal. First of all, the racial attitudes of white women have been difficult to ascertain because studies of racial thought in America rarely differentiate between the sexes. However, two categories of studies are the most useful for a discussion of white female attitudes toward black women—those that deal with racism within the women's rights movement from its inception in 1848 to its demise in the 1920s after the passage of the Nineteenth Amendment, and those that deal with northern teachers who went south after the war to provide for the educational needs of freedmen.[10]

Anti-black female sentiment among white women in the women's rights movement and the women's club movement during the nineteenth century has been well documented, as the sources cited in Note ten illustrate. In a recent monograph on black women and feminism, the first study of its kind, Bell Hooks makes the surprising point that nineteenth-century white female reformers harbored more intense racist attitudes toward black women than they did toward black men, which is ironic in light of the "bonds of womanhood" thesis that other historians have advanced in their attempt to explain alliances between black and white women in various reform movements.[11] Hooks argues that it was fear of contamination and sexual competition that caused white women to resist cooperation with black women.

. . . black men were more accepted in white reform circles than black women. Negative attitudes toward black women were the result of prevailing racist-sexist stereotypes that portrayed black women as morally impure. Many white women felt that their status as ladies would be undermined were they to associate with black women: No such moral stigma was attached to black men. Black male leaders like Frederick Douglass, James Forten . . . and others were occasionally welcome in white and social circles. . . . Given . . . the history of white male sexual lust for black females we cannot rule out the possibility that white women were reluctant to acknowledge black women socially for fear of sexual competition. . . . White women saw black women as a direct threat to their social standing—for how could they be idealized as virtuous, goddess-like creatures if they associated with black women who were seen by the white public as licentious and immoral?[12]

A persistent theme in the analyses of racism on the part of white women in the movement is that at some point nearly all of the major white suffrage leaders, most of whom were women, compromised their support of suffrage for black women, allegedly because of their desire not to alienate southern suffragists who were, almost without exception, supporters of white supremacy and states' rights.

Several studies that do not fall in the categories mentioned above also deal, but to a lesser extent, with the attitudes of white women toward black women.[13] Beth Day's *Sexual Life Between Blacks and Whites* pays more attention to this subject than most other studies dealing with interracial sex. Here she discusses the rivalry between the white wife and the black mistress (or concubine) during slavery.[14] In a chapter entitled "Miss Ann, The Hysterical Virgin," she alludes to the envy white women had of black women's sexual freedom, independence, and strength.

In contrast to the dependent white Southern women, the black woman was eons ahead in strength, durability, and independence. If she had survived, it had been through the protection, support, or strength of no man, educational system, or body of law. It had been by her own nature, strength, wit, and gut wisdom. . . . In the rough side of life the white woman has never ever been tested. She has never learned to survive in the world on her own.[15]

Furthermore, she says that white women believe that black women are less delicate than they are, have a greater tolerance for pain, especially during childbirth, are careless about personal hygiene, and are looser in their morals.

In her discussion of the Women's Committee on Work of the Committee on Interracial Cooperation (CIC)—which grew out of the Tuskegee and

Memphis Conferences (1920), when southern black and white women met to explore means by which they could work together to solve the race problem—Jacquelyn Hall discusses, rather briefly, white female attitudes toward black women. Despite efforts to form a lasting coalition, Hall concludes that CIC white women were not fundamentally opposed to the caste system but "their deeply ingrained hierarchical attitudes" prevented the development of a real sisterhood between them and black women.

> Their assumption of superiority made it difficult for white women to distinguish between interracial cooperation and charity. . . . As the earliest attempt to build a women's organization in the South explicitly devoted to overcoming the barriers of race, the Woman's Committee . . . was shaped by the hierarchical social order from which it emerged, and the goal of meeting as equals the "psychological basis" of motherhood had proven easier to assert than to accomplish. . . .[16]

Secondary sources dealing with black women's attitudes about themselves (or about issues of particular concern to their group) during this period are even more scarce. Exceptions to this generalization would be studies dealing with the black women's club movement, black feminist thought, and black women's history.[17]

The most obvious question raised by this study is how to get at attitudes toward a particular group at a given time.[18] For views of black women at the turn of the century, a variety of sources required analysis. The bulk of them were nonfiction material—speeches, pamphlets, manuals, sermons, articles, and books. This material, much of it unexplored for the purposes outlined here, and some of it ignored for any purpose, consists of numerous documents in the category of "race literature" generated by whites and blacks (mainly males) on the popular subject of "the Negro question."[19] These writers felt that the gravest question confronting the nation at the turn of the century was "The Negro Problem." A wide range of ideas purporting to be solutions was expressed in numerous books, periodicals, newspapers, and even fiction, all of which reveal a lack of uniformity in the response to the problem. The published proceedings of the many conferences convened during the period to grapple with "the Negro problem" would be one example of such material. This period also witnessed an unprecedented growth in black publications, especially newspapers, journals, and magazines, that contain information on both the race question and, to a lesser extent, the woman question. Similarly, the woman's club movement began and flourished during the period, resulting in an outpouring of documents by black and white women on issues of particular concern to women. And finally, a number of influential and productive black intellectuals and/or activists—most notably Frederick Douglass, W. E. B. Du Bois, Booker T. Washington, Alexander Crummell, Anna J. Cooper, Mary Church Terrell, and Fannie Barrier Williams—were speaking and writing about a number of racial and women-related matters. These documents, a virtual gold mine for the student of late nineteenth-century intellectual history (especially on matters relating to race and women), have been underutilized, if examined at all, in the studies undertaken on blacks and/or women during the period under consideration.

Fiction, and to a lesser extent poetry, are also used here, a method that departs from most studies of this kind. While the relationship between literature and society is complex and remains problematic, the idea that literature does indeed reflect society is at least as old as Plato, according to Albert Albrecht, who critically examines various viewpoints and theoretical assumptions about the relationship between literature and society. His thesis is that literature does reflect the norms and values of a culture.

> At one time or another literature has been thought to reflect economics, family relationships, climate and landscapes, attitudes, morals, races, social classes, political events, wars, religion, and many more other more detailed aspects of environment and social life. . . . Probably the commonest conception has been that literature reflects predominantly the significant values and norms of a culture.[20]

For this study it seemed particularly imperative to exploit Albrecht's theory. An examination of the complex literary portrait of a black female (for example, Roxy in Mark Twain's *Pudd'nhead Wilson*) illuminates the ironies and contradictions embedded, but unacknowledged, in the prevailing attitudes and stereotypes about black women found in non-literary sources. By dealing with literary reflections of racial and sexual assumptions, one can further get at dominant racial attitudes as they are expressed in a fictional character. In addition, an exploration of recurring themes in the fiction of the period as they relate to black women can reveal much about prevailing attitudes toward this particular group. Needless to say, then, in order to explore attitudes toward black women it is crucial to employ an interdisciplinary perspective, for it is only through an examination of the social and intellectual history of the period, as well as its belles-lettres, that one can begin to approach this topic. The objective then is not merely to summarize these attitudes, but also to relate them to currents in the larger stream of American social and intellectual thought (especially racial and sexual) prevalent during this period.

In this regard, attitudes toward black women cannot be viewed as distinct from the racial attitudes that dominated American thought at the turn of the century. Many scholars have analyzed the white supremacist ideology rampant in America during the period under consideration; but perhaps the most concise description of this ideology can be found in the "racial creed" of southerners, which one of its most outspoken advocates, Thomas Pearce Bailey, espoused in 1914.

1. "Blood will tell."
2. The white race must dominate.
3. The Teutonic peoples stand for race purity.
4. The negro is inferior and will remain so.
5. "This is a white man's country."
6. No social equality.
7. No political equality.
8. In matters of civil rights and legal adjustments give the white man, as opposed to the colored man, the benefit of the doubt.
9. In educational policy let the negro have the crumbs that fall from the white man's table.
10. Let there be such industrial education of the negro as will best fit him to serve the white man.
11. Only Southerners understand the negro question.
12. Let the South settle the negro question.
13. The status of peasantry is all the negro may hope for, if the races are to live together in peace.
14. Let the lowest white man count for more than the highest negro.
15. The above statements indicate the learnings of Providence.[21]

George Frederickson, in *The Black Image in the White Mind*, also outlines the fundamentals of this white supremacist ideology, which was shared by most white Americans at the turn of the century. His summary of a racial creed, on which there was "almost universal agreement,"[22] is quite similar to the one above. Similarly, Forest Wood in his *Black Scare* reaffirms this widely held belief in Anglo-Saxon superiority. Moreover, these views were buttressed, he asserts, by scientific arguments from anthropologists, ethnologists, eugenicists, naturalists, and clergymen. Richard Weiss echoes many of these same points in his discussion of "the cult of Anglo-Saxon superiority," especially the fact that racist thinking intensified during the era of industrialization.[23] He says that "by the eve of World War I, American racism had achieved as much refinement as an ideology as it would ever develop" and that a "belief in the innate inferiority of the nation's largest oppressed minority continued to dominate both popular and scientific thought."[24] Furthermore, what most Americans feared—especially southerners—was social equality between the races. This fear resulted in the 1880s and 1890s in the establishment of Jim Crow laws and practices and of segregation as the American way of life.

Conceptions of the True Woman, the cultural expression of the Victorian image of woman that prevailed during the nineteenth century,[25] also had a crucial impact on attitudes toward black women. Barbara Welter, in her classic article on this cultural phenomenon, argues that "Woman, in the cult of True Womanhood . . . was the hostage of the home." The attributes of True Womanhood were piety, purity, submissiveness, and domesticity.[26] A contemporary historian has summarized the most essential elements of this ideology, which had such a profound effect on nineteenth-century American social thought.

> The cult of true womanhood was a compound of four ideas: a sharp dichotomy between the home and the economic world outside that paralleled a sharp contrast between female and male natures, the designation of the home as the female's only proper sphere, the moral superiority of woman, and the idealization of her function as mother.[27]

A few widely held assumptions about women in nineteenth-century America were related to these notions of the True Woman: (1) Though women were inferior to men physically and intellectually, they were thought to possess "finer sensibilities" and a "special nature" that made them not only different from men but also morally superior.[28] (2) Women were thought to be endowed with certain traits that were peculiar to their sex: delicacy, frailty, emotionalism, spirituality. They were thought to exhibit the softer and more gentle virtues, described by such adjectives as beautiful, delicate, tasteful, refined, and sensitive.[29] (3) Women were thought to have little interest in sex and to exhibit such virtues as chastity and modesty. A woman's duty was to subdue male passions, not to arouse them.[30] (4) God and nature had assigned a separate sphere for women—the home—for which they were temperamentally suited. Marriage and motherhood enabled women to have their most profound influence on society. In addition, the ideal was that the wife be fully engaged in taking care of the family rather than gainfully employed outside the home.

The most significant aspect of this nineteenth-century cult of domesticity or True Womanhood (whose values were internalized by women and men alike) was the strong belief that women and men should occupy separate spheres of activity; this belief has been described with considerable clarity.

> At the heart of the cult of domesticity were a rigid conceptual distinction between the home and the economy and a determination to preserve that separation. . . . The world outside the home, the man 's sphere was the scene of . . . economic struggles. . . . From this world, man retreated to the home, the woman's sphere, for physical and spiritual refreshment. Here he found shelter from the anxieties of modern society and a sanctuary for moral and spiritual values that could not survive outside the domestic circle. Presiding over this veritable temple was woman. . . . life in the home had to express the highest moral and Christian values.[31]

It must be borne in mind that the code of behavior prescribed by this ideal was more relevant to the life-style of white middle- and upper-class women, whereas poor women, especially black women, were unable to act out this model of womanhood even if they embraced the ideology.

Herein lies the main problem of the study—to ascertain what attitudes were about black women in the private and public spheres as they are revealed in what was published during the period. During the nineteenth century the appropriate sphere of activity for women (of a certain class) was considered to be the home, while the public sphere was considered to be the appropriate domain for men. The wide range of attitudes expressed by black and white men makes it difficult to generalize about what their overall attitudes were. This is especially true for black males, who, as could be expected, had more to say about black women and in so doing revealed a greater diversity of thought. The study will focus on the most important and frequently discussed issues or questions surrounding the debate about black women in several clearly defined areas. Arguments pertaining to the domestic sphere revolved around the question of morality and the black woman and that of her critical role as mother in preserving the integrity of the race. The significance attached to her role as nurturer not only in her own household but also in the households of whites is revealed in discussions about the black mammy. Second, debates relating to black women and the public sphere tended to focus on three major issues: the feasibility of higher education for black women, especially the issue of industrial vs. liberal

11

education; granting the vote to black women; and the nature of their role in the work force. A less frequently discussed subject, which is related to the first and last issues, was whether they should be ordained in the ministry. In other words, the roles of black women in politics, education, the economy, and the church were the areas in the public sphere around which divergent opinions were expressed.

The major argument of the dissertation is that the dominant attitudes toward black women expressed by whites (men and women) are traceable to their acceptance of two widely held ideologies—the cults of white supremacy, or Anglo-Saxonism, to use Weiss's term, and True Womanhood—and that these ideologies influenced arguments about blacks and women with peculiar consequences for notions about black women. Black male attitudes related to their own racial philosophy, which was in many ways a reaction to notions of white supremacy. Ironically, their attitudes were also shaped by their acceptance of the True Womanhood ideal and their realization that black women, because of their historical circumstances, could not be expected to conform totally to this ideal; but, black males argued, black women could provide a new model of the ideal woman and could be seen as an alternative to the dominant cultural ideal of womanhood. Similarly, black women (especially the elite) were outraged over the persistent attacks on their character and the refusal of the larger society to recognize their womanhood. Internalizing the values of the cult of domesticity, they also felt that the elevation and protection of women were critical to the survival of the black race. Despite these divergences in the thoughts of blacks and whites about black womanhood, both groups viewed motherhood as the most essential function of women, thereby seeing women as a means to an end rather than as ends in themselves. Almost no one, in other words, rejected this apt description of the prevailing philosophy about woman's proper function during the period.

Under woman's reigning presence, the domestic realm was made the source of personal virtue and social adjustment, the preserve of Christian morality. "The Home," and the beatific rituals and emotions supposed to take place within it, attracted an almost fetishistic concern. . . . Woman's thorough fulfillment of her responsibility to the members of her family—imbuing them with her own morality, self-sacrifice, and Christian love—became her contribution to society.[32]

The heated debate about black women tended to revolve around two diametrically opposed notions about the nature of black womanhood. Most whites, male and female, maligned the black woman on the grounds of racial make-up and questionable moral character, which resulted in her inevitable conceptual deviation from the True Womanhood ideal. Blacks, on the other hand, agreed that she departed from the ideal, but not because she was morally defective; rather, she was the victim of sexual abuse and exploitation and could therefore not be blamed for circumstances beyond her control. Instead of being damned, the argument continued, she should be perceived as a new model of the True Woman because of the unique qualities she had developed surviving in a hostile environment.

This study was inspired by my reading of W. E. B. Du Bois who was, in my opinion, the most passionate defender of black women, to whom he referred as "daughters of sorrow" in his moving tribute to the mothers of the race in an essay entitled "The Damnation of Women." It was Du Bois' contempt for the South's "wanton and continued and persistent insulting of black womanhood"[33] that I found refreshing during the past decade and a half when notions about the black matriarchy and theories about the emasculation of black men by black women seemed to overshadow concerns about the special burdens of black women. It is this last point that is for me the most instructive about an examination of past attitudes toward black women. During the period covered by this examination, there is little disagreement among the groups examined that black women experience a unique array of problems because of their race and sex. This consensus among blacks and whites about the "double jeopardy"[34] experienced by black women existed despite radical differences in their attitudes about many other aspects of the black woman question. Furthermore, their sensitivity to the plight of black women and the need for special attention to their peculiar status are only now, nearly a hundred years later, being manifest again and mainly among black women themselves. Contemporary counterparts of Douglass and Du Bois are yet to emerge as the debate over the nature of black womanhood and the appropriate roles for black women continues. The emergence of renewed controversy surrounding "the woman question" as a result of the contemporary women's movement also makes an examination of present attitudes toward black women a timely subject for scholarly inquiry.

TWO

Daughters of Sorrow: Historical Overview of Black Women, 1880-1920

If any would gain a true knowledge of the inner soul of black folks, let him contemplate the position of their women, whose pathetic situation must fill the soul with infinite pity.

Kelly Miller, 1908

. . . the American Negro woman is the most interesting woman in this country. . . . She is the only woman in America who is almost unknown; the only woman for whom nothing is done; the only woman without sufficient defenders when assailed; the only woman who is still outside of that world of chivalry that in all the ages has apotheosized womankind.

Fannie B. Williams, 1904

The world that wills to worship womankind studiously forgets its darker sisters.

W. E. B. Du Bois, 1920

The history of black women from 1880-1920 is better understood through a consideration of both African American history and women's history, though both have, until recently, underemphasized the black female experience. This scholarly neglect of the history of black women is nowhere more apparent than in works that either focus on women in the nineteenth and early twentieth centuries or include a considerable amount of material on the subject. This generalization includes such works as Nancy Cott's *The Bonds of Womanhood, Woman's Sphere in New England, 1780-1835*; Thomas Woody's *A History of Women's Education in the United States*; Sara Delamont and Lorna Duffin's *The Nineteenth Century Woman: Her Cultural and Physical World*; Ann Douglas's *The Feminization of American Culture*; Anne Scott's *The Southern Lady, From Pedestal to Politics, 1830-1930*; and Sheila Rothman's *Woman's Proper Place, A History of Changing Ideals and Practices, 1870 to the Present*. Similarly, though the "cult of domesticity" received considerable attention from women's studies scholars in the 1970s, their assumption seems to have been that black women were irrelevant to such a discussion. Though black women had important familial roles (both in their own communities and in the white community) within the domestic sphere, they are virtually absent from the scholarly discourse surrounding the cult of True Womanhood.[1] A partial explanation for this situation has been offered by one historian.

> . . . the class nature of the cult of domesticity as a behavioral model must be underscored. In the United States, the life-style that this ideal prescribed was accessible only to white, middle- and upper-class women in more settled areas of the country. Its code of behavior took no account of the problems and harsh necessities of poor women, women on the frontier, and slave women. Indeed, one could argue that a privileged elite was able to translate the model of true womanhood into social reality solely because a large number of less fortunate females existed to be exploited sexually, and as domestic servants.[2]

Though this is certainly a sound argument, it overlooks the impact of this ideology on, at the very least, the beliefs and values of blacks, especially the elite, during the period following slavery. It also fails to take into consideration the significance attached to motherhood, a central element in the cult of domesticity, in the black community both during slavery and afterwards. Moreover, while it is less difficult to document the public lives of highly visible black women, women's history scholars have not been as interested in documenting the activities of black women in reform movements, social welfare, the professions, or the church, for example, as they have been in exploring such activities for middle-class white women. This generalization does not include the work of Professor Gerda Lerner, whose pioneering documentary history *Black Women in White America* (New York, 1973), paved the way for the new scholarship on black women conducted over the past several years.[3]

The period under consideration is an especially provocative one to examine because critical changes were occurring in the lives of women and blacks, so that many contradictions are apparent as one considers the history of black women. The purpose of this historical overview is to provide an appropriate context for the analysis of attitudes toward black women in the chapters to follow. Specifically, this chapter highlights those aspects of black women's history that are germane to an understanding of the complex nature of the attitudes toward black women from 1880 to 1920. The discussion focuses on significant occurrences in black women's history, such as the founding of Spelman Seminary in 1881, highlights of the black women's club movement, and the involvement of black women in various reform movements, professions, and educational ventures. The chapter also includes a brief profile of the African American woman that includes her occupational and educational status and other important demographic data.

These years were eventful ones for both blacks and women in the United States. Although the nineteenth century was a period of reform movements and organized struggle for human rights on a variety of fronts (the abolition movement comes to mind), the late nineteenth and early twentieth centuries were disillusioning years for blacks. The South, home for the majority of blacks, had been devastated by the Civil War, embittered by the demands of Reconstruction, and plagued by the fate of four million ex-slaves still in its midst. The obstacles facing blacks, only twenty years out of bondage, were tremendous, for the majority were impoverished, landless, and illiterate. To be sure, the last decade of the nineteenth century and the opening decades of the twentieth "marked the nadir of the Negro's status in American society," according to a well-known historian.[4] The notion of the inherent inferiority of blacks was accepted by the majority of Americans who sat quietly as the political, legal, and social rights of the freedmen and freedwomen continued to erode. The 1890s was an especially dismal decade for blacks as they witnessed the defeat of the Blair Bill for federal aid to public education and the Lodge Bill for federal supervision of federal elections. In addition, the southern states amended their constitutions, starting with Mississippi in 1890, and the disfranchisement of blacks was accomplished by 1910. The Supreme Court in the famous 1896 *Plessy* vs. *Ferguson* case gave legal sanction to the already widespread practice of Jim Crow when it ruled that separate but equal public facilities were constitutional. Blacks were being lynched in record numbers, and between 1900 and 1910, six major race riots occurred throughout the nation, which signaled growing racial hostility in the North and South. Blacks and whites inhabited two separate worlds, and the chasm between them was deep and ever widening.

Furthermore, despite rapid industrialization and urbanization throughout the rest of the nation, the former slaves and their children remained concentrated in the rural South, unable to extricate themselves from an exploitative labor system of sharecropping. By 1900, nine out of ten blacks still lived in the South, primarily in the Cotton Belt, 80 percent of whom resided in rural areas. Since a woman's race, class, ethnic background, and geographical location determined in many ways the nature of her daily experiences—her participation in the labor force, her household duties, her access to education, and her life expectancy, etc.—it is not surprising that the lot of black women in the South was in many ways different from that of their female counterparts elsewhere, since race was the dominant factor in determining one's status during the years under consideration.[5]

Black women, the majority of whom were sharecroppers, lived in a quite different world from both white upper-class women and those in the urban working class. The wives of businessmen and other professionals, freed from the need to earn a living, their household chores lightened considerably by store-bought products and domestic servants, had leisure time to spend as they wished. Philanthropy, education, and social reform often engaged their interest. Before marriage, native-born and immigrant white women worked to support themselves and other family members and were employed in offices, factories, and sweatshops. They were often able, especially in the South, to bypass the most menial, lowest paid, and least desirable jobs, which were reserved for black women. In the South, black women were domestic servants, laundresses, and cooks, for the most part. When they were allowed to work in factories, they performed the most hazardous and demeaning jobs available, in tobacco factories and seafood processing plants, and they were even denied the jobs poor white women were able to get in textile mills. In 1910, 95 percent of black women aged sixteen and over were field workers on farms, laundresses, or domestic servants, whereas only half of all white women employed were in these categories. In other words, black women were either planting or harvesting cotton on family farms, taking in laundry at home, or performing domestic chores in white households.[6]

Not only did black women's work differ from the work of other women, but their labor force participation rate also departed in significant ways from their white female counterparts.

In 1900 only three out of every hundred married white women held paid employment; in 1920 still only six out of every hundred were gainfully employed. Nearly all white women, then, worked until they were married, and gainful employment represented a stage in their life before marriage. . . . Nearly half of all black women, however, could expect to work most of their adult life. . . . In 1900 and 1920, more than 40 percent of all black women regardless of age worked. . . . In 1910, twenty-six out of every hundred black married women worked; in 1920, thirty-three out of every hundred.[7]

In other words, the marital status of black women did not affect their labor force participation rate, as was the case with white women, and over one-third of all black women continued to work as field laborers or wage earners even after they reached sixty-five.[8]

According to federal census data for 1880-1910, the typical black household included both a husband and a wife (86.4 percent in the 1880 sample and 82.5 percent in the 1900 sample included both spouses) and contained four to five members.[9] A description of the typical sharecropper's dwelling illustrates the harsh conditions under which rural black families in the South lived.

. . . constructed by the white landowner (usually many years before), the one or two-room log or sawn-lumber cabin measured only 15' or 20' square. It lacked glass windows, screens . . . running water, sanitary facilities, artificial illumination, cupboard and shelf space, and adequate insulation as well as ventilation. Most of the daily business of living—eating, sleeping, bathing—took place in a room where 'stale and sickly odors' inevitably accumulated. . . . Most families owned a few pieces of heavy furniture; modest earnings were often invested in a mule ox, plot, or wagon. . . . Sharecroppers' households also lacked artifacts of middle-class life, such as a wide variety of eating and cooking utensils, books, papers, pencils, bric-a-brac, and clocks.[10]

A typical day for the female sharecropper went as follows. She usually arose at 4 a.m., and prepared over an open fire a breakfast for the family, which included fried salt pork, molasses, and cornbread. During the planting season, she worked alongside other family members in the fields, where she was assigned particular tasks. During harvest time, which was reminiscent of slavery days, she picked cotton from August to December. Around 11 a.m. she would leave the fields in order to prepare for the noon meal, which included gathering firewood and the difficult task of securing water. The family consumed this low-protein meal and the woman returned to the fields, usually leaving the house untidy. After a twelve-hour day, she returned to the cabin to prepare the evening meal.[11] The "inexorable" rhythms of the black wife's life have been poignantly described:

> Few rural women enjoyed respite from the inexorable demands of day-to-day household tasks or the annual cycle of cotton cultivation. Nursing a newborn child and cooking the family's meals; digging, hoeing, and chopping in the fields—these chores dictated the daily and seasonal rhythms of a black wife's life. But they represented only the barest outline of her domestic obligations. On rainy days, or by the light of a night-time fire, she sewed quilts and mended clothes. During the day she had to carve out time to grind corn for meal, bathe the children, weed the garden, gather eggs, milk the cow, and do the laundry. Periodically, she devoted an entire day to making soap out of ashes and lard or helping with the hog butchering.[12]

Equally as dismal was the plight of the black domestic servant, whose life of toil is revealed in the autobiography of a southern black woman who told her story to a magazine reporter in 1912:

> For more than thirty years—or since I was ten years old—I have been a servant in one capacity or another in white families. . . . I frequently work from fourteen to sixteen hours a day. I am compelled . . . to sleep in the house. I am allowed to go home to my own children . . . only once in two weeks, every other Sunday afternoon—even then I'm not permitted to stay all night . . . I don't know what it is to go to church . . . I live a treadmill life. . . . I am the slave, body and soul, of this family. And what do I get for this work—this lifetime bondage? The pitiful sum of ten dollars a month![13]

According to David Katzman, black female domestics increased by 43 percent between 1890 and 1920 while their white female counterparts declined by one-third. By 1920 black women comprised 40 percent of all domestics. Similarly, by 1920, 73 percent of all laundresses outside laundries were black. Only 0.5 percent in 1910 and 1.4 percent of black women in 1920 were employed in such non-agricultural occupations as clerks, bookkeepers, saleswomen, and telephone operators, which was due in part to the fact that these occupations were underdeveloped, in general, in the South.[14] The extent to which black women became disproportionately represented in the servant category during this period has been well documented by a number of other scholars as well.[15]

The negative impact of poverty was apparent in other ways as well. The fertility rates of black women declined by one-third from 1880-1910 as a result of, among other factors, poor nutrition; the life expectancy at birth for black men and women was only thirty-three years; a black mother could expect to see one out of three of her children die before age ten and to die herself before the youngest left home. Health conditions were deplorable, there was a shortage of black doctors, and hospitals were almost non-existent.

By contrast, this same period might be considered a high point in women's history generally. In fact, many enlightened women, some of whom were black, felt that a new day had dawned for the American woman as a result of "a great national and international movement . . . based on the inherent right of every . . . soul to its own highest development . . . making for Woman's full, free, and complete emancipation."[16] Anna Julia Cooper, one of the most outspoken black feminists during this era, went on to acknowledge the new challenges beckoning the women of her day:

> She stands now at the gateway of this new era of American civilization. . . . To be alive at such an epoch is a privilege, to be a woman then is sublime . . . changes of such moment are in progress, such new and alluring vistas are opening out before us, such original and radical suggestions for the adjustment of labor and capital, of government and the governed, of the family, the church and the state, that to be a possible factor . . . in such a movement is pregnant with hope and weighty with responsibility. To be a woman in such an age carries with it privilege and an opportunity never implied before.[17]

This feeling of hopefulness and excitement, if not euphoria, can be explained by several important occurrences. In 1877 the U.S. Senate was presented with a petition for the Sixteenth Amendment, which was to grant women the vote. On January 25th the first vote on woman suffrage was taken and, though it was defeated, a new era in women's political history began. The Anthony Amendment, as it was called, ultimately became the Nineteenth Amendment. The most concrete illustration of the political "coming of age" of women occurred in 1890 when the two major woman suffrage organizations—the National Woman Suffrage Association (led by Elizabeth Cady Stanton and Susan B. Anthony) and the American Woman Suffrage Association (led by Lucy Stone and Henry Beecher)—merged and became the National American Woman Suffrage Association.

The national women's club movement, which skyrocketed in the 1890s, was another manifestation of the emergence of women as a group with potential power. The organization of the General Federation of Women's Clubs in 1890 signaled the beginning of significant transformations in the lives of middle-class white women. This was indeed the era during which women's organizations came of age.

> Whatever the specific direction . . . women took as they emerged from domestic confinement it led them to mass organizations headed by members of their own sex. By the second decade of the twentieth century, women had formed a veritable army composed of many well-organized divisions, strategically linked, and positioned on the outer flank of the home. By 1920 it was estimated that the General Federation of Women's Clubs had perhaps 1 million members; the Women's Christian Temperance Union 800,000; the YWCA 500,000; there were 400,000 union members; and as many as 2 million women participated in the suffrage campaign. The seeds of the major contemporary women's organizations, from the PTA to the American Association of University Women, were planted before 1920.[18]

Significant improvements in the domestic lives of middle-class urban women were also taking place as a result of modern technological innovations that freed them from the drudgery of many household tasks and significantly altered their daily routines. Hot and cold running water in the home and the washing machine, for example, made one of the middle-class woman's most demanding domestic tasks—the weekly wash—an entirely new experience. Other labor-saving and time-saving devices that transformed the housewife's life included the sewing machine, the refrigerator, the gas stove, the sink, and the vacuum cleaner. Commercial canning and mass-produced products, such as biscuits, also freed the housewife from time-consuming kitchen chores. In fact, by 1900, 90 percent of urban households, which were mainly outside the South, were using bread prepared by commercial bakeries.[19]

This period also witnessed increased educational opportunities for these same women, the growth of women's colleges, and growing numbers of women in diverse professions. Job opportunities for women also increased, especially in offices, department stores, and public schools. Women, under a mandate to "tame society,"[20] also became more involved in an impressive array of reform activities—temperance,[21] social purity, settlement work, slum removal, child welfare, consumers rights, and protective legislation for working women and children. Schools such Bryn Mawr, as well as coeducational universities, cleared the way to professional careers for women between 1900 and 1920. During that period the number of professional women increased 226 percent, almost triple the rate of male advancement. While the majority of professional women were teachers at the elementary school level, some women made substantial inroads into traditionally male spheres. By 1920, 5 percent of the nation's doctors were women, 1.4 percent of the lawyers and judges, and 30 percent of the college presidents, professors, and instructors.[22]

The history of black women during this period can be seen as a reflection of the paradoxes that are apparent in an analysis of black and women's history. While black women experienced all of the hardships that beset their race during the period, they were also affected by what was taking place in the women's movement, which is apparent in several key areas. First, their involvement in racial uplift activities can be viewed not only as a manifestation of their obligations to their race (as most scholars have interpreted it), but also as an indication of the extent to which they had taken quite seriously their obligations as women to join the "domestic crusade," as Mary Ryan describes it. In her most extensive discussion of the cult of domesticity, Ryan analyzes this crusade, which began during the antebellum period and continued throughout the nineteenth century:

> The wife's conjugal function was defensive and rehabilitating. . . . Innumerable magazine articles on "woman's influence" summoned females to their collective social responsibility. . . . The theory of domestic influence promised women the power to set the course of society without leaving home. By sustaining her mate through the discomforts of the modern work situation, and gently restraining him from anti-social behavior, a wife did her part to ensure the national morality.[23]

Though Ryan, as is the case with other women's history scholars, does not include black women in her discussion of the cult of domesticity, a careful analysis of the racial uplift work and writings of professional black women during the post-Reconstruction era will reveal the impact of this ideology on their philosophies and values. The habit on the part of many women's studies scholars to think of black women mainly in racial terms and to fail to recognize their gender identity causes them to ignore significant aspects of the history of American women. Similar interpretations of the organizational work of black women, especially their club activity, are also absent from traditional black history texts, which tend to include the involvement of black women in the race uplift movement only within a racial context. A consideration of the black woman's awareness of her gender obligations would render obsolete such a narrow view of, for example, the black women's club movement in the 1890s. One of the most articulate spokeswomen for the peculiar burdens of the black woman because of her race and her gender was Anna Julia Cooper, who revealed on many occasions her awareness that being black and female dictated a dual set of responsibilities. In fact, the grandiose statements that many black female writers made can be seen as examples of what Ryan has observed among white women writers of an earlier period, whom she refers to as "the literary generals of the domestic crusade"; their role was to inspire wives to "send forth living and refreshing streams to fertilize and make beautiful the moral wilderness of the world."[24] The following statement by Cooper (who has been ignored by scholars studying the cult of True Womanhood) illustrates her acceptance of her role as a literary general of both the domestic crusade and the race uplift crusade, which for her were inseparable.

> To be a woman in such an age carries with it a privilege and an opportunity never implied before. But to be a woman of the Negro race in America, and to be able to grasp the deep significance of the possibilities of the crisis, is to have a heritage, it seems to me, unique in the ages. . . . What a responsibility then to have the sole management of the primal lights and shadows. Such is the colored woman's office. She must stamp weal or woe on the coming history of this people. May she see her opportunity and vindicate her high perogative.[25]

Cooper argued that black women should work within the domestic sphere to upgrade the quality of the home and the family. This would improve the moral fiber of the race. However, she felt that black women must also become involved in the public sphere, but not just as wage earners.

> No plan for renovating society, no scheme for purifying politics, no reform in church or in state, no moral, social, or economic question . . . is lost on her. . . . no woman can possibly put herself or her sex outside any of the interests that affect humanity. All departments in the new era are to be hers.[26]

This desire to purify the home and society was seen by Cooper and other black women to be a part of their definition of race uplift, but it was also consistent with efforts on the part of reform women in general to uplift the entire society.

The black woman's club movement that emerged on the national level in the 1890s must also be seen as a manifestation of black women's race *and* gender obligations. Black women's clubs were established not only because white women's clubs prohibited their membership (except in New England), but also because black women felt they had special and unique problems to

Anna Julia Cooper (1858-1964), educator and intellectual, wrote in 1892 a book, *A Voice from the South by a Black Woman from the South*, which has the distinction of being the first black feminist analysis of the condition of blacks and women. Cooper (A.B., 1884, A.M., 1888, Oberlin College) became the principal of M Street High School, Washington, D.C., in 1901 after having been a teacher there for fourteen years. In 1925, at the age of 65, she was awarded the Ph.D. degree from the Sorbonne.

solve. These special agenda items were alluded to when the First National Conference of Colored Women convened in Boston on July 29, 1895:

> . . . we need to talk over not only those things which are of vital importance to us as women, but also the things that are of especial interest to us as *colored* women, the training of our children, openings for our boys and girls, how they can be prepared for occupations . . . what *we* especially can do in the moral education of the race . . . our mental elevation and physical development, the home training it is necessary to give our children in order to prepare them to meet the peculiar conditions in which they shall find themselves, how to make the most of our own, to some extent, limited opportunities, these are some of our own peculiar questions to be discussed.[27]

They also felt that there were general questions that as women they should address: "temperance, morality, the higher education, hygienic and domestic questions. . . ."

The specific catalyst for this first national convention came as a result of a letter that Florence Belgarnie, an officer of the Anti-Lynching Committee in London, received from an American newspaper editor, John Jacks, president of the Missouri Press Association. Angry over her anti-lynching activities, which had been encouraged by the crusade of black activist Ida Wells-Barnett[28] during her speaking tours in England, Jacks wrote Belgarnie a letter in which he defended the white South by maligning black women for their immorality. Belgarnie in turn sent a copy of the letter to Josephine St. Pierre Ruffin, a member of the largely white New England Women's Club and founder of the black Woman's Era Club. In 1895 she convened a group of black women at the Charles Street A.M.E. Church in Boston, resulting in the formation of the National Federation of Afro-American Women. Later she distributed the letter to black women's clubs throughout the nation and called for a national conference that eventually led to the formation of the National Association of Colored Women (NACW). In 1896 the Association was established when the National Federation of Afro-American Women (Margaret Murray Washington, president) and the National League of Colored Women (Mary Church Terrell, president) combined, with Terrell becoming the NACW's first national president. At this historic gathering, Mrs. Mahammitt, a delegate of the Omaha Women's Club, stressed the importance of vindicating the honor of black women and denouncing Jacks:

> We are sent almost across the continent, to Boston, to this convention of American colored women to vindicate the honor of colored women, wantonly

traduced by a cowardly writer in a southern paper. . . . There was a time when our mothers and sisters could not protect themselves from such beasts as this man Jacks and it is to him, and his kind, that the morality of colored women has been questioned. But a new era is here and we propose to protect and defend ourselves.[29]

The illustrious group of women present included Margaret Murray Washington; Anna G. Brown, widow of the well-known writer William Wells Brown; Selena Sloan Butler of Atlanta, Georgia (also Spelman alumna), who some years later would organize the black Parent Teachers Association; and Victoria Earle Matthews, journalist and writer, who in 1897 founded the White Rose Industrial Mission for the purpose of assisting black females who migrated to New York from the South. Other black female journalists there included Miss Lewis of the Boston *Herald*, Mrs. Cooper of the Washington *Post*, and Florence Lewis of the Philadelphia *Press*.[30] In a glowing tribute to these women gathered in Boston, a journalist covering the convention had this to say:

> . . . a convention of colored women, planned and carried through to a successful end by themselves, with all dignity, decorum and a thorough knowledge of all that is essential in parliamentary law, is not merely a novelty, it is far more, it is a demonstration complete in itself of the capacity of the American Negro, taken from his supposed weakest left side. These women educated, crude, earnest and thoughtful, showed their ability to think upon and grapple with all the subjects of vital interest to their race, capable of defending themselves from scurrilous attacks and answering the sneers of the thoughtless. . . .[31]

The crowning achievement of the conference was the formation of the Federation. Greener credits Victoria Matthews and Mrs. Ridley of Boston with this tour de force:

> . . . the South and West were true to their aggressive characters, and fought for everything in sight and it looked at one time as if they would have got all had it not been for the untiring vigilance of the New York delegation under the skillful leadership of Mrs. Matthews who proved herself a true Napoleon of attack and defense. She broke the back of the movement in favor of the Washington organization to hitch the convention to their national cart. She led the movement which selected Mrs. Washington as president of the new organization, declining peremptorily all mention of herself. But it was she [Mrs. Ridley] who made the conciliatory speeches at opportune times which softened the factions. At the supreme moment . . . when the scholarly Wellesley graduate made the point of order that none of the business left over

by the Convention could properly come up at this meeting she promptly moved the formation of a National Federation of Colored Women and carried it by storm. Here was seen again on this arena that combination of qualities so rare in the world in man or woman.[32]

Black women were also pioneers in the establishment of important educational institutions during the period. To date, however, there is no study that documents the history of black women in education. Only a few outstanding black female educators have been mentioned in Afro-American history sources, though ironically these same names rarely appear in women's history sources, even in the numerous ones on the history of women's education in America. The most recent special issue of *The Journal of Negro Education* (Summer 1982), which is devoted to "The Impact of Black Women in Education," is the first attempt to deal in a scholarly way with this important though neglected topic. What follows is a historical overview of the diverse efforts of black women to respond to the critical educational needs of the race after the Civil War.

The story of the struggle to establish schools throughout the South for the education of nearly four million newly freed slaves is a heroic one. The African-American family's profound respect for education and its strong desire that children avail themselves of formal learning made this monumental task less difficult. While the history of the development of educational institutions in the South following the Civil War is well documented and generally well known, much that is written focuses on the hordes of northern missionaries, many of whom were single white women, who came South to assist in the struggle to provide education for the masses of illiterate blacks fresh out of slavery. While their efforts were indeed praiseworthy, as were the efforts of black men, much remains to be written about the struggles of black women, especially southerners, to provide for the educational needs of the race. Like their white counterparts, black women were attracted to the teaching profession and helped to make up the 70 percent of women workers who were teachers in 1900 and the 80 percent in 1910.[33]

The work of several post-Civil War school founders will be mentioned briefly. While southern public education systems instituted during Reconstruction survived after 1876, they did not include black children except on the lowest levels. In many rural counties in the South, where most blacks resided, schools for black children were open only a few months out of the year, and higher education was accessible to only a select few. It is not surprising then that southern blacks, many of whom were women, would feel compelled to start their own schools. One example was Emma J. Wilson, a graduate of Scotia Seminary (founded by Presbyterians for black women in Concord, North Carolina, in 1867), who returned to her hometown, Mayesville, South Carolina, in 1892 and opened a school with ten pupils in an abandoned cotton-gin house. She accepted eggs and chickens as tuition, and later her efforts resulted in the founding of Mayesville Institute (from which Mary Bethune graduated). Cornelia Bowen, a Hampton Institute graduate, founded Mt. Meigs Institute in Montgomery, Alabama, which was a rural school for black children. Like other pioneers she gained the support of the black community, churches, and white philanthropies.[34]

More well known are the efforts of several pioneering educators who served as presidents of the institutions they founded. Lucy Laney, an 1873 graduate of Atlanta University (the first graduating class of the Normal Department) founded Haines Normal and Industrial Institute in Augusta, Georgia, in 1886, in the basement of Christ Presbyterian Church with five students; by the end of the second year over two hundred were in attendance. Referred to by Du Bois as "the dark vestal virgin who kept the fires of Negro education fiercely flaming," Laney was recognized in her day as the leading woman educator among southern blacks if not in the nation.[35]

Charlotte Hawkins Brown was another pioneer. After attending Salem State Teachers College and taking courses at Harvard and Wellesley, Brown opened a school in Sedalia, North Carolina, in 1902, having raised the initial funds by signing and speaking in summer resort hotels in Massachusetts. The school, named the Palmer Memorial Institute, was initially a rural grammar school that emphasized agricultural and manual training. Brown was its president from 1904 to 1953, during which time it became one of the leading preparatory schools for blacks in the South. Nannie Burroughs founded the National Training School for Women and Girls in 1907 in the nation's capital for the purpose of producing missionaries, Sunday school teachers, stenographers, bookkeepers, musicians, cooks, laundresses, housemaids, and other skilled workers.[36] Rigid moral codes were enforced by Burroughs, who wanted to develop strength of character in the women. Domestic training and the art of homemaking were also emphasized.

Mary McLeod Bethune, the most well known of this group and "the only woman identified by most history texts as having played a significant role in the building of a black educational institution," founded the Daytona Educational and Industrial Training School, which evolved into a four-year college known as Bethune Cookman, where she served as president from 1904 to 1942.[37] Born in 1875 in Mayesville, South Carolina, the youngest of seventeen children of farmers who were ex-slaves, Bethune walked five miles to a school started by Emma Wilson, a young black female missionary of the Northern Presbyterian Church. At age seventeen, she was given the rare opportunity to further her education at Scotia Seminary in Concord, North Carolina. Later she attended Moody Bible School in Chicago, from which she graduated in 1895. Denied a missionary post in Africa, she reluctantly accepted a teaching position at Haines Institute in Augusta, Georgia. This marked a turning point in her life, for she realized from President Laney's example that her life's work was at home and not in Africa. In 1904 she went to Florida after learning about the Florida East Coast Railroad's demand for black construction workers. Her dream was to start a school and on October 3, 1904, she opened its doors with five black girls and her own son. It was later named the Daytona Normal and Industrial School for Negro Girls. Four years later boys were admitted. In desperate need of a permanent site, she learned that a dumping ground called Hell's Hole was for sale for $250. In order to raise the requisite $5.00 down payment, she sold ice cream and sweet potato pies to the construction workers. Later she made appeals among the contractors for gifts of sand and bricks to construct a building on the newly acquired grounds. She also asked local mechanics, carpenters, and plasterers to donate a few hours of their time in the evening on the construction of the building in exchange for sandwiches and tuition for their children and themselves to attend her school. Eventually Faith Hall was built on the new campus.[38]

Another important event in black women's education, ignored in chronicles of both black and women's educational histories, took place during this period as well. The story begins in February of 1880 when Sophia B. Packard, a white female, went to the South as a representative of the Woman's American Baptist Home Mission Society (WABHMS)[39] of New England so that she might gain a better knowledge of the plight of the freedmen. During her travels, she was disturbed by the extremely difficult conditions under which blacks were living and especially by the status of black women. A product of female seminaries and a former teacher and administrator at several outstanding New England academies, she was particularly sensitive to the lack of educational opportunities for black girls. When she became ill after reaching New Orleans, she sent out an urgent call to her long-time friend, Harriet E. Giles, who was then teaching in Boston.

Lucy Craft Laney (1854-1933), educator, was in the first graduating class of Atlanta University (1873). She taught in the public schools of Augusta, Macon, Milledgeville, and Savannah, Georgia, before founding in 1886 the Haines Normal and Industrial Institute in Augusta. Mary McLeod Bethune began her teaching career there in 1895. The school offered liberal arts courses, a nurses' training department and the first kindergarten for the city of Augusta.

31

Giles was equally appalled at the condition of black women during her stay in the South, and both became convinced that God had called them to work for their elevation. They returned to Boston in late April, determined to start a school in the South for black females. Though they overcame overwhelming obstacles, these courageous women have never received the national recognition they deserve as pioneers in the cause for women's education, especially black women's education. Their largely unexamined writings provide a rich source of information on white female attitudes toward black women during the period under consideration, and will be examined in detail.

When they returned to the North in April, Packard and Giles solicited aid from the WABHHMS, whose members listened with interest to their plans, but decided that while the work was necessary the magnitude of the task was overwhelming. To a young organization with little money in the treasury, the suggestion that they immediately establish a school for black girls seemed impractical, if not impossible. Persisting in their efforts, however, Packard and Giles took their plan in March 1881 to the First Baptist Church of Medford, Massachusetts. At a prayer meeting, the congregation became enthusiastic over the prospect of such a school as the women had envisioned and pledged their support of $100. With this encouragement, Packard and Giles returned to the WABHMS and successfully solicited their support. On March 29, 1881, they left for Georgia. This state had been chosen because the American Baptist Mission Society (ABMS) had made no provision for the education of young black females there, though they supported a school to train black ministers. Packard and Giles finally decided on Atlanta in part because of their familiarity with teachers at the Mission-supported Atlanta Baptist Seminary (later Morehouse College). After arriving in Atlanta on April 1, 1881, an unusually cold, bitter Friday night, they contacted Dr. Shaver, a white teacher at the Seminary, who took them the next day to visit Reverend Quarles, the most influential black Baptist in Georgia and the pastor of Friendship Baptist Church. Because of Father Quarles's sensitivity to the needs of blacks, Dr. Shaver indicated that he could best advise them on how to go about organizing a school for black women. Giles revealed in an April 1881 diary entry the details of that fateful day, April 1, 1881, during which they picked up a few pebbles and tossed them at the window of Father Quarles's study.

Dr. Shaver knocked and there was no response for some time. At last Father Quarles opened the door, invited us in, and on our being introduced and stating why and from whence we had come, he said, 'While I was praying, the Lord answered. For fifteen years I have been asking the Lord to send Baptist teachers for our girls and women.' He further said, 'I do not know where you will teach, but there is the basement. You are welcome to that,' and leading the way, he took us down to that room. It was indeed dark and cheerless, but we were glad for even that place.[40]

On April 4, Father Quarles brought together local black ministers to meet Packard and Giles and encouraged them to give the women all the help they could. Besides making personal calls and appealing to numerous church organizations, the ministers printed and distributed circulars and handbills announcing the opening of the school. The assistance given by this committee and their encouragement to Packard and Giles in these early days cannot be over-emphasized. Their efforts are indicative of the willingness of enlightened members of the black male population to do all they could to assist in efforts to provide black women with a sound education, an essential ingredient for racial uplift.

After a week of getting settled and calling on black families to recruit students, Packard and Giles convened the first class of the Atlanta Baptist Female Seminary, which was held in the basement of Friendship Baptist Church on April 11, 1881. The class consisted of eleven pupils of all ages, though most were women out of slavery who were eager to learn to read the Bible and to write well enough to send letters to their children. Packard and Giles had only a Bible, a pad, and a pencil at the beginning of this ambitious undertaking. Within three months, however, the enrollment had increased to eighty and those under fifteen years were turned away. Within a year there were two hundred students ranging in age from fifteen to fifty-two. In a letter to supporters describing the first year of their work, Packard and Giles alluded to the great sacrifices that students were making to attend school and the joy they experienced at being able to read their Bibles for the first time. Some walked eight or nine miles to and from school, and they took in washing to support themselves. One mother came with her four daughters and was overwhelmed with excitement. "I reckon I am the happiest woman in town. One year ago I did not know a letter; today I can read my Bible and I am going on fifty-two years old."[41] Fifty years after the founding of Spelman, a journalist made this observation on the editorial page of *Opportunity*: "If there is any nobler achievement in the annals of American womanhood than the founding of Spelman College for Negro women . . . we confess that we know not of it."[42]

Though the period under consideration was indeed a difficult time for the majority of blacks, a privileged group of black women, beneficiaries of increased educational opportunities for blacks and women, were convinced that it was possible to improve the conditions under which the other members of their race lived. Encouraged by the potential of women and their ability to affect the progress of the human race during this "new era," Anna J. Cooper—who entered Oberlin College the same year Spelman Seminary was founded, earned a doctorate at the age of sixty-seven from the University of Paris in 1925, and became president of Frelinghuysen University in Washington, D.C. in 1930—was one of the most eloquent spokeswomen for black women during the 1890s.[43] Despite the fact that the majority of her sisters were poor, illiterate and faced innumerable obstacles, Cooper believed strongly that the future of the race was in the hands of black women and that the more enlightened ones must assume the major responsibility for providing the leadership for the difficult struggle ahead.

> Now the fundamental agency under God in the regeneration, the re-training of the race, as well as the ground work and starting point of its progress upward, must be the *black woman*. With all the wrongs and neglects of her past, with all the weakness, the debasement, the moral thralldom of her present, the black woman of today stands mute and wondering at the Herculean task devolving upon her. But the cycles wait for her. No other hand can move the lever. She must be loosed from her bands and set to work.[44]

The history of black women from 1880-1920 is in large part the story of black women's work in the midst of extraordinary hardships, not the least of which was a conglomeration of attitudes that might have rendered them mute and immobile. That they were able to carry out their work—which included self-improvement, race work, and women's work—under these circumstances is remarkable. No one was more aware of the difficulties of their "Herculean task" than W. E. B. Du Bois who felt compelled to memorialize these "daughters of sorrow":[45]

> . . . I honor the women of my race. . . . No other women have emerged from the hell of force and temptation which once engulfed and still surrounds black women in America with half the modesty and womanliness that they retain. I have always felt like bowing myself before them in all abasement, searching to bring some tribute to these long-suffering victims, these burdened sisters of

W.E.B. Du Bois (1868-1963), scholar/activist, Pan-Africanist, and women's rights spokesperson, has the most distinguished career of any black leader. A founder of the NAACP, he edited its publication *The Crisis* from 1910 to 1934, which contained extensive analyses of the woman suffrage issue. An outspoken advocate for black women throughout his life, his book *Darkwater: Voices Within The Veil* (1920) provided the inspiration for this study and its title.

mine, whom the world loves to affront and ridicule and wantonly to insult. . . . This, then,—a little thing—to their memory and inspiration.[46]

THREE

Sinner or Saint?: Antithetical Views Concerning Black Women and the Private Sphere

The struggle of the colored woman toward purity and refinement involves as deep and as dark a tragedy as any that marks the history of human strivings.

Kelly Miller, 1908

. . . while in the eyes of the highest tribunal in America she was deemed no more than a chattel . . . the Afro-American woman maintained ideals of womanhood unshamed by any ever conceived.

Anna J. Cooper, 1893

. . . the American Negro woman is the most interesting in this country. . . . She is the only woman in America who is almost unknown; the only woman for whom nothing is done; the only woman without sufficient defenders when assailed; the only woman who is still outside of that world of chivalry that in all the ages has apotheosized womankind.

Fannie B. Williams, 1904

W ithin the past decade, anthropologists, employing a feminist perspective in their analyses of culture, have advanced the argument that "an asymmetry in the cultural evaluations of male and female, in the importance assigned to women and men, appears to be universal."[1] This universal asymmetry of sex roles is due in part, the argument continues, to the woman's role as mother, which leads to a clear identification of women with the domestic sphere and of men with the public sphere. Moreover, this opposition between the domestic and the public provides a framework for examining male and female roles in all societies and for understanding the nature of female subordination. In other words, "the domestic orientation of women is felt to be the critical factor in understanding her social position," which is to be contrasted with the "extra-domestic, political, military spheres of activity and interest primarily associated with men."[2] Because men are not expected as fathers to bond with their children in the same way that is expected of mothers, they are free to pursue activities in the larger society away from the confines of home.

This public sphere/private sphere dichotomy also provides a useful framework for examining attitudes toward black women during the period under consideration. Since the cult of True Womanhood held that a female's natural sphere of activity is the home and her roles as mother, wife, and daughter are her most important functions, it is not surprising that many discussions about women, even black women, focused on the domestic sphere during this period. However, it must be pointed out that interest in black women and the domestic sphere was a new phenomenon, as Fannie B. Williams, outspoken clubwoman, observed in 1903 in a discussion of the black women's club movement. For the past thirty-five years, she argued,

. . . colored women as mothers, as home makers, as the center and source of the social life of the race have received little or no attention. These women have been left to grope their way unassisted toward a realization of those domestic virtues, moral impulses and standards of family and social life that are the badges of race respectability. They have had no special teachers to instruct them. No conventions of distinguished women of the more favored race have met to consider their peculiar needs. There has been no fixed public opinion to which they could appeal. . . . Certain it is that colored women have been the least known, and the most ill-favored class of women in this country. Thirty-five years ago they were unsocialized, as either maids or matrons.[3]

Arguments about women's moral and spiritual influence, as is evident from the remarks above, were also related to the domestic sphere since the prevailing notion was that though women had a moral role to play in society, it must be kept outside of the sphere of political power. In fact, women's moral nature ill suited them for participation in social and political matters, where a different set of values was needed. Moreover, competition between women and men in the public arena would destroy women's special moral sensibilities. It was essential, therefore, that women focus their attention on the domestic sphere so that they could fulfill their special role of preserving the moral conscience of Victorian society.[4]

At the center of the debate about black women during this period were arguments about her moral character, which can be seen as an outgrowth, among other factors, of the general preoccupation with women's moral nature on the part of Victorian society. As one might expect, whites and blacks were generally, but not always, at opposite ends of the pole on this issue. The most persistent theme in the writings of white men is the devaluation of the black woman, which is ironic given the high valuation of American women generally during this time.[5] In a recent monograph on the impact of sexism on black women's lives from slavery to the present, written by a young black feminist, an explanation is given for this change in male attitudes toward white women during the nineteenth century:

> With the shift away from fundamentalist Christian doctrine came a change in male perceptions of women. 19th century white women were no longer portrayed as sexual temptresses; they were extolled as the "nobler half of humanity" whose duty was to elevate men's sentiments and inspire their higher impulses. The new image of white womanhood was diametrically opposed to the old image. She was depicted as goddess rather than sinner; she was virtuous, pure, innocent, not sexual and worldly. By raising the white female to a goddess-like status, white men effectively removed the stigma Christianity had placed on them. White male idealization of white women as innocent and virtuous served as an act of exorcism, which had as its purpose transforming her image and ridding her of the curse of sexuality. The message of the idealization was this: as long as white women possessed sexual feeling they would be seen as degraded immoral creatures. . . . Once the white female was mythologized as pure and virtuous, a symbolic Virgin Mary, white men could see her as exempt from negative sexist stereotypes of the female.[6]

This shift from the image of woman as sinner to woman as saint or virtuous lady in the minds of white men did not apply to black women, however. In fact, the black woman was devalued not only because of her racial traits but also because she departed from whites' conception of the True Woman—which is indicative of the degree to which prevailing notions about race and gender interacted in the minds of whites and resulted in a particular set of attitudes about black women. Many whites felt that notions about the "ideal woman" did not apply to black women because the circumstances of slavery had prevented them from developing qualities that other women possessed and from devoting their lives to wifehood and motherhood. A contemporary historian has commented on this phenomenon.

> . . . femininity and domesticity were not held sacred by slave owners. Such amenities were outlawed by a system of forced labor, where men, women, and children were considered agricultural machinery, valued primarily for their muscle, endurance, and productive capability. . . . Aside from procreation, black women were assigned few exclusively female roles. Wifely service remained rudimentary. . . . Motherhood might be reduced to giving birth, interrupting work in the field to nurse the infant, and . . . cooking frugal meals for the young. . . . The slave master felt few compunctions to model the black family after the cult of domesticity.[7]

Additionally, the "devaluation of black womanhood" is traceable to the sexual exploitation of black women during slavery.[8] Moreover, the black woman's allegedly innate racial traits tended to cancel out those uniquely feminine traits that white women were supposed to possess.[9]

The theme of the devaluation of black women has several component parts. While most of the works by white males that address the "Negro Problem" do not distinguish between males and females in their discussion of Negro traits and behavior, they frequently allude to the immorality of black women, especially in discussions of the deteriorated condition of the black family and the criminality of the race (which is more applicable to black men). Though these comments vary in length, they constitute a much repeated refrain in the seemingly endless paragraphs on the degradation of blacks.

According to Rev. A. H. Shannon, a southern Methodist minister, the immorality of the black mother is one of the causes of the degraded home life among blacks.[10] William Pickett, a northerner who advocates the removal of blacks from the country as the solution to the "Negro Problem," refers to the criminality of blacks because of their defective moral sense and especially the failure of black women to develop "the qualities of personal chastity" as the primary cause of the "gravest deterioration in the moral standards of the community where such class exists."[11] A similar comment is made in 1905 by William Smith, a professor at Tulane University, concerning the greater serious harm done to a community when its women are morally lax. He says that the absence of chastity in women (especially lacking in black women) is worse than the sexual irregularities of men because "the offense of men is individual and limited while that of women is general and strikes mortally at the existence of the family itself."[12] In a curious lack of logic, but a perfect illustration of the interaction of racial and sexual assumptions, he goes on to say that if a white man fornicates with a "negress," he only debases himself and dishonors his body, but he in no way impairs the dignity or integrity of his race. "He may sin against himself and others, and even against his God, but not against the germ-plasma of his kind."[13] That is to say, because a man's sin is individual, as opposed to a woman's larger sins against the family and race when she commits sexual transgressions, it is of little consequence that white men fornicate with black women, for they do not contaminate the white race. This line of reasoning helps to explain why it is the black woman who is consistently singled out for scorn. Her frequent sexual transgressions are perceived as having dire consequences for the integrity of the black race since it is women, not men, who bear the burden of keeping a race pure.

Howard Odum, a professor at the University of North Carolina at Chapel Hill, blames the weakness of black schools on the lack of moral strength in their black female teachers. In an entire chapter entitled "The Home Life, Diseases and Morals of the Negro" in his influential book on racial traits written in 1910, he blames the immoral black mother, among other factors, for the poor home life of blacks (one of the most frequently discussed Negro problems of the time). Moreover, though black women are held in high esteem by their own males, because they are good workers and providers for their families, they are not held to the same standards of morality as other women. "The worst comment of the negroes upon their women is the fact that they are not expected always to be faithful and that they are often considered unclean."[14] While this statement reveals the extent to which male-defined standards are considered the relevant ones, it also indicates that at least one white male feels that black men do not adhere to the prevailing ideology of True Womanhood in their assessments of their own women. Odum's perception of black male standards of womanhood is not borne out in the writings of many black men, however.

In an influential study published in 1889, Philip Bruce, a Virginia historian and son of a wealthy planter, who has the most to say about black women, devotes two chapters to a discussion of the various shortcomings of black women as a result of their defective moral sense. This virtually ruins relationships between them and their children and husbands and renders the black family degenerate. Though slave parents were incapable of providing moral instruction to their children, the situation is worse now.

> On the whole the parents of the present day are still more imperfect as ethical teachers and exemplars, because greater unsteadiness and laxness of conduct prevail among them under the freedom of the new regime. . . . They are now at liberty to act upon all the impulses of their nature. . . . The average father and mother are morally obtuse and indifferent, and at times even openly and unreservedly licentious. Their character is such . . . that they have no just conception of the parental obligation or the onerous duties that it should lay upon them. . . .[15]

What is worse, black mothers fail to instill in their daughters (the hope of the race) those virtues that females are supposed to possess.

> . . . their mothers do not endeavor to teach them, systematically, those moral lessons that they peculiarly need as members of the female sex; they learn to sew in a rude way, to wash, to iron, and to cook, but no principle is steadily instilled that makes them solicitous and resolute to preserve their reputations untarnished. Chastity is a virtue which the parents do not seem anxious to foster and guard in their daughter; she has no abiding sense of personal purity. . . .[16]

Furthermore, while slavery did nothing to "raise the dignity of marriage or to improve the relation of the sexes," the moral condition of black women has since deteriorated further.

> . . . they [blacks] celebrate their various entertainments . . . with so much spirit. These are . . . distinguished for low debauchery, which encourages a course of subsequent intercourse . . . that breaks down the last barrier between the sexes, the effect being peculiarly demoralizing to the character of the women, who properly should be bulwarks of sobriety and conservatism . . . whereas they are . . . the floodgates of the corrupting sexual influences that are doing so much to sap and destroy it. The number of illegitimate children born to unmarried negresses is becoming greater every year.[17]

Contrary to the standards that prevail in the white community, however, this situation is no obstacle to their marrying because black males do not fret about immorality in their women, which only makes the situation worse.

> . . . a life of gallantry on the part of females . . . cannot be said to jar upon the sensibilities of the men in general, for they have apparently no sense of delicacy. . . . As a rule, they marry the most indiscreet of the other sex with as much unconscious satisfaction as the purest. . . . This state of mind . . . with respect to the conduct of the women they marry, is very injurious to the moral tone of the unmarried women, for it removes the most powerful influence that could . . . make them prudent, inasmuch as the thoughtless and wanton can secure husbands with the same ease as the virtuous and circumspect.[18]

Even her own women do not censure her because of her behavior.

> A plantation negress may have sunk to a low point in the scale of sensual indulgence, and yet her position does not seem to be substantially affected even in the estimation of the women of her own race, who . . . if we followed the analogy of women of all other races . . . would be even unjustly severe on her contempt for decency. . . . The truth is that neither the women nor the men . . . look upon lasciviousness as impurity. . . .[19]

That is, black women do not have to live up to a standard of morality (or adhere to the cult of True Womanhood) because no such values exist in the black community. Furthermore, black men never even have to rape their women, because of the women's constant willingness to engage in sex.

> He is so accustomed to the wantonness of the women of his own race that it is not strange that his intellect, having no perception of personal dignity or the pangs of outraged feeling, should be unable to gauge the terrible character of this offense against the integrity of virtuous womanhood. . . . The rape of a negress by a male of her own color is almost unheard of, a fact that is a strong proof of the sexual laxness of the plantation women as a class; for if they attached any importance to sexual purity, and strenuously resisted all improper encroachment upon it, the criminal records of the negro men would contain details of many such assaults.[20]

He implies, in perhaps the most degrading comments made about black women, that they are so thoroughly debased sexually that they willingly give their bodies to men, making rape a crime with which they are totally unfamiliar. Bruce, in keeping with dominant racial attitudes, leaves his readers with the impression that the average wife is responsible for the degradation of the institution of marriage among blacks and that unless a fundamental change occurs in her character, the race is doomed to extinction.

A similar argument is made by Eleanor Tayleur, a southern white woman, who also feels that the destiny of a race is inextricably bound to the moral character of its women and that, since the black woman is "the most anomalous and portentous figure in America today," the Negro race is doomed.[21] She attributes the decadence of "the new negro woman," a post-Civil War phenomenon, to the deterioration of home life (present during slavery because the masters provided it), her disdain for honest work, especially domestic labor, and her loss of close personal contact with white women (also present during slavery).

> Before the war the negro woman was brought into intimate contact with the refined and educated women of the dominant race. . . . they copied the manners and the morals of the mistress they served. Many a black woman was a grande dame who would have graced a court. . . . The modern negro woman has no such object-lesson in morality or modesty, and she wants none.[22]

Now, she is jealous of white women, treats them with childlike brutality, and when she imitates white women, she imitates only their worst qualities.

> She copies her extravagance in tawdry finery that is a grotesque exaggeration of fashion, she copies her independence in utter abandon of all restraints, she copies her vices and adds to them frills of her own.[23]

Furthermore, she is an unfit mother because of defects in her character and is even criminal in her treatment of infants. This charge is ironic given the mammy role for which black women were constantly praised during slavery.

> For her children she has fierce passion of maternity that seems to be purely animal, and that seldom goes beyond their childhood. When they are little, she indulges them blindly when she is in good humor, and beats them cruelly when she is angry; and once past their childhood her affection for them appears to be exhausted. She exhibits none of the brooding mother-love and anxiety which the white woman sends after her children as long as they live. Infanticide is not regarded as a crime among negroes, but it is so appallingly common that if the statistics could be obtained on this subject they would send a shudder through the world. The story of many negro midwives, who are veritable female Herods, is not a thing to be told.[24]

Echoing other whites mentioned earlier, Tayleur indicates that immorality in women is not frowned upon in the black community, so that there is no incentive for black women to develop moral qualities.

There is no public opinion to be defied, no society to turn the cold shoulder upon her. She loses no caste changing husbands, as the whim seizes her, and no odium is attached to the possession of what she graphically . . . described as a "bandanna family"—meaning thereby one in which each child is a different color.[25]

The black woman is also the best example to be used to demonstrate the fallacy of the theory of free love for, with no support from the men with whom she freely engages in sex, "the negro woman stands at the gate of the garden of free-lovism, and cries out that it is a false paradise—that all of its fruits are apples of Sodom, and that nowhere else is a woman's sorrow so inescapable, and her lot so bitter." (p. 220) So it is ridiculous that the black woman, "with the brain of a child and the passions of a woman, steeped in centuries of ignorance and savagery, and wrapped about with immemorial vices," (p. 270) should hold the destiny of the Negro race in her hands. Since the real uplift of the race and the solving of the race problem are impossible without first arousing "this lethargic giantess to a sense of her responsibilities," it is incumbent upon white women to proceed with this overwhelming task, or else their own race is also threatened.

> The mission of the white woman of this country is to the black woman. If ever there was a God given and appointed task set to the womanhood of any people, it is to the women of America to take these lowly sisters by the hand and lift them out of the pit into which they have fallen . . . for be assured unless we succor these Hagars who have been thrust out into the desert of their own ignorance and superstition and sin, they will raise up Ishmaels whose hands shall be against our sons forever.[26]

Here, her desire for racial uplift seems to be motivated more by concern for the white race. In fact, despite her apparent desire to help black women, the overwhelming tone of the article is quite negative if one examines closely the imagery and allusions used. Black women are compared to Frankenstein and Herod, both of whom are despicable male figures. The extent to which the black woman is defeminized throughout the article is revealed in analogies between her and males. Ironically, Tayleur overlooked comparable female figures, which underscores the black woman's negative masculine traits.

She also attributes the particular plight of black women to the inability of black men, on whom they cannot rely for protection or support, to live up to the True Manhood ideal.

45

No other woman among civilized people is so little protected, so little cherished, and evokes so little chivalry from the men of her race. All the hardships that other men endure she bears, and more. She loves, but no sense of loyalty, no convention of faithfulness, binds her lover to her. She may marry, but with no certainty of the tie being permanent. She bears children, but with . . . no husband's hand to even provide the food and clothing. When she toils, it is only too frequently to have her meager wage taken from her by a drunken brute. No other race in the world shows such a number of men supported by women as does the negro race.[27]

Perhaps the most vicious attack on black women, one totally void of any sympathy for her plight, is an article written by an unidentified southern white woman in a series on the race problem that appeared in *The Independent* in 1904 following a race riot in Ohio. The article begins with a discussion of the author's fear of black men who are a menace to all southern white women, but her most scurrilous remarks are reserved for black women, who must be blamed for the crimes against white women that black men commit. Ironically, she accuses black women, because they belong to the weaker sex, of being even more depraved than their men.

And so degeneracy is apt to show most in the weaker individuals of any race; so negro women evidence more nearly the popular idea of total depravity than the men do. . . . They are the greatest menace possible to the moral life of any community where they live. And they are evidently the chief instruments of the degradation of the men of their own race. When a man's mother, wife and daughters are all immoral women, there is no room in his fallen nature for the aspiration of honor and virtue. . . . I sometimes read of virtuous negro women, hear of them, but the idea is absolutely inconceivable to me. . . . I can not imagine such a creature as a virtuous black woman.[28]

Similarly, another southern white woman, who also writes of her fears of "the negro brute," alludes to the immorality of black women, the increase in illegitimate children since slavery, and to the fact that "the most prominent women in their religious enthusiasms are oftenest public prostitutes."[29] And finally, an Alabama woman indicates that though she has spent thirty-five years in the South, she has met only one chaste black woman. All of her female servants had illegitimate children and were born out of wedlock themselves. Furthermore, slavery cannot be blamed for the immorality of black women, which is an innate racial trait that education cannot alter.[30] She also refers to black women as stupid and deceitful and is especially hostile to mulattoes to whom she refers as "yellow Jezebels" and prostitutes.[31]

In the article that ends the series, a northern white woman who has moved South disagrees with the thesis of the article above and argues that "it is the prejudice of the white man more than the worthlessness and depravity of the blacks which has given us a negro question."[32] She also argues that southerners' ignorance of white servants makes them "ascribe solely to colored women what, unfortunately, is not unknown among white ones of the same class."[33] That is to say, immorality in women is more a function of class than of race.

The theme of the sexual promiscuity of black women is also treated in the fiction of white women.[34] Gertrude Stein's *Three Lives*, written from 1905-06, is appropriate for a brief discussion here because it is one of the few narratives by a white woman during the period that focuses entirely on a young black woman and her relationships with her female friends and lovers.[35] Though the novella focuses on Melanctha, a turn-of-the-century tragic mulatto, when the story opens, the focus is Melanctha's good friend, Rose, "a real black, tall well-built, sullen, stupid, childlike, good looking negress" who has married Sam, "a tall square shouldered, decent, a serious straightforward, simple, kindly colored workman," whom she had met at church.[36] An argument that appeared frequently in the nonfiction of the period—that immorality is no deterrent to black women marrying—is illustrated dramatically in Rose's case. Despite moral laxity, she is still able to attract a decent husband and the assumption is that black men do not perceive immoral women to be unsuitable marriage partners.

The use of black women characters as embodiments of white myths and fantasies is even more apparent in the portrait of Melanctha, a mulatto with a black father and a white mother. Addison Gayle, the noted critic of black novels, comments on prevalent stereotypes that appeared in the fiction of the period and what they revealed about whites:

> Never before in the history of civilization have men bent their energies more toward denigrating a race of people; no other century, save the nineteenth, witnessed the purposive attempt of a nation to transform a people into images of its own fantasy.[37]

Paule Marshall, the contemporary black novelist, also comments on the use of black women as embodiments of myths and fantasies "that have little to do with her and much to do with the troubled and repressed conscience of the country, which has reached so far down in the national psyche that not even the best of the white writers have escaped it."[38] Gertrude Stein, who "also adhered to the old images," is no exception to the generalization. Marshall goes on to say that while the story is a philosophical one dealing with the conflict between instinct and reason, Stein relies on conventional types to illustrate her theme.

> Instinct is the sullen, stupid promiscuous Rose, to use Miss Stein's adjectives. Reason is the graceful, pale yellow, intelligent, attractive Melanctha.[39]

Melanctha manifests schizophrenic behavior, which is typical of mulattoes[40]—due presumably to the warring of black and white blood in her veins. Addison Gayle sums up this "schizophrenic inheritance" in Melanctha rather succinctly:

> From her mother, she inherited the civilized virtues, correct standards of living, proper manner, and ladylike qualities: from her savage black father, she inherited nuances and rhythms of her jungle past.[41]

While Stein's fictional portrait merely suggests that a primary cause of immorality in black women is their inherent animalism, the writings of southern white men contain an explicit treatment of this theme. The black woman as animal stereotype is to be distinguished from the more frequently discussed "brute Negro" stereotype which was prominent in the minds of Americans, especially southerners, at the turn of the century, but which applied to the black male. White writers thought that this animal sexuality that black women possessed did not result in criminal behavior on their parts (as was the case with black men who raped white women), but could be used to justify their sexual exploitation at the hands of white men. In other words, white men could turn to them for the uninhibited sex that was denied them by white women. Thomas Bailey, a southern dean at the University of Mississippi, comments on this phenomenon.

> Southerners do not ordinarily have the biological and aesthetic repulsion that is usually felt by Northerners toward the Negro. . . . The memory of ante-bellum concubinage and a tradition of animal satisfaction due to the average negro woman's highly developed animalism are factors still in operation. Not a few "respectable" white men have been heard to express physiological preference for negro women.[42]

Her animality is also manifest in the anger she expresses during quarrels and fights with other women, which are frequent and violent occurrences in the black community. Savage animal imagery pervades the following description:

> . . . such negroes are raving amazons . . . apparently growing madder and madder each moment, eyes rolling, lips protruding, feet stamping, pawing, gesticulating. . . . This frenzied madness . . . seems beyond control. . . . With the men the manifestations are less violent.[43]

Animal imagery is also used in William D. Howells' *Imperative Duty* (published in 1892), a novella about a white girl who learns that she has Negro ancestry (her mother was an octoroon), immediately flees to Boston's black neighborhoods, and ends up at a black church so she can "surround herself with the blackness from which she had sprung."[44] Her descriptions of the women in the church (as well as the black fellows in the streets) contain animal overtones.

> . . . Rhoda distinguished faces, sad, repulsive visages of a frog-like ugliness added to the repulsive black in all its shades. . . . One old woman . . . opened her mouth like a catfish to emit these pious ejaculations . . . as the church filled, the musky exhalations of their bodies thickened the air, and made the girl faint; it seemed to her that she began to taste the odor; and these poor people whom their Creator had made so hideous by the standards of all his other creatures, roused a cruel loathing in her . . . . "Yes," she thought, "I should have whipped them, too. They are animals; they are only fit to be slaves." But when she shut her eyes and heard their wild, soft voices, her other senses were holden. . . . (p. 197)

The black woman's ugliness, rather than her sexuality, is being emphasized in the references to her animality. In sum, the black woman's promiscuity and physical unattractiveness—overt manifestations of her animal-like traits—cause her to be devalued because she is unable to reach the standard of feminine beauty and behavior required of "ideal" women.

While the devaluation of black women is illustrated most frequently by references to their immorality, what is interesting is the lack of agreement concerning who or what to blame for this condition. Most whites seemed to feel that immorality was an inherent racial trait in American blacks because of their savage African ancestors and that black women were especially guilty. However, some whites questioned the charge or blamed themselves or the environment, rather than defective genes. In this regard, Ray Stannard Baker, a northern journalist, bemoaned the plight of black girls, especially southerners, because of their sexual exploitation by white men and the peculiar conditions under which they lived.

> It is remarkable . . . that the Negroes should have begun to develop moral standards as rapidly as they have. For in the South few people *expect* the coloured girl to be moral: everything is against her morality. In the first place, the home life of the great mass of Negroes is still primitive. They are crowded together in one or two rooms, they get no ideas of privacy, or of decency. The girls are the prey not only of white men but of men of their own race. The highest ideal before their eyes is the finely dressed prosperous concubine of a white man. . . .
> When the coloured girl grows up, she goes to service in a white family . . . or goes home at night. In either event the mistress rarely pays the slightest attention to her conduct. . . . It may be imagined how difficult it is in such an atmosphere for Negroes to build up moral standards, or to live decently. If there ever was a human tragedy in this world it is the tragedy of the Negro girl.[45]

Similarly, W. D. Weatherford, a liberal southern white male, argued in 1915 in a book with an interesting history[46] that the sexual immorality among blacks (which was also causing health problems, including infant mortality and venereal diseases) was related to substandard and crowded housing. Weatherford cited statistics from Du Bois' Atlanta University studies, for example, that indicated that in 1897, 117 families lived in single-room dwellings. In the seventh ward of Philadelphia in 1899, 828 families (35 percent) lived in one-room houses. Environmental conditions, then, are to be blamed for the moral decadence of blacks.

> So long as people are huddled together in filthy houses . . . so long will they be lacking in that pride and self-respect which makes for morality. A man living on a clean street . . . is a more decent and moral man than he would be were he living on a back alley. A man who has had a bath is surely more apt to have clean thoughts than the man who never bathes. . . . Further, people cannot be moral so long as they are herded together like cattle without privacy or decency. . . . If a mother, a father, three grown daughters, and men boarders have to sleep in two small rooms, we must expect lacks of modesty, promiscuity, illegitimacy and sexual diseases. . . . No nation in modern times can work and sleep, bring forth children and come to death in one-room cabins.[47]

He also argues that another solution to the race problem (especially race degeneracy) would take place when "white men ceased their ravages of colored girls."[48] Since many of the incidents that he cites concerning this problem came from the black males present at the meeting, it seems safe to assume that Weatherford was made more sensitive to this issue because of the presence of black men who were apparently quite vocal about this evil "which is the plague of white and black alike."[49] In fact, he goes on to say that when white men exploit black girls it is an even more horrendous crime than their exploitation of white girls because of the greater vulnerability of black girls.

> It is a crime as black as night when a man robs a white girl of her purity, even though she consents—but she is his equal in moral strength and has powers of self-protection. The negro girl, however, has no such equal chance in the struggle; so, when a white man takes advantage of one who is socially down, who cannot protect herself, he is a fiend of the blackest die. . . . If we expect the black man to respect our women—and he must—then we must force our white men to keep hands off the negro girl—whether she be pure or impure. There must not be any mingling of the races.[50]

Though Weatherford may actually be more disturbed by race mingling than the sexual abuse of black women, he does shift the blame from black women to white men in his discussion of what can be done to improve the plight of blacks in the South.

Similarly, in an unusual short story entitled "The White Brute" written in 1907, Mary White Ovington, a northern white liberal, portrays the southern white male as the culprit. The race problem is presented as having nothing to do with the immorality of black women but rather with the sexual depravity of white men. In this particular story a recently married black couple is traveling by train in Mississippi on a Jim Crow car. While Sam and Melinda are waiting to change trains, two white men approach, force Melinda to leave her new husband for two hours, and rape her despite the pleas of her husband and his desire to protect her.

> I's worked for the white boss, I's ploughed and sowed and picked for him. I's been a good nigger. Now I asks you, masters, to play fair. I asks you to leave me alone wid what's mine. Don't touch my wife![51]

Fearing that he will be lynched and that his new wife will be even more vulnerable to such sexual exploitation, he permits his wife to be whisked away. The story is a perfect illustration of the sensitivity of some white women to the sexual exploitation of southern black women by white males and the utter powerlessness of their men to protect them given the potential consequences of such action.

John James Holm, an atypical writer from Wisconsin who believed in the equality of the races, also blames his own race for the moral laxity of blacks and rejects the notion of the inherent criminality of blacks. "As long as there is no respect for the colored womanhood of America, by the white man of the country, so long will it be impossible to cultivate and infuse a higher moral tone in the race."[52] His solution to the race problem, especially the degradation of black women, is to remove the barriers preventing the legal marriage of whites and blacks. First, he blames "our civilization" for its depleted sense of decency. Later, he appeals to white women to help their wronged sisters and pays tribute to black women for having endured all manner of debasement.

> . . . the African woman has gone with the white man through an enforced vale of tears, degradation and shame, and has not once shrunk from the care, responsibility and duty of rearing . . . her illegitimate children by him. She unreservedly deserves the laurels of a superior womanhood for so faithfully and lovingly, under the most trying circumstances, caring for her white babies and thereby improving her race. She has done more than her duty.[53]

Similarly, an unidentified journalist from New England who traveled in the South after the Civil War wrote about his personal experiences there in a prominent literary magazine. He blames the white man for the immorality of black women and claims that the purity of southern women has come at their expense.

> Young men . . . always dwell with proud and endless iteration on "the superior purity of Southern women." . . . They do not recognize the fact . . . that the women of another race, formerly helpless and now degraded, have always formed a protecting barrier between the licentious passions of Southern white men and the women of their own race. I do not suppose the best women of the South have any superiors on earth, but, their immunity from temptation and wrong has cost other women dear.[54]

It seems that at least some non-southerners rejected many of the racial attitudes that prevailed in the South at the turn of the century.

Perhaps because she is female, Eleanor Tayleur is also sensitive to the plight of black women and does not blame them *entirely* for their moral decadence. She argues that the black woman is a monster created by society for whom sympathy is in order because she is doubly victimized by her racial and sexual identity. Tayleur also realizes that black women should not be judged by standards that apply to white women.

> As she exists in the South today the Negro woman is the Frankenstein product of civilization, a being created out of conditions of sectional hate and revenge. . . . There is no other figure so forlorn and pathetic as she. Doubly cursed by her color and her sex, on her has fallen alike the heaviest burden of the negro and of the womanhood. Shut out by her sex from the opportunities of the Negro man, she is the victim of every injustice of society. . . . She has always been hapless sacrifice to the lust of man. . . .[55]

Ironically, this article, cited earlier because of its references to the debased nature of black womanhood, contains intense anti-black female remarks at the same time that it reveals a sensitivity to the unique status of black women in white America. It advances the "double jeopardy" argument that contemporary black feminists have popularized, while it also refers to black women as ignorant creatures and "kinky-headed little coons." This ambivalence can be attributed perhaps to her unconscious racism and to her identification, at the same time, with black women because of their common gender identity. As a southerner, it would have been difficult for her to transcend the racial attitudes that pervaded the region.

Lily Hammond, the liberal daughter of slave-holding parents, argues on the other hand that white women themselves must share some responsibility for the plight of their darker sisters. The destiny of the Negro race is in the hands of privileged white women who must see "the recognition of womanhood as a thing deeper even than race, a thing for all women to protect."[56] The "race question" will be solved only when white women reach out to black women and help them improve their homes.

> . . . the foundation of all morality is the home. . . . and the full prosperity of Southern industry and commerce waits . . . upon the moral status of the Negro home. It is the privileged white women who alone can fix this status for the entire community, building it up in white respect, and helping the better class of colored women to build it up in colored life. . . . To perform it they are adventuring into the unknown, discovering their cooks and washerwomen as women beset by womanhood's clamorous demands and utterly unable to meet them without help and sympathy.[57]

In other words, the "bond of common womanhood" should propel black and white women to work together toward common goals, which is the only solution to the race problem, and of course white women must assume the lead since they represent the more highly developed race.

> The status of the Negro woman and the Negro home in the minds of the privileged white women will determine the status of the race. Among all races, in all times, it has been the lot of the women to bear the unbearable things. As they have won respect and protection the race has climbed toward freedom and self-control. There is no way to raise Negroes except by this world-old process and no one can set it in motion as can our Southern white women.[58]

Furthermore, Hammond reminds her audience of some comments made by a southern Methodist elder blaming white women for perpetuating immorality among blacks.

> "You white women," he said, "are the main obstacle to Negro morality. You teach us men, and your children—your sons—that morality in a Negro woman is beneath a white person's notice." You refuse to give a Negro wife her legal title of 'Mrs.' . . . You Christian women refuse it to women sufficiently handicapped . . . without this added difficulty. I'm not talking about your cooks; in the kitchen a woman of no race would expect the use of her legal title; but you refuse it to the race. You make no distinction between the Christian wife and the mother of half-a-dozen haphazard mulattoes; they're 'Sally' to you. You say, in effect, that morality in a Negro doesn't count. You teach your sons that from babyhood. The Negro women pay for it; but by God's law your sons pay, too—pay a debt more yours than theirs. And the daughters they marry pay, too."[59]

That is to say, when white women refuse to respect black women by addressing them with appropriate titles or refuse to make distinctions between moral and immoral black women, then inadvertent messages are sent to other whites, especially men, who then grow up to disrespect black women. Everyone involved is hurt by this situation, however, including the women white men marry who must presumably experience the pain associated with the knowledge that their husbands are sexually involved with black women (whom they have been taught by their mothers to disrespect).

In her 1914 book on race relations, in which she blamed environmental factors rather than defective genes for the "Negro question," she discussed at length the injustices that blacks suffered in her native South, and she was particularly disturbed by the indignities to which both refined and poor black women were subjected. Near the end of her analysis, she delivered an eloquent plea to her southern sisters, on the basis of all women's common identities as mothers, to see themselves linked to all women of the world and to especially respect black women.

> Being a woman goes deeper than being of this race or that. . . . Have we not reason to stand together, we women of the world? A Chinese girl hawked publicly by her owner on the streets of Shanghai . . . Negro girls whom men of no race reverence—where is the difference. They are women, women all; and women bore them. . . . We need to see . . . the women of our poor as women first, and black afterwards. We need to think of negro womanhood as sacred, as the womanhood of all the world must be.[60]

While it is not surprising given the widespread acceptance of Negro inferiority throughout the nation during this time that white writers, male and female, would advance the thesis that black women, for a variety of reasons, were morally defective, it is shocking that some blacks also accepted the dominant culture's definitions of the race. This group tended to be educated, of mixed blood and victims of "cultural schizophrenia."[61] The most obvious and extreme example of this phenomenon is to be found in a scathing attack on black women by William Hannibal Thomas, a mulatto teacher who was frequently cited by racist whites as support for their arguments.[62] The sins of the black woman that Thomas enumerated were presumably more difficult to deny since they had been observed by an insider. He argued that the destiny of a people is tied to its women and therefore blacks are doomed because of their immoral women.

> . . . not only are fully ninety percent of the negro women of America lascivious by instinct and in bondage to physical pleasure, but . . . the social degradation of our freed-women is without parallel in modern civilization. . . . The moral status of a race is fixed by the character of its women; but, as moral rectitude is not a predominant trait in negro nature, female chastity is not one of its endowments.[63]

In the area of sexual behavior the black woman is especially wicked.

> It is . . . almost impossible to find a person of either sex, over fifteen years of age, who has not had carnal knowledge. . . . Innate modesty is not a characteristic of the American Negro women. On the contrary, there is . . . a willing susceptibility to the blandishments of licentious men, together with a widespread distribution of physical favors among their male friends. . . . Marriage is no barrier to illicit sexual indulgence, and both men and women maintain such relations in utter disregard of their plighted troth. . . . Women unresistingly betray their wifely honor to satisfy a bestial instinct.[64]

55

These traits, moreover, are not peculiar to the lower classes, "but are equally common among those who presume to be educated and refined."[65]

Especially disturbing to Thomas is the fact that black women fail as wives and mothers, the most important function women have.

> Negro women . . . have but dim notions of the nature and obligations of wifehood. . . . So visibly universal is the strife for personal adornment that Negro mothers cannot be held blameless for the immoralities of their daughters, and there is at least ground for believing that sexual impurity is deliberately inculcated in them, since . . . their maternal guardians appear to be never so pleased as when the physical charms of their daughters have procured for them dress and jewels . . . negro women are . . . weak in purpose, timid in execution, superstitious in thought, lascivious in conduct, and signally lacking in those enduring qualities which make for morality, thrift, and industry. . . . Negro motherhood is not animated with profound convictions of truth and duty. The freedwomen evidently do not realize that they are the custodians of the souls as well as the bodies of their children, and the first and chief teachers in life of purity . . . of right-doing . . . and the God-ordained creators of *true manhood and womanhood* [emphasis added]. On the contrary, they bring to the discharge of their domestic duties illiterate minds, unskilled hands, impetuous tempers, untidy deportment, and shiftless methods.[66]

In other words, black women have not internalized any traits that characterize the True Woman ideal, the main components of which Thomas fully endorses. Black women are especially inept in the domestic sphere, the assigned place for women in the nineteenth-century order of things. In his most damaging indictment, he blames black women for whatever differences exist between whites and blacks.

> . . . there is a fundamental difference in the racial character, habits, integrity, courage, and strength of negro and white Americans. What makes it? The answer lies in one word—their women. . . . Girls of the two races will grow up side by side, attend the same schools . . . enjoy equal mental advantages, yet the chances are two to one that the negro girl at twenty will be a giggling idiot and lascivious wreck, while her white companion . . . has blossomed out into chaste womanhood, intelligent in mind and accomplished in manner. This difference between them becomes of fundamental significance when we reflect that each girl represents the future maternal life-blood of her respective people.[67]

He has accepted the conventional notion that black women are not only hopelessly degenerate unless they make basic changes in their character, but also that white women are paragons of virtue and models of womanhood whom they should emulate. He concludes by saying that whites must assume responsibility for uplifting blacks who are incapable of redeeming themselves. Northern white women must especially be "aroused to a sense of the needs and wants of a degraded black sisterhood" and should train young black women to abhor immorality and aspire to chaste living.[68]

In an attempt to counter increasing attacks, such as the one above, which served to "magnify the moral weakness of Negro womanhood,"[69] black women wrote many articles for popular magazines in defense of the character of black women. In answer to the question "Whence comes all this talk about the immorality of the Negro woman?" Mrs. Hunton, president of the Atlanta Women's Club, responds by saying that the "unmerciful criticism" heaped on black men comes from persons who "know little or nothing of that best element of our women who are quietly and unobtrusively working out the salvation of the race."[70] In other words, the attackers are generalizing about all black women based upon their own limited experiences with and observations about a particular class of black women. This intense class consciousness made middle-class black women especially perturbed over the tendency among whites to be blinded to differences among black women. Frequently paternalistic in their attitudes toward their less fortunate sisters, elite women such as Hunton, Margaret Murray Washington (the wife of Booker T. Washington) and Fannie B. Williams felt it was their duty, however, to inform the general public about the educated class of black women and their mission of racial uplift among the masses.

> It is the credit of the higher usefulness of the colored club woman that she has taken the initiative in doing something to reach and help a class of women who have lived isolated from all the regenerating and uplifting influences of freedom and education. It is the first touch of sympathy that has connected the progressive colored woman with her neglected and unprogressive sister.[71]

Whatever shortcomings these less privileged black women have, however, it is also imperative that those who would slander them be informed of the struggles as well as the strengths of black women in the face of adversity which make them a special breed of woman.

> . . . in the face of all this ignominy—all this immorality and cruel oppression—she has staggered up through the ages ladened with the double burden of excessive maternal care and physical toil, and she has . . . thrown off much of the dross and become more chastened and purified, conforming

herself as fast as possible to the demand for upright Christian living. . . . in spite of all accusations the Negro woman has been the motive power in whatever has been accomplished by the race. She early realized that the moral and conservative qualities of a race reside in its womanhood, and with this realization came a longing and a reaching after a virtuous home life; hence, we have thousands of homes. . . . citadels of purity and virtue, presided over by women of intelligence and house-wifely care.[72]

Additionally, the American public should know about the new Negro woman, "the real new woman in American life," who is a revelation for those "knowing only the menial type."[73] Well educated, refined, courageous, and involved in every profession "not prohibited by American prejudices," she is a credit to the nation as well as to her race.

> This woman, as if by magic, has succeeded in lifting herself as completely from the stain and meanness of slavery as if a century had elapsed since the day of emancipation. This new woman . . . has come to the front in an opportune time. . . . This woman is needed as an educator of public opinion. She is a happy refutation of the idle insinuation and common skepticism as to the womanly worth and promise of the whole race of women. She has come to enrich American life with finer sympathies, and to enlarge the boundary of fraternity and the democracy of love among American women. She has come to join her talents, her virtues, her intelligence, her sacrifices and her love in the work of redeeming the unredeemed. . . . She has come to bring new hope and fresh assurances to the hapless young women of her own race. . . . They have begun to make the virtues as well as the wants of the colored women known to the American people.[74]

The continued sexual assault of black women after slavery in both the North and the South prompted black men and women alike to write popular magazines articles appealing to the American public to put a stop to this abuse. In a 1912 issue of *The Independent*,[75] a southern black nurse from Georgia, who for thirty years was a servant in white households, recounts, after describing in detail the horrible conditions under which she worked, an experience she had of being fired when she refused "to let the madam's husband kiss me."[76] She was young and newly married then but learned quickly "that a colored woman's virtue in this part of the country has no protection" (p. 198). She heard about similar incidents from other women and concluded that "nearly all white men take undue liberties with their colored female servants—not only the fathers, but in many cases the sons also" (p. 198). What is worse, this moral debasement is sometimes encouraged by their white wives who preferred for their husbands to sleep with black women rather than sleep around with outside white women." In other words, they preferred "to keep their husbands straight" rather than encourage the morality of black women. She ends by an appeal to southern white women to realize that it is in their best interest to come to the defense of black women, who, in their roles as mammies, have such an influence on white children.

> If none others will help us, it would seem that the Southern white women themselves might do so in their own defense, because we are rearing their children . . . and it is inevitable that the lives of their children will in some measure be pure or impure according as they are affected by contact with their colored nurses.[77]

Similarly, in a series of articles on "the race problem" published in *The Independent* in 1904, a southern black woman alludes to her father's desire after the war to support his family by his own efforts so that his wife and daughters would not have to "be thrown in contact with Southern white men in their homes." When she grew up, married, and had daughters of her own she vowed that she would protect them in the same way her father had protected her.

> There is no sacrifice I would not make, no hardship I would not undergo rather than allow my daughters to go in service where they would be thrown constantly in contact with Southern white men, for they consider the colored girl their special prey.[78]

A variety of factors can explain why most blacks took a radically different stance from most whites in the debate over the alleged immorality of black women. As a response to their deteriorating status in America at the end of Reconstruction, blacks developed a philosophy of self-help, racial pride, and solidarity.[79] Many of the attitudes, therefore, that blacks expressed with respect to black women can be viewed within the context of this broader canvas of racial thought, since many of their comments were intended to foster in their community a sense of pride and solidarity by paying tribute to their women at a time when they were being publicly humiliated.

Jack Thorne, journalist and Pullman porter in New York, reiterates in a pamphlet the abuse that black women have suffered at the hands of white men and pleads with black men to develop a chivalrous posture toward them as all strong men must do with their weak women.

> . . . it is our duty to begin the work of properly safeguarding the mother of our children. . . . When we have advanced to that stage where the intrinsic worth of the purity of womanhood is known and appreciated we will then realize the degrading influence of American slavery. . . . No men of any race have the right to boast of education or wealth whose women are under the control and domination of the men of another race. . . . Have the Negro woman [sic] remembered that in these wild shoutings for the protection of womanhood she is not considered; if she is to be protected, honored . . . it is to be done by the men of her own race. . . . If he is to hold his own and be counted among those who shall survive as "the fittest" it is to be through the chastity and purity of the woman. . . . That time is past when concubinage should be winked at. . . .[80]

That is, black men must safeguard the virtues of their women, as other men do, so that they can attain the virtues appropriate to the True Woman.

In order to counter the charge that black women were immoral, many black men shifted the blame to the institution of slavery and its aftermath. Alexander Crummell, prominent Episcopalian minister and outspoken intellectual, and W. E. B. Du Bois, whose glowing tributes to black womanhood and whose sensitivity to the plight of these "daughters of sorrow"[81] are without parallel, were the most eloquent in their delineation of one of the most destructive aspects of slavery—the stripping away of the womanhood of the female slave. Crummell has this to say in a pamphlet, *The Black Woman of the South: Her Neglects and Her Needs*, which he published in 1881 and distributed himself:

> In her girlhood all the delicate tenderness of her sex has been rudely outraged. . . . No chance was given her for delicate reserve or tender modesty. From her childhood she was the doomed victim of the grossest passion. All the virtues of her sex were utterly ignored. If the instinct of chastity asserted itself, then she had to fight like a tiger for the ownership . . . of her own person. . . . When she reached maturity, all the tender instincts of her womanhood were ruthlessly violated. At the age of marriage . . . she was mated as the stock of the plantation were mated. . . . There was no sanctity of family, no binding ties of marriage, none of the fine felicities and the endearing affectations of home. . . . Instead thereof a gross barbarism which tended to blunt ·the tender sensibilities to obliterate feminine delicacy and womanly shame.[82]

Similarly, a persistent theme in the writings of Du Bois is the victimization of black women, which he believes is the most terrible injustice of slavery.

Alexander Crummell (1819-1898), abolitionist, teacher, scholar, missionary, and minister, was active in the Negro Convention Movement. He founded St. Luke's Church in Washington, D.C., taught at Howard University from 1895 to 1897 and organized the American Negro Academy that same year. His book *Africa and America: Addresses and Discourses* (1891) contains an extensive discussion of the plight of black women.

I shall forgive the white South much in its final judgement day; I shall forgive its slavery, for slavery is a world-old habit. . . . I shall forgive its so-called "pride of race," the passion of its hot blood, and even its dear, old, laughable strutting and posing; but one thing I shall never forgive . . . its wanton and continued and persistent insulting of the black womanhood which it sought and seeks to prostitute to its lust.[83]

His poem "The Burden of Black Women" also deals with the evils of white men, to whom he refers as "spoilers of women" and "shameless breeders of bastards."[84] He is especially critical of their sexual exploitation of the black woman, whom he describes as "a prisoned soul a-panting to be free" of "the White Man's Burden of Liquor and Lust and Lies!" In a poem with a remarkably similar title, "The Black Woman's Burden," Daniel Webster Davis describes the double sexual exploitation that black women, "ye daughters of a long downtrodden race,"[85] suffer at the hands of both black and white men, though he is more critical of the latter:

Hard is the task to battle 'gainst the lust
Of thine own blood, whose lecherous men
So oft thy truth would try. Thy Scylla this,
And they Chyribdis is the sinful aim of those
Of yet another race, whose men oft feel
Thy virtue is their lustful prey.

What emerges from these vehement protests on the part of Crummell, Du Bois, and Thorne, however, is an idealized image of black womanhood. She becomes the black counterpart of the "ideal woman" to whom so many nineteenth-century males paid homage. A careful analysis of this tendency on the part of black activists to idolize the black woman, in much the same way that southern white men "paid homage to the shrine of womanhood,"[86] will reveal the extent to which black men subscribed to the notion that since women are the weaker sex they must be protected by their men from the evils of the world. This protection is even more critical for black women, since their predators also include lecherous white men who would rob them of their virtue with impunity. The more intense vulnerability of the black woman means that black men must assume an even greater chivalrous posture than white men and place black women even higher on their pedestals than white women. However, it is because of "this history of insult and degradation" that the black woman has emerged as a model of "efficient" and strong womanhood, the spiritual heir of Harriet Tubman and Sojourner Truth.[87] She should receive praise rather than scorn:

No other woman on earth could have emerged from the hell of force and temptation which once engulfed and still surrounds black women in America with half the modesty and womanliness that they retain. I have always felt like bowing myself before them in all abasement, searching to bring some tribute to these long-suffering victims . . . whom the world, the wise, white world, loves to affront and ridicule and wantonly to insult. I have known the women of many lands . . . but none have I known more sweetly feminine, more unswervingly loyal, more desperately earnest, and more instinctively pure in body and in soul than the daughters of my black mothers.[88]

If these comments seem exaggerated, one should be reminded of the prevailing stereotypes of black women that Du Bois and others were attempting to counteract. Crummell was also aware that the glorification and the new freedom for women that characterized their era did not apply to black women. Despite their degradation, however, he also recognizes their uniqueness.

The Negress is one of the most interesting of all the classes of women on the globe. . . . For, humble and benighted as she is, the black woman of the South is one of the queens of womanhood. If there is any other woman on this earth who in native aboriginal qualities is her superior, I know not where she is to be found. . . . in tenderness of feeling, in genuine native modesty. . . . in sweetness of disposition and deep humility, in unselfish devotedness, and in warm, motherly assiduities, the Negro woman is unsurpassed by any other woman on this earth.[89]

This attempt to place black women on a pedestal should be seen against the backdrop of the elevation of the white woman. Black men wanted their women to be worshipped in the same manner.

Further attempts to place black women on pedestals are manifested in two chronicles of their achievements by black males. Both were published in 1893 and were written in part to combat negative stereotypes about black womanhood.[90] Lawson A. Scruggs, a physician, says in his preface to *Women of Distinction* that the world does not fully appreciate the mind and character of the women of his race whose achievements should engender race pride. In a chapter on "Influence of Negro Women in the Home," he compliments black women for "preserving, maintaining and purifying the home," despite difficult circumstances (p. 376).

Similarly, Sutton Griggs,[91] unheralded novelist and social critic, was equally disturbed by the vulnerability of black women, which is apparent in both his fiction and nonfiction. In *Wisdom's Call* (1911), a book on the race problem, especially in the South, he devotes a chapter to a discussion of the southern black woman. Echoing Thorne, he illustrates, through the use of real-life examples that have been related to him, her lack of protection, a condition that her white counterparts are spared.[92] Though the black man should be her natural protector, circumstances in the South make this dangerous, if not impossible, so that the black woman hesitates to call on him. She must rely on statesman-like white men to protect her chastity (a solution that Thorne would reject) or white women who instill in their sons respect for black women. He ends his argument with an impassioned plea to the white race to work for the protection of black women so that blacks' dream of a pure race can be realized:

> . . . every interest of the white race . . . calls for the protection of the Negro woman. She should be encouraged to speak out. The courts should be thrown wide for her protection. She should not be left alone in her struggle to save her daughter from the wooers of the other race. The entire white South looking out for the ultimate purity of its own blood should . . . sound the slogan that the colored woman must have as sacred atmosphere to surround her and her daughters as the best civilization affords.
>
> Respect for the colored woman might be taught in the home, preached from the pulpit, advocated in the daily press and provided for by legislative enactments.[93]

Some black men were so disturbed by this lack of protection that they saw it as one of the most serious problems in the black community. Reverend R. A. Adams, president of the National Home Purity League, wrote an entire book, *The Negro Girl* (1914), which is full of advice to parents. He hoped the book would halt the degeneration of the womanhood of the race.[94] The young black servant girl who works in white homes is a particular concern. After describing in detail (through the use of stories from real life) the unique problems that young black girls face, especially in the South, he addresses his comments to black men.

> I wish I could arouse these Negro men to a sense of their duty to the womanhood of the race. . . . In the interest of the white girl there are organizations, statutes and volunteers to help, protect and save them. . . . If you think of the poor Negro girl, you realize she is not considered, but is left to suffer, and to die with little concern manifested for her.
>
> It is this condition of affairs which has induced me to write . . . which I hope will be a warning to young women who are sought as prey. . . . I

earnestly hope it will reach the Negro men, and awaken them to their duty, their responsibility, and their accountability.[95]

He goes on to remove the blame from black women for illicit relations between them and white men, despite accusations to the contrary.

> . . . that the Negro women in general are so anxious to be with white men . . . is one of the blackest lies ever told. . . . The Negro girl . . . does not seek the white man and seduce (?) [sic] him, but she is sought by him, and for him, and is made a prey in order to satisfy his awful, insatiate desire for the unlawful use of lawful things. She is the victim![96]

What is worse, this is done so the white girl can be saved—so that her purity and chastity can remain intact.[97]

The exploitation of black women and the need for black men to defend them are persistent twin themes for the many writers who used the novel as a vehicle of social protest. *Out of the Darkness*, published in 1909, dramatizes the numerous problems blacks faced after the Civil War and is perhaps the most explicit of the novels of the period in its defense of black women. Early in the narrative, the plight of black female domestics is revealed through an incident involving Leonora, a slave girl who finally succumbs to the uninvited advances of her master, for whom she later bears a son. This incident underscores the immorality of white men as opposed to the promiscuity of black women. Later, in a sermon, a black minister asks black men to respect their women who have had difficult lives.

> . . . you can nevah be truly brave or manly twell you learns ter 'spect yohselves, an' ter 'spect an' defend yoah wimmen. Our wimmen has hahd road ter travel. . . . Dey is de prey uv de white man an' many uv our own men. We do not guard an' 'spect de virtue uv our wimmen as we should. Dese things we has got ter learn ter practice an' teach ter ouah chillun. We is poah, an' ouah wimmen an' gals is compelled ter wurk wha dey is constantly beset by bad white men, who look 'pon dem as dahr lawful prey. No race can be great ur gran', whut does not honah it wimmen an ' is not willin' ter die fer dahr pertecshun . . . twell we learns ter treat ouah good wimmen wid dat 'spect dat is due ter 'onerable wimmen, we can't 'spect others ter 'spect dem, ur ter regahd us as a race uf true men.[98]

When Mr. Norris's daughter, Marie, is attacked by the white superintendent who has offered her a job, Norris shoots her attacker, but explains why he must defend her honor:

> Although my daughter is as pure as an angel, your juries would laugh at the idea that a Negro woman is virtuous. They would infer that she was there in your office for immoral purposes. So that I must, like you, take the law into my hands.[99]

Norris's friend Professor La Prade, who had rescued Marie from the attack, was later tried and found guilty as an accessory to the murder and sent to prison, but is content that he did his duty. "To die to save our poor, abused and misused womanhood from the blight of villainous outrage ought always to be sweet to true manhood" (p. 171).

Sutton Griggs also uses his novels to convey his strong belief that racial progress can be attained by black men adopting chivalrous behavior toward their women. In Griggs's first novel, Belton Piedmont, one of two main characters, suffers embarrassment and risks getting in trouble with the law in an incident involving his inability to pay the cab fare for a fellow female student once they arrive at the train station. When the driver suggests that the girl pay the difference, Belton reacts angrily and prevents him from asking the girl for money. This incident causes him to reflect on the impact of his recent college training, which enables Griggs to convey a message to his readers about the importance of respecting women.

> At Stowe University, Belton had learned to respect women. It was in these schools that the work of slavery in robbing colored women of respect, was undone. Woman now occupied the same position in Belton's eye as she did in the eye of the Anglo-Saxon.
> There is hope for that race or nation that respects its women. It was for the smile of a woman that the armored knight of old rode forth to deeds of daring. . . .
> The Negro race had left the last relic of barbarism behind, and this young negro . . . was but a forerunner of the negro, who, at the voice of a woman, will fight for freedom until he dies fully satisfied if the hand that he worships will only drop a flower on his grave.[100]

When Belton is older, in an attempt to learn what whites think of blacks, he disguises himself as a nurse and gets a job in the home of a prominent white family, where he experiences first-hand the indignities to which the black female domestic is subjected. Similarly, in Griggs' fourth novel, *Hindered Hand*, a black married couple are burned at the stake, which prompts Ensal, a main character, to bemoan the fate of "poor Negro womanhood."[101] Her men are unable to protect her, which suggests a paradox in the treatment of women in American society; white women are of course protected, but there is no limit to what society will do to black women.

Afro-American fiction was also used as a vehicle to counteract negative stereotypes of black women by presenting black female characters who could serve as models of black womanhood, for they were paragons of virtue and seriously committed to racial uplift.[102] In fact, many of these novels are thinly disguised social criticism or "arguments in the guise of fiction," according to Sterling Brown.[103] He comments further on their function.

> After the long years of caricature and contempt, it was natural that Negro novelists of the first generation after slavery should write as apologists. Not literary men, with the exception of Du Bois and Johnson, but most often preachers and teachers, they had a charge to keep instead of a story to be told. . . . The race problem, at the core of their work, turns their novels into tracts. . . . All are concerned with refutation of Thomas Dixon and his school.[104]

In keeping with this goal, a number of novelists—most notably Sutton Griggs, J. W. Grant, and J. McHenry Jones—filled their narratives with idealized portraits of beautiful, chaste, near-perfect heroines, in order to combat the notion that black women were morally lax and irresponsible.

The physical descriptions of Griggs' and Jones' heroines call attention to the beauty and queenliness of the black woman, though, as Arlene Elder points out, these descriptions also reveal the extent to which black men have accepted the conventional white standard of beauty. Marlene in Griggs' *Unfettered* is described as follows by the narrator:

> A wealth of lovely black hair crowning a head of perfect shape and queenly poise, a face, the subtle charm of which baffles description; two lustrous black eyes, wondrously expressive, presided over by eyebrows that were ideally beautiful; a neck which . . . descended and expanded so as to form part of a faultless bust; as to form, magnificently well proportioned; when viewed as a whole, the very essence of loveliness.[105]

Reginia, Jones' mulatto heroine, is described similarly:

> Her complexion was a cream, into which some fairy's hand had deftly mixed the first rays of the morning's sun. Of medium height, her form was the perfection of symmetry. Her face, of classic mold, was almost severe in its hauteur. . . . A wealth of dark brown hair hung in natural ringlets above her oval forehead.[106]

Both Marlene's and Reginia's character traits are also similar. They are modest, virtuous, and unselfish. They also have a strong sense of commitment to the black community, which is manifested in their teaching the poor. Unlike their white counterparts in nineteenth-century sentimental fiction, however, they do not have a purely ornamental function and are not confined to the domestic sphere. They become actively involved in the race struggle along with their men. For example, Tiara of Griggs's *Hindered Hand*, after discovering her Negro ancestry, devotes her life to blacks by doing temperance work and going on the lecture circuit. Elder indicates that these heroines, who are interchangeable because of the similarities in their traits and physical appearance, represent the potential for refinement in black women. Furthermore, she says, they are the "ultimate in sentimental, romantic heroines and a propaganda device intended to educate whites to black possibilities and to inspire blacks to self-development."[107] They are sources of inspiration then, not only because they embody conventional feminine traits, but also because they are role models for black women who must be concerned about racial uplift. These novelists demonstrate that one can be feminine and active in race work at the same time. Griggs' description of a school teacher who later marries Belton, one of two protagonists in *Imperium in Imperio*, illustrates this point.

> Antoinette Nermal was famed throughout the city for her beauty, intelligence and virtue. Her color was what is termed a light brown skin. . . . She was of medium height, and for grace and symmetry her form was fit for a sculptor's model. Her pretty face bore the stamp of intellectuality, but the intellectuality of a beautiful woman, who was still every inch a woman despite her intellectuality.[108]

In this novel, Griggs also attempts to counteract the dominant society's ideal of white beauty by emphasizing the beauty of his dark-skinned heroine, Viola Martin, though she does have white ancestry. She is described thusly when Bernard, fresh out of Harvard Law School, first meets her at a reading circle reception in Norfolk, Virginia:

> She was a small, beautifully formed girl with a luxuriant growth of coal black hair that was arranged in such a way as to impart a queenly look to her shapely head. Her skin was dark brown, tender and smooth in appearance.[109]

Struck by her beauty, he turns to his friend and asks, "Pray, who is that girl that met you at the door? I really did not know that a dark woman could look so beautiful" (p. 98). The friend responds by saying that men in general acknowledge her beauty. "Her picture is the only Negro's picture that is allowed to hang in the show glasses of the white photographers downtown. White and colored pay homage to her beauty" (p. 98). She is also educated, talented, witty, brilliant, religious, unassuming, and best of all *chaste*. In other words, she is almost perfect and "a universal favorite" (p. 100). As one might expect, a courtship between Bernard and Vie develops, and at the end of two years, he proposes marriage, at which point she faints. A few days later, after promising to tell Bernard why they cannot marry, she writes three letters—one to her mother, one to her father, and the other one to Bernard—and then commits suicide. In her lengthy letter to Bernard, she reveals her intense fear that her white ancestry will taint future generations of the race if they marry and produce off-spring. Determined that she must promote race purity at all costs after reading a book about the dangers of race mingling to the black race (not to the white race!), she vowed two years earlier that she would never marry a mulatto (which Bernard is) since miscegenation was destroying her race. She also worked hard to put an end to relationships between black women and white men.

> My other and greatest task was to persuade the evil women of my race to cease their criminal conduct with white men and I went about pleading with them up on my knees to desist. I pointed out that such a course was wrong before God and was rapidly destroying the Negro race.[110]

Viola's decision to remain sexually pure to the point of choosing death above her love for Bernard is another indication of her unusually high moral standards. This idealized portrait of a black woman who is without any shortcomings reaches its pinnacle when she choose the supreme sacrifice—her own happiness and life—in order to preserve the integrity of her race.

A recent study of black women novelists analyzes the relationship between the images of black women held at large in society and the black novelist's "struggle to refute these images" during the late nineteenth century.[111] A persistent stereotype in the antebellum literature of southern whites was the "lewd" and "impure" black woman who emerged as a result of the planters' belief that "black women, unlike white women, craved sex inordinately."[112] The "loose black woman" had the same physical traits:

> She is brown-skinned . . . voluptuous . . . and she possesses a sensuous mouth and a high behind. She is known to have an 'evil' disposition . . . which is

contrasted with the sweet demeanor of the lady. She is good looking and passionate, but never beautiful, for her animal nature rather than her human qualities are foremost in her makeup. She ensnares men with her body rather than uplifting them with her beauty. Her corresponding image, the chaste lady, would function as a vessel of beauty, that spiritual flower who could aid men in their ascent toward God and culture.[113]

Heroines created by Griggs and Jones conformed to the latter stereotype of the white southern lady, ironically, and were antithetical to the more common image of the black woman as lewd and impure.

In their attempt to refute prevalent stereotypes about black women, however, black men revealed their own acceptance of the larger society's definitions of womanhood. Their attitudes must be seen then as manifestations of the extent to which as males they had internalized the dominant cultural notions about appropriate sex roles.[114] The ascendancy of "motherhood" as *the* definitive point for most arguments pertaining to women in the nineteenth and early twentieth centuries led some blacks and whites, especially males, to be aligned in the continuing debate over black women, though they probably would have disagreed about most other racial issues. The ideas that this diverse group of writers expressed should be viewed within the context of the development of the cult of motherhood or the "rise of the moral mother," which occurred in the early nineteenth century and is intimately tied to the cult of True Womanhood discussed earlier.[115] This increase in the importance of mothers (the primary child rearers) resulted in their being ultimately held responsible for producing a better world since they were also the mothers of the race. In her analysis of the writings of late nineteenth-century social theorists, such as Herbert Spencer, Lorna Duffin comments upon the concept of motherhood as a social responsibility that women must accept despite the sacrifices they will incur.

> . . . the campaign for motherhood was part of more general pressure to keep women within their traditional role.
> . . . The eugenicists offered women a *positive* role—that of motherhood—and insisted that it was not only the duty of women to fulfill this role but also that it would be entirely fulfilling for all women. The duty of women was clear: the future of the human race depended on them; 'the destiny of the race rests with women'; 'the *racial* importance of motherhood cannot be exaggerated'.[116]

The most eloquent and detailed defense of black womanhood written by a white male came from the pen of B. F. Riley, a southern minister, in

1910.[117] Unlike most of his white contemporaries, Riley assumed that prevailing notions about womanhood—especially the "deification of motherhood" which Robert Riegel, a contemporary historian, describes,[118]— must also be applied to black women.

> The mother and wife are the vital source of power in the home. That accumulated and mysterious influence is the leaven which has lifted and expanded, or the element which has contracted and shriveled, in proportion to the character of woman. The lesson of the position providentially assigned to the sex has never been lost to the world. No less applicable is the principle to the Negro race.[119]

He also attempted to convince his readers that black women must be put on the same pedestal with white women since "a race or nation is just as good as its women," who are "the arbiters of the destiny of a people."[120] Because of the conditions that prevailed during slavery, when white men had free access to black women (an argument echoing Du Bois and others), it is especially essential now, he argues, that chastity for black women be the idea toward which the race strives if they are to preserve their integrity.

> Rigid safeguards must be placed above the persons of their growing womanhood. Chaste womanhood for the Negro, as well as for every other race, is indispensable if the race . . . is to be preserved. Virtue must be the angel with flaming sword, guarding first of all the portals of the home. More than anything else . . . must be the moral strength of Negro womanhood. . . . The protection of the womanliness of woman in the Negro race is the bulwark of Negro race integrity.[121]

In fact, he indicates that this increase in "moral excellence" on the part of black men and women is already taking place and that the improvement in their home life is the root cause of Negro progress. The most critical improvement, however, is the moral uplift of the women of the race. That is, to the extent that black women are able to approach the American ideal of womanhood (especially where chastity is concerned), then the elevation of the race is assured. Herein lies the key to its survival. Just as the white woman is the hope of the white race, so is the destiny of blacks tied to the moral posture of its women. As mentioned earlier, many white women made arguments similar to those of this white clergyman.

Black men also revealed their acceptance of the cult of True Womanhood, with its attendant emphasis on the importance of motherhood. Though very few men in the history of America were as opposed to male supremacy as was Du Bois, even he was not totally free of conventional ideas about women's roles, especially where domesticity was concerned. Du Bois can also illustrate how one can be in favor of equal rights for women but still hold tenaciously to the ideology of motherhood. In a speech to a group of Spelman students in 1902, he emphasized that "the first and greatest function of their lives" was the duty of motherhood.[122] The "spiritual" duty of homemaking was their second most important function, though he realized that there was a tendency among some women, given their new ideas about women's roles, to shrink from this responsibility. The conservative Kelly Miller, a college professor and later dean of Howard University as well as a prolific essayist, expressed typical views about feminine traits in an article opposing woman suffrage that he submitted to *Crisis* in 1915.

> . . . sex is the one fixed and unalterable separatrix of mankind. . . . The bearing and rearing of the young constitute the chief duty and responsibility of the female. . . . Woman's sphere of activity falls mainly within while man's field of action lies largely without the domestic circle.
>
> Woman is physically weaker than man and is incapable of competing with him in the stern and strenuous activities of public . . . life. . . .
>
> As part of her equipment for motherhood, woman has been endowed with finer feelings and a more highly emotional nature than man. She shows tender devotion and self sacrifice for those close to her by ties of blood. . . . She is far superior to man in purely personal and private virtue, but is his inferior in public qualities and character.[123]

Here, Miller clearly articulates the conventional argument concerning the naturalness and appropriateness of the private sphere for all women and, conversely, the appropriateness of the public sphere for men.

Many black male leaders held similar views. In a number of articles and editorials that appeared in *A.M.E. Church Review*, a popular black magazine and the official organ for the A.M.E. Church from 1884-1917, several ministers revealed their acceptance of many of the tenets of the cult of True Womanhood.

> Being made a "helpmeet" for man, she was endowed with peculiar qualities—made softer, sweeter, and milder than he; being made the "mother of all living," she was made to be clearly understood and respected. . . . She was given a tender heart and plastic hand, that she might "rock the cradle and rule the world." She was constituted to manage the intricate affairs of the family circle. . . . She has patience and perseverance in illuminating home-life; in extending the influence of the Church; in intensifying the excellency of

character; in improving the condition of the world. She, in this respect, stands as a striking contrast with man, the outdoor agent, made for sterner work.[124]

William Alexander, a historian, expresses similar views about women's special nature and alludes to the function that black women should serve.

> Women are formed to become instructors. . . . It is through her children that a woman rules posterity; that she leaves, for good or for evil, indelible marks on the universe. . . . Just in proportion as Colored Mothers train aright their children, so we will see the race advance, and not until then. . . . It is the glory of a woman, that for this she was sent into the world, to live for others rather than for herself; to live, yes, and often to die for them. Surely this is woman's calling—to teach man . . . to temper his fiercer, coarser, more self-assertive nature by the contact of her gentleness, purity, self-sacrifice.[125]

These special feminine qualities to which many black men allude especially suit black women for their primary responsibility—carrying the burden of the race by becoming good mothers and thereby creating a better home life. When black women uplift themselves, the race will be uplifted. This theme is repeated with such frequency that it appears to be a battle cry. It also represents a point at which black and white attitudes intersect, for both groups agree that the prestige of a race is tied to the character of its women. Echoing Riley and others, Crummell argues:

> I am anxious for a permanent and uplifting civilization to be engrafted in the Negro race in this land. And this can only be secured through the womanhood of a race. If you want the civilization of a people to reach the very best elements of their being . . . you must imbue the *womanhood* of that people with all its elements and qualities. . . . Without them, [females] no true nationality, patriotism, religion, cultivation, family life, or true social status is a possibility.[126]

Du Bois agrees with Crummell and others that because of the special problems in the black community (especially an impoverished home life), it is critical that black women, especially the more privileged, realize the importance of their duties as mothers and as custodians of the moral fiber of the race.

Black women were even more vocal than other groups about the importance of a healthy moral atmosphere in black homes and the critical role of mothers, especially, to the future of the race. In the second annual conference held at Atlanta University on the condition of blacks in cities, a black female graduate of the institution alludes to this very point.

> If it is true, that of the three main factors in the make-up of the individual—the home, the school and the church—the greatest is the home, and since it is true that the home is what the parents make it, the mother by nature having the larger share in the making, then it follows that the destiny of the Negro race is largely in the hands of mothers.[127]

Moreover, a critical component of the black women's club movement since its inception on a national level in 1895 was Mother's Meetings and Conferences, whose primary purpose was the imparting of information about ways of improving the domestic life of the race to the masses of ordinary black women by the "superior class of Negro women."[128] The meetings dealt with such practical and moral matters as dressmaking; the laws of sanitation; economic cooking; care of babies; proper dress; handling the physical, mental, and moral needs of childhood; preventive health care; prenatal care; teaching a boy to protect women; and instilling high moral standards in girls and boys—to name a few. Mrs. Fannie Barrier Williams, a member of the Chicago Woman' s Club, describes the goals of club activities in this area.

> Home-making has been new business to the great majority of the women whom the women's clubs aim to reach and influence. For this reason the principal object of club studies is to teach that homes are something better and dearer than rooms, furniture, comforts and food. How to make the homes of the race the shrines of all the domestic virtues rather than a mere shelter, is the important thing that colored women are trying to learn and teach through their club organizations. . . . The mothers' meetings . . . have probably had a more direct and beneficial influence on the everyday problems of motherhood and home-making than any other activity.[129]

In fact, a major objective of the black women's club movement was to persuade poor rural black women in the South to embrace the sexual morals of the Victorian middle class. This approach to racial uplift that the middle- and upper-class leaders of the club movement took was a domestic feminist one, according to the author of a recent analysis of the movement during its early years. This approach emphasized the idea that enlightened women should focus their activities on the domestic sphere in order to upgrade the morality of home life in the black community.[130]

During the Negro Young People's Christian and Educational Congress held August 6-11, 1902, in Atlanta, Georgia, much attention was given to discussions of "moral and social reform questions among the race." Numerous talks were given by both males and females concerning the improvements to be made in the home life of the Negro. Special attention was also given to the role of the black mother and especially her role in teaching her daughters and sons social purity.[131] What this reveals is the extent to which blacks themselves felt that their home life, especially motherhood, was critical to the survival of the race. Margaret Murray Washington (wife of Booker T. Washington) underscores this point in her article "The Negro Home and the Future of the Race":

> . . . we have many things in common with all the other citizens of the community, and one of these is a love of family life, a desire and yearning to bring our children up in a wholesome and clean atmosphere, a growing desire to create for ourselves an ideal which expresses itself more and more in decent living, our homes and the future of our race and of both races would be happier[sic].[132]

Similarly, in a book devoted entirely to the rearing of black children, Mrs. Hackley, a southerner and prominent concert singer, indicates that the black mother has an even heavier burden to bear because of the peculiar problems of the race, but she can also experience a greater sense of accomplishment when she is successful at her difficult task of motherhood.

> To assume the position of colored motherhood is the greatest privilege and responsibility that can come to any woman in this age. The colored mother beautiful carries a heavy burden—the weight of future generations of a handicapped, persecuted people. She may bless or curse each succeeding generation; she may change race history; she may make a more beautiful race with the beauty that comes from beauty of character and right living.
> What a privilege to carve the destiny of a race! How glorious to look into the future and see lines of ancestry influenced and advanced by her thought and example. . . .
> The time has come when each colored girl must prepare herself for this race privilege, when she must distribute her powers and talents for race good.
> Whatever the colored mother is, millions of colored children will be. A colored mother lives not only for herself and for her own children, but she must live for the race. A colored mother is a success as she measures up to her relation and obligation to the race.[133]

Frances E. W. Harper, antislavery lecturer, poet, women's rights advocate, prominent clubwoman, and novelist, also talks about the need of an "enlightened motherhood" among her race in an address delivered before the Brooklyn Literary Society in 1892.

We need mothers who are capable of being character builders, patient, loving, strong, and true, whose homes will be an uplifting power in the race. This is one of the greatest needs of the hour. No race can afford to neglect the enlightenment of its mothers. If you would have . . . a manhood without honor, and a womanhood frivolous, mocking, and ignorant, neglect the education of your daughters. But if, on the other hand, you would have strong men, virtuous women, and good homes, then enlighten your women, so that they may be able to bless their homes by the purity of their lives, the tenderness of their hearts, and the strength of their intellects.[134]

It is interesting to note, however, that black women felt that it was their responsibility and not the responsibility of white women (as others had argued) to bring about such racial uplift in their communities. An article written by Mary Blauvelt, a white woman who attended the meetings of the Michigan State Federation of Colored Women's Clubs, reported that in order to foster race pride, black women preferred to rely on themselves primarily for the betterment of the race. This was also why they supported a separate women's club movement because they felt they had special work to do that was in many ways different from the goals of the white women's club movement (they were also, of course, prohibited from joining many white clubs).

For it is necessary to the development of self-respect that colored women should prove to themselves and to the world that they can do things without the help of white women—that they are capable of organized effort. . . . "We need," said one, "each one to believe in herself, and then to believe in others of her race. We must raise ourselves, if we are to rise. Our white sisters wish to help us, and do help us, but we ourselves do a great share of the work, and we must do it among ourselves, and by ourselves."[135]

The extent to which the ideology of motherhood has influenced the views of whites toward black women, even when they disagree about other aspects of the "Negro Problem" is revealed in their persistent references to the black mammy. In an astute analysis of the evolution of the mammy figure, "one of the most dominant images to emerge in southern life and literature," Barbara Christian argues that one cannot fully understand the mammy stereotype without a consideration of the lady stereotype, which was also a manifestation of the South's reverence for motherhood.[136]

A lady was expected to be a wife, a mother, and a manager; yet she was supposed to be delicate, ornamental, virginal, and timid. . . . But given a system of mistress and slave, she need not nurse, be chained to her babies'

Frances E. W. Harper (1825-1911)was an outspoken anti-slavery crusader and women's rights activist and the most popular and prolific black woman writer of her day. In addition to publishing five volumes of poetry, the first at the age of 21, she has the distinction of having published the first short story by an American black and the second novel (*Iola Leroy, or Shadows Uplifted*, 1892) by a black female.

continuous demands, or do heavy housework, elaborate cooking. . . . If the image of the delicate alabaster lady were to retain some semblance of truth, it would be necessary to create the image of another female who was tougher, less sensitive, and who could perform with efficiency and grace the duties of motherhood for her mistress and of course for herself. The image of the southern lady, based as it was on a patriarchal plantation myth, demanded another female image, that of the mammy.[137]

Furthermore, because the mammy figure is by definition both black and female, she embodies the convergence of both racial and sexual stereotyping in its most overt form. Christian's description of the mammy, a persistent stock character in white antebellum and Reconstruction fiction, reveals both the racist and sexist components of this stereotype.

Enduring, strong, and calm, her physical characteristics remain the same. She is black in color as well as race and fat, with enormous breasts that are full enough to nourish all the children of the world; her head is perpetually covered with her trademark kerchief to hide the kinky hair that marks her as ugly. Tied to her physical characteristics are her personality traits: She is strong. . . . She is kind and loyal, for she is mother; she is sexless, for she is ugly; and she is religious and superstitious, because she is black.[138]

In his blatantly racist polemic on black degeneracy, Thomas Nelson Page, a popular southern novelist, attempted to memorialize the mammy, the figure that looms large in the southern imagination.

So, no one can describe what the Mammy was, and only those can apprehend her who were rocked on her generous bosom, slept on her bed, fed at her table, were directed and controlled by her, watched by her unsleeping eye, and led by her precept in the way of truth, justice, and humanity. She was far more than a servant. She was a member of the family in high standing and of unquestioned influence. She was her mistresses's coadjutress and her wise adviser. . . . After forty-five years, I recall, with mingled awe my mammy's dignity, force, and kindness. . . .[139]

In an otherwise atypical response to the Negro problem because of its call for equality between the races, there is a similar attitude revealed on the part of Lewis Blair, a liberal southerner, though his motive for evoking the black mammy is quite different from Page's. In order to counter the widespread notion that blacks will demoralize whites if allowed to mix socially with them (especially in schools), Blair reminds whites of their intimate association with mammies from earliest childhood and of the positive effect of their

Margaret Murray Washington (1865-1925) became the third wife of Booker T. Washington in 1893 after having come to Tuskegee in 1889 as "lady principal." An institution builder at Tuskegee, she was responsible for programs relating to female students. A prominent clubwoman, she was also founder of the International Council of Women of the Darker Races of the World and president of the National Association of Colored Women (NACW) from 1912 to 1916. She also edited and supported *National Notes*, the official organ of the NACW.

association with these surrogate mothers, whose influence was anything but demoralizing.

> . . . Most of us above thirty years of age had our mammy. . . . Up to the age of ten we saw as much of the mammy as of the mother, perhaps more, and we loved her quite as well. The mammy first taught us to lisp and to walk . . . taught us who made us and who redeemed us, dried our tears and soothed our bursting hearts. . . . The mother might grow weary and faint, but the faithful mammy seemed never to weary, but was always patiently and lovingly at her post. . . . In the hands of the Negro mammy were we as clay to the potter, but did she demoralize us? Thousands who are scattered over the land, and in whose memory the mammy holds a tender and an honored place, have but one response, "no."[140]

Oswald Villard, a liberal northerner, argues in a speech before the National Negro Business League that the race problem would be alleviated if efficient, well-trained domestic servants were available to southern white households; his position, he says, is based on the fact that over 80 percent of black women are engaged in household service. Specifically, he would like trained black mammies (as in slavery) to reappear so that race relations in the South would be improved.

> Is not the Colored race recreant to its duty if it fails to produce thousands of mammies . . . ? Is not such a servant one of the best intermediaries or missionaries between the races? Is not her efficiency of a cash as well as a sentimental value to the race? . . . I could tell . . . of a young college president who said . . . that he would as soon fail to kiss his mother as to fail to embrace his mammy when he returned home on his college vacation.[141]

Near the end of the article, in an attempt again to get blacks to alleviate the servant problem, he quotes a southern white preacher who had evoked the black mammy.

> The fine spirit of the old slave and black mammy, at whose breast many of us nursed, is not wholly dead and it can be brought to ascendancy again.[142]

He also pleads for household training for black women in the form of increased educational opportunities, specifically, domestic science courses like those afforded their white counterparts at Bryn Mawr, so that the race will be uplifted.

Southern white women, in particular, bemoaned the passing from their midst of beloved mammies who were so indispensable in their own households. Eleanor Tayleur recalls with nostalgic longing this group of women who are "among the most cherished recollections of the Old South . . . between whom and their owners existed a bond of affection that only death could sever." She goes on to paint a vivid and perhaps romanticized portrait of super-mothers.

> . . . the Aunt Dinahs, ample of girth, clad in clean cottonade . . . who at dinner would poke an anxious head through the doorway to hear the compliments bestowed upon their art, are almost as extinct as the dodo. Gone, too, are the neat housemaids in guinea-blue calicoes . . . whose ministrations were benedictions, so filled were they with loving care and solicitude. Gone also, are the old black mammies on whose broad breasts childish sorrows sobbed themselves to sleep and broken baby hearts were mended.
>
> In their places is an ignorant creature in dirty finery, the first article of whose faith is a settled determination not to work.[143]

Lily Hammond, a northern liberal white woman, felt, on the other hand, that southern white women should assume responsibility for racial uplift among black women. She argued that one solution to the race problem would be the protection of black women, which could be accomplished through, among other things, burying "the old Black Mammy."[144]

> She may still be loved and honored. . . . She deserves a funeral, bless her. . . . Her removal will clear the atmosphere and enable us to see the old soul's granddaughters, to whom we must in justice pay something of the debt we so freely acknowledge to her. We must lay aside the mental attitude of the past—the attitude of a people toward a slave race—and face the present with a forward look.[145]

Some southerners were so committed to the southern way of life, of which the Mammy was a symbol, that efforts were made to establish monuments of endearment to this highly esteemed member of the black community. Perhaps, the most extreme example of this phenomenon was the founding in Athens, Georgia, of the Black Mammy Memorial Institute.[146] The Institute was the result of attempts by whites to memorialize the "old black Mammy" and the desire of a black high school principal, Samuel Harris, to promote himself and his idea of industrial training for blacks. In 1909, he and four other black men started an independent evening industrial school and one of the courses provided cooking instruction for prospective black cooks in white homes. In 1911, the Athens white newspaper, *The Banner*, reported on a southern movement to establish monuments and memorials to the "old Black Mammies of the South." This "Black Mammy Memorial Movement" had inspired leading white citizens in Athens in 1910, according to *The Banner*, to form the Black Mammy Association. One of its major functions was to solicit contributions to support the Black Mammy Memorial Institute. D. C. Barrow, chancellor of the University of Georgia, was credited with the idea of the monument and the name of the Institute, which was originally Harris's evening industrial school for blacks. Harris and the founders of the evening school cooperated with the white association members and established the Black Mammy Memorial Institute, with Harris becoming its first principal.

These similar responses toward the black mammy among whites whose racial views were radically dissimilar reveal the extent to which they were unable to rid themselves of filial feelings toward the black women with whom they came in close contact as they were growing up and, in the case of the women, with whom they interacted in a mistress/servant relationship. In 1949 Lillian Smith, who was born in the South in 1897, published her memoirs describing those experiences that "most white southerners born at the turn of the century share with each other."[147] She refers to "this tender and tragic relationship of childhood—the white child and his colored nurse" as "one of the profound relationships of my life."[148] She also asserts boldly that one must understand this "primal experience" between the mammy and child, which "powerfully influenced the character of many southerners of the dominant class," if one is to really comprehend the South.[149] She writes endearingly of her beloved mammy whose expertise at mothering was profound.

> . . . she was a necessary part of these big sprawling households; her knowledge, alone, of how to grow children was too precious a thing to throw away lightly. . . . She nursed old and young when they were sick, counseled them when they were unhappy . . . and in crises her biologically rooted humor had a magic way of sweeping white clouds away. She was nurse, witch doctor, and priest, conjuring off our warts, our stomach-aches and fears. . . . following her precepts we prospered as did her own children.[150]

As one might expect, most blacks revealed a different perspective on the black mammy: while whites tended to romanticize her in their fiction and nonfiction, blacks saw her as a tragic object of abuse. A notable exception was Booker T. Washington; at the opposite pole from Du Bois on several major racial issues (especially the feasibility of industrial vs. classical education for blacks), he also held different views about the black mammy issue. Unlike Du Bois, he spoke fondly of the southern whites' relationship with their mammies.

> The simple hearted devotion of the Negro slave woman to their masters . . . was one of the redeeming features of Negro slavery in the South. . . . I know of scarcely anything more beautiful than the tributes I have heard Southern white men and women pay to those old coloured mammies, who nursed them as children, shared their childish joys and sorrows and clung to them through life with an affection that no change of time . . . could diminish.[151]

Du Bois was perturbed, on the other hand, by southerners' worship of the black mammy because he realized that there was no concern for her mothering role in her own home. Having read Thomas Page's sentimental account of his mammy, Du Bois offered a counter-proposal to the suggestion that a statue be erected in the national capital to honor the black mammy:

> Let the present-day mammies suckle their own children. Let them walk in the sunshine with their own toddling boys and girls and put their own sleepy little brothers and sisters to bed. As their girls grow to womanhood, let them see to it that . . . they do not enter domestic service in those homes where they are unprotected, and where their womanhood is not treated with respect. In the midst of immense difficulties, surrounded by caste, and hemmed in by restricted economic opportunity, let the colored mother of today build her own statue, and let it be the four walls of her own unsullied home.[152]

Similarly, James Weldon Johnson published in 1915 a poem in *Crisis* bemoaning the fate of the black mammy, the "foster-mother" of the white race, who, ironically, might have to witness the harm done to her own child at the hands of whites though she has nurtured and sheltered their children.

> O foster-mother in whose arms there lay
> The race whose sons are masters of the land!
>
> . . . .
>
> In times of old
> It was thy breast that nourished them to
>   strength.
> So often hast thou to their bosom pressed
> The golden head, the face and brow of

snow . . .
came ne'er the thought to thee, swift
  like a stab,
That it some day might crush thine own
  black child?[153]

Although Du Bois and Johnson reject the adulation of the mammy and are opposed to the abuse of black mothers in white households, they nonetheless embrace the ideology of motherhood, for they believe in the fundamental values associated with the mammy—home, nurturance, and maternal influence. In other words, black mothers should be removed from white homes so that they can devote themselves full time to the needs of their own homes.

A former mammy and wet nurse (who served more than a dozen white children) prefers to emphasize the hardship under which household servants work, a condition she describes as similar to slavery. She is also disturbed by the infrequency with which she sees her own children.

> I frequently work from fourteen to sixteen hours a day. . . . I am allowed to go home to my children . . . only once in two weeks. . . . I live a treadmill life. . . . I am the slave, body and soul, of this family. And what do I get for this work—this lifetime bondage? The pitiful sum of ten dollars a month.[154]

What she would like to see is not memorials to black mammies but a better life for this abused segment of the black female population.

> . . . whether in the cook kitchen [sic], at the washtub . . . behind the baby carriage, or at the ironing board, we are but little more than pack horses, beasts of burden, slaves! In the distant future . . . a monument of brass or stone will be erected to the Old Black Mammies of the South, but what we need is present help, present sympathy, better wages, better hours, more protection, and a chance to breathe for once while alive as free women.[155]

Unlike Du Bois and Johnson, she sees the solution to their problem to be better working conditions; she knows that black women will need to continue to provide financial support for their families since, whether married or single, most black women must work for a living.

A similar kind of empathy for the black mammy is also revealed in at least one portrait of her that appears in a novel written by a major white writer of the period. The preoccupation with the black mammy on the part of whites was widely reflected in their literary portrayals of black women.

Because of the dominance of the Plantation Tradition[156] in the fiction of the times, black mammies appear more than any other type in the fiction of both white male and female writers, with the possible exception of the tragic mulatto.[157] Black female characters, when they appear in this fiction, are minor figures generally portrayed in one or the other of these stereotyped roles. The notable exception is Roxy in Mark Twain's *Pudd'nhead Wilson*. His depiction of a full-scale, multi-dimensional black heroine distinguishes him from other white writers. Unlike the conventional mammy types, Roxy is treated as a complex character. Her characterization illuminates the paradoxes that create the dilemma of the black woman as mother. Roxy's uniqueness has been underscored frequently by critics.

> . . . at the center of the motion and the plot, stands the figure of the slave-girl Roxana, precisely the black mammy of Poe's sentimental editorializing, who has held at her breast both her own child and her master's, black and white milk-brothers. Roxana, however, defies all cliches; she is no gross, comfortable, placid source of warmth, all bosom and grin, but a passionate, complex and beautiful mulatto, a truly living woman distinguished from the wooden images of virtue and bitchery that pass for females in most American novels.[158]

Leslie Fiedler argues that her character transcends prevailing racial and sexual stereotypes. She does not conform to the True Woman stereotype, who lacks her passion and vibrancy and does not conform to the racial stereotype of the mammy figure, who is a passive, uncomplicated source of warmth and comfort.

While other aspects of Roxy's character are significant, especially her own ancestry and her racial attitudes, my interest here is in what her character reveals about white male attitudes toward the black mammy. Through the character of Roxy, Twain, the literary artist, is able to dramatize the central role that black women played in white families during slavery and the paradox of being a mother but at the same time being unable to function as a mother; the conventional mammy figure, on the other hand, transcends these paradoxes. Interestingly, there are no important white females in the story. Mrs. Percy Driscoll, Thomas Driscoll's real mother, dies within a week after her and Roxy's sons are born, and the weakness of the white woman is underscored in the contrast between her and Roxy.

> On the 1st of February, 1830, two boy babies were born in his house; one to him, the other to one of his slave girls, Roxana by name. Roxana was

twenty years old. She was up and around the same day, with her hands full, for she was tending both babies.

Mrs. Percy Driscoll died within the week. Roxy had her own way, for Mr. Driscoll soon absorbed himself in his speculations and left her to her own devices.[159]

Roxy's most important qualities reveal a curious mixture of traits associated with both the mammy figure and the True Woman, which sheds further light on the interaction of racial and sexual assumptions in conceptions of black women. Roxy's most outstanding character trait is not loyalty to her white family, which is usually the case in depictions of black mammies, but love for her own child; this is what motivates her to switch children in the cradle—she does not want her child to be sold down the river. This image of the black mother as more concerned about her own children is in keeping with the thinking of many black males during the period, especially Du Bois, who felt that black mothers should perceive their own families as their first priority. Another of her traits is self-sacrifice, a trait that the True Woman is supposed to possess. When, after being freed, Roxy volunteers to be sold back into slavery so that her son, the false Thomas, can use the money to pay off gambling debts, she reminds him of a mother's nature when he questions her sincerity.

Ain't you my chile? En does you know anything dat a mother won't do for her chile? Dey ain't nothin' a white mother won't do for her chile. Who made 'en so? De Lord done it. En who made de niggers? De Lord mad 'em. In de inside, mothers is all de same.[160]

For Twain, then, race does not obliterate the maternal "instinct" to protect one's child at all cost. Moreover, the extent to which Roxy's mothering function is perceived to be the most important aspect of her character is underscored by the lack of attention paid to other aspects of her character. That is, Twain rarely permits his readers to see her interact with persons other than her children. This emphasis on her maternal role and self-sacrifice also relates to the tenets of the cult of True Womanhood, especially because of its emphasis on domesticity, which other commentators endorsed during the period under consideration.

Roxy does not conform to all aspects of the stereotype, however, for she is not submissive, a cardinal virtue of the True Woman. Despite the general powerlessness of slaves, Roxy, because of her role in the white family, is portrayed as a powerful figure. First, she has the power to alter the fate of her son and her master's son (which of course would have been impossible without the miscegenation that had taken place). Despite having to appear meek and humble in the presence of whites, she possesses the grandeur and stature of a queen, which is probably also a result of the predominance of white blood in her.

> She was of majestic form and stature; her attitudes were imposing and statuesque, and her gestures and movements distinguished by a noble and stately grace. . . . She had an easy, independent carriage—when she was among her own caste—and a high and 'sassy' way withall.[161]

Much later in the story, after she tells Thomas that he is really her son, she gets pleasure from lording over him. "Her nature needed some thing or somebody to rule over, and he was better than nothing. Her strong character and aggressive and commanding ways compelled Tom's admiration" (p. 120).

To underscore her power, the queenly imagery is repeatedly used in descriptions of her, which is paradoxical given her lowly station in life. After confronting Thomas with the truth about his ancestry, she sinks back and enjoys his humiliation.

> Roxy knew her conquest was complete! . . . She went and sat down on her candle box, and the pride and pomp of her victorious attitude made it a throne. . . . Under the inspiration of her soaring complacency the departed graces of her earlier days returned to her, and her bearing took to itself a dignity and state that might have passed for queenly if her surroundings had been a little more in keeping with it.[162]

Leslie Fiedler has commented on Roxy's power and the function she serves in the narrative as a symbol of black women as the real mothers of the South.

> Though the men of Dawson's Landing, being Virginians, are potent still, their white women, who languish and retreat and die, are latter-day Americans, almost asexually genteel, so that only the Negress can match the vigor of fathers with a corresponding fertility and power. Roxy is just such a Negress, and her union with Cecil . . . Essex represents not only a sociological but a symbolic truth. If the fathers of the South are Virginia gentlemen, the mothers are Negro girls, casually or callously taken in the parody of love, which is all that is possible when one partner to a sexual union is not even given the status of a person.[163]

Another critic makes a similar observation about Roxy's function:

Small wonder that in the slave South of Mark Twain's memory the Negro women became the Mammies who were the real mothers in a society so obsessed with innocence that divested, figuratively if not literally, its ordained mothers of their vitality. The white women of the privileged classes could not be real mothers at all . . . and were relieved of the odious obligation as soon after the travails of childbirth as possible. . . . She [Roxy] is the dark queen, but the real queen nevertheless in the social order which Twain envisions. . . . Roxana alone has the magic power to create drama and to become a primary force in the world she serves.[164]

Both of these comments underscore another critical way in which Roxy departs from the True Woman ideal. Because of the racial dynamics in the South between masters and slave women, she lacks purity, an absolutely essential trait of the nineteenth-century Ideal Woman. That is, her sexual involvement with men without the benefit of marriage sets her apart from the "asexually genteel" white females who lack the vitality and power of the black woman. Furthermore, she also departs in a number of ways from the asexual mammy ideal because of her physical appearance because she is only one-sixteenth black. Unlike the conventional Mammy, she has not been desexualized by being made to appear dark-skinned, fat, and therefore ugly by the dominant culture's standards. Because of her mixed blood, she has some of the typical traits of the tragic mulatto type, but Twain does not present her as the melancholy tragic mulatto, irrevocably caught between two worlds. Secondly, unlike the conventional mammy who prefers her master's children to her own because "as a member of a lower species, she acknowledges almost instinctively the superiority of the higher race,"[165] Roxy prefers her own child.

Though Roxy is a victim of the sexual exploitation of white males—a phenomenon that was scorned by black and white males alike—she is presented by Twain as a positive figure, even as she deviates from the True Woman ideal; her passion and vitality and independence make her a real woman, which white women, if they conformed to the True Woman ideal, were unable to achieve. Twain's characterization of Roxy reveals, then, the inability of the True Woman ideal and the mammy stereotype to encompass the complexities of the black woman's experiences. While Roxy's life can illustrate the tragic consequences of the sexual abuse of the black woman by the white male, the qualities she develops as a result of the harsh circumstances of her life—strength, aggressiveness, determination, even independence—can be seen as a positive alternative to the prevailing model of womanhood that relegates women to a submissive, child-like status. As many black males pointed out, black women, because of the peculiar circumstances of their lives, can be looked upon with admiration for having developed qualities alien to other women.

Though Roxy becomes a surrogate mother to Tom, her real son, she is unable to function as a real mother would because of the racial barriers that dictate certain behaviors on both their parts. Paradoxically, though he is dependent on her for many of his needs, she is denied the respect and rewards that accrue to mothers because the institution of slavery perverts the normal mother/son relationship. She is also unable to function as a mother to her supposedly real son, who is ignored through much of the narrative as if he did not exist. This situation can shed light on the anger expressed by many black males during the period, who see the black mother's inability to function on a full-time basis in her own home as the real tragedy for the black community. Though Twain stands almost alone among his race, he has created in Roxy a portrait that supports this contention and makes him the ally of many black male writers on the issue of the peculiar plight of black women. In the May 1912 issue of *Crisis*, Du Bois discusses a letter by Twain which was published in the *Ladies Home Journal*. In this unusual letter, Twain spoke of artists who spoil the Virgin Mary by making her fair "and *white*, which she wasn't."[166] When his daughter questioned him about the truth of his implication that the Virgin Mary was "colored," Twain replied that during Mary's day most of the world was indeed colored. He concluded by saying that "to my mind one color is just as respectable as another: there is nothing important, nothing essential about a complexion." However, he continued, God apparently did not share his view and made the madonna black because "he doesn't think much of white people. He prefers the colored." These statements by Twain, which obviously claimed Du Bois's attention, may shed some light on the unconventional racial attitudes which are apparent in his portrayal of Roxy.

Finally, the complex character of Roxy sheds light on the paradoxical nature of black womanhood. Her departure from many aspects of the True Woman ideal at the same time that she takes seriously the sacred duty of motherhood is indicative of the extent to which the categories of sinner and saint are inappropriate when one is evaluating black women, though these images pervade the writings of blacks and whites during the period under consideration.

In general, a careful consideration of both the fiction and nonfiction of the period indicates that blacks and whites, irrespective of their gender identity, had similar ideas about the nature of womanhood, especially the importance of motherhood. Yet, also in general, their attitudes toward black women were dissimilar, especially on the moral question, as one would expect given their drastically different vantage points from 1880-1920. This period represented a high point for the native-born white and the "nadir" for blacks. That blacks and whites, both males and females, had similar conceptions of womanhood with respect to the importance of the domestic sphere is indicative of the extent to which members of a given culture, despite their ethnic and gender identity, accept, at least to some degree, the sex-role stereotypes fostered upon them by virtually every aspect of society. In the nineteenth century the cult of True Womanhood, with its emphasis on woman's natural place in the domestic sphere, affected the thinking of black and white men as well as black and white women. It is also ironic that white women, even those who realized that the key to achieving equality and freedom for women was tied to a weakening of the cult of domesticity, were not able to transcend conventional racial attitudes and forge a bond with black women as equals on the basis of their common gender identity. When they were sometimes sensitive to the plight of black women, they assumed a maternalistic posture. They arrogantly concluded that without the generosity and cooperation of white women, black women and by extension the entire race were doomed. Black women themselves were also painfully aware that they were devalued, no matter what their strengths might be, and that the cult of True Womanhood was not intended to apply to them no matter how intensely they embraced its values.

> The colored girl may have character, beauty and charms ineffable, but she is not in vogue. The muses of song, poetry and art do not woo and exalt her. . . . Man's instinctive homage at the shrine of womanhood draws a line of color, which places her forever outside its mystic circle. . . . The women of other races bask in the clear sunlight of man's chivalry, admiration, and even worship, while the colored woman abides in the shadow of his contempt, mistrust or indifference.[167]

Despite the "tyranny of race prejudice" that makes the lot of black women more difficult than any other group of women in America, however, they remain "irrepressible" and a credit to their race.[168] Many black men were also convinced, in spite of the peculiar nature of the black woman's burden, that it was possible for these "daughter of a long down-trodden race"[169] to throw off their yokes and reach or even surpass the True Woman ideal.

FOUR

Books, Brooms, Bibles, and Ballots: Black Women and the Public Sphere

Nothing in the present century is more noticeable than the tendency of women to enter every hopeful field of wage-earning and philanthropy, and attempt to reach a place in every intellectual arena.

Lucy Laney, 1899

Nothing in the whole progress of humanity is more interesting and more suggestive of the persistence of rightness than the steady gain of womankind in those larger relationships of human life and civilization in which the stronger as well as the gentler virtues, are tending to increase her importance.

Fannie Barrier Williams, 1895

Fifty years ago woman's activity according to orthodox definitions was on a pretty clearly cut "sphere," including primarily the kitchen and the nursery. . . . The woman of today finds herself in the presence of responsibilities which ramify through the profoundest and most varied interests of her country and race.

Anna J. Cooper, 1892

While the prevailing attitude about women during the nineteenth-century was that social stability could be maintained only if women confined themselves to the home, women became more visible in the public sphere during the latter quarter of the century as educational and job opportunities for them expanded and as reform work became more acceptable. Moreover, increased numbers of women, many of whom had been involved in the abolitionist struggle, were becoming more dissatisfied with the status quo, and as their feminist consciousness awakened, their defiance of Victorian notions about women's proper sphere intensified. In fact, an important aspect of the controversy surrounding "the woman question" was the debate that ensued during the latter quarter of the nineteenth century concerning the appropriate roles for women as progressive ideas about the "new woman" emerged. Journalists and popular novelists presented a fairly consistent image of the "new woman" ideal at the turn of the century.

> The New Woman was self-reliant. She was determined to live her own life and to make her own decisions. She was eager for direct contact with the world outside her home. She held independent views. . . . She was well educated. . . . She wanted to stand in a new relation to man, seeing herself as a companion—an equal—rather than as a subordinate or dependent.[1]

Furthermore, these "new women" were leaving the confines of home; going to college; joining clubs, settlement houses, the professions, and even unions; and entering the labor force in larger numbers. By 1920, eight million women were gainfully employed outside the home. Domestic workers accounted for the largest percentage and workers in manufacturing establishments (mainly textile mills) were second by as early as 1900.[2] Middle-class, native-born white women, on the other hand, entered the labor force as elementary school teachers, social workers, nurses, and clerical workers. It was among this class that motherhood or women's special sensibilities (aspects of the cult of domesticity) were used to justify activities in the public sphere that were perceived, in some cases, as extensions of one's maternal influence in the home. Ryan refers to this group as "social housekeepers" because of their acceptance of the values associated with the cult of True Womanhood.

> Jane Addams clothed settlement work in maternal metaphor, an expression of "the great mother breast of our common humanity." Women's clubs were founded under the motto "Now show a more glorious womanhood a new unit, the completed type of the mother-woman working with all as well as for all." Of course, the suffrage movement resorted to maternal rhetoric, asserting that "the mother of the race . . ." must keep watch over the ballot box. . . . The most honored woman in the labor movement was "Mother" Jones, whose route of agitation was littered with sentimental images of the plight of angelic children.[3]

The involvement of black women in certain pockets of the public sphere (mainly the labor force) was never questioned since the slave system had demanded that black women work alongside men in the fields. Even after slavery, black women were expected to stay in the work force and perform similar tasks as domestic servants, agricultural laborers, and laundresses, to name a few occupations relegated to black women. Du Bois commented on the plight of the black female worker in one of his numerous apologias for black women during the period.

> . . . these black women toil and toil hard. There were in 1910 two and a half million Negro homes in the United States. Out of these homes walked daily to work two million women and girls over ten years of age—over half of the colored female population as against a fifth in the case of white women. These, then, are a group of workers, fighting for their daily bread like men; independent and approaching economic freedom. They furnished a million farm laborers, 80,000 farmers, 22,000 teachers, 600,000 servants and washerwomen, and 50,000 in trades and merchandising.[4]

In fact, an essential aspect of the lives of black women is an historical tradition of working. It is one of the variables that distinguishes them from white native-born women. Several contemporary analyses of the black female experience in America have alluded to the connection between women's work role in Afro-American culture and the perpetuation of alternative notions of womanhood that are antithetical to those prevalent in the majority culture. In other words, the historical role of the black woman as laborer or "beast of burden" is contradictory to the American ideal of domestic womanhood.[5] The extent to which black women themselves have been aware that the life-style of the ideal American woman has been inaccessible to them is revealed dramatically in the perceptive though untutored response of a character in Zora Neale Hurston's classic novel about what it has meant to be black and female in America. Janie, the novel's heroine, is being lectured to by her grandmother, a victim of white male sexual exploitation and hard work.

> De nigger woman is de mule uh de world so fur as Ah can see . . . Ah was born back der in slavery so it wasn't for me to fulfill my dreams of what a woman oughta be and to do. . . . Ah didn't want to be used for a work-ox and a brood-sex. . . . Ah wanted to preach a great sermon about colored women sittin' on high, but they wasn't no pulpit for me.[6]

While the black woman worker was a generally accepted phenomenon, attitudes did vary during the period concerning what constituted appropriate work for black women.

The feasibility of higher education for women was another issue involving the public sphere about which attitudes diverged concerning black women. The Freedmen's Bureau (established in 1865 to address the myriad problems of ex-slaves and disbanded in 1871) had been most successful in the area of education for men and women, having supported hundreds of schools for blacks, including several colleges, among them Fisk, Howard, Atlanta University, and Hampton. Southern whites were especially resentful of the Bureau's educational activities and the horde of northern educators who flocked South to teach the newly freed slaves. However, education was perceived by philanthropists and missionaries alike, especially in the North, as the panacea for the problems of blacks. The pursuit of education also came to be a major preoccupation of freedmen and freedwomen that was evidenced by the extent to which black parents were willing to make sacrifices in order to provide schooling for their children so that they might escape the problems and indignities that were so much a part of the daily lives of the masses of blacks during the post-Reconstruction era.

There was a desperate need for schools to train teachers who could in turn go to common or normal schools to teach reading, writing, and ciphering to the masses of illiterate blacks who had been denied even the rudiments of education during slavery. In fact, the major catalyst for the education of black women after the Civil War was the increasing demand for black teachers. The federal government, denominational boards, mission societies, and church organizations were the first to come to the aid of blacks, and by 1910 there were a hundred colleges established, most of them in the South. Gradually, large education foundations, among them the General Education Board, the John F. Slater Fund, the Phelps-Stokes Fund, and the Anna T. Jeannes Fund, broadened their base of support to include southern black education.[7] This period was indeed an age of philanthropy (responsible for the establishment of white institutions as well), without which the growth of black education in the South would have been virtually impossible.

Another area outside the home in which women were becoming increasingly more involved was the political arena. The women's rights movement[8] in America is generally thought to have begun in 1848 when Elizabeth Cady Stanton, wife of an abolitionist leader, and Lucretia Mott, founder of the first Female Anti-Slavery Society, and three other Quaker women convened the Seneca Falls, New York, woman's rights convention for the purpose of discussing the "social, civil, and religious rights of woman."[9] A Declaration of Sentiments and Resolutions, which revealed the disadvantaged status of women and offered solutions to their problems, was drafted for approval. Though according to one of its chief historians, the women's movement "was essentially from beginning to end a struggle of white, native-born middle-class women for the right to participate more fully in the public affairs of a society the basic structure of which they accepted,"[10] there was always black participation in it, however minimal, from its inception to its demise in 1919 once the vote was won. For example, Frederick Douglass, the famous ex-slave and abolitionist leader, was the most prominent male at the Seneca Falls deliberations and the only one who supported the unpopular resolution of Stanton that women should vote.[11] Though woman suffrage was never as crucial or primary an issue to blacks generally as lynching, Jim Crow, or disfranchisement, to name only a few problems facing them during the years under consideration, the attitudes toward suffrage for black women enlighten us about prevailing notions concerning black women as political beings during a period in which the political rights of blacks in general were being seriously challenged.

Before discussing attitudes about black women and the public sphere, it is important to delineate the general context in which these attitudes were expressed. Progressive black women, even when they embraced the cult of True Womanhood (which many did), felt that it was necessary to extend themselves beyond the home and to work for the improvement of the race through community building and other activities in the public sphere. They were also aware that they were living during a critical era—a "woman's century." For the first time the notion of equality between the sexes was being affirmed among certain groups and women were able to exert their influence in a wider range of areas. Anna J. Cooper, an 1884 Oberlin graduate and teacher for forty years at M Street High School and later Dunbar High School in Washington, D.C., in an 1892 book-length, feminist analysis of the condition of blacks, especially women, spoke eloquently on the subject.

> Fifty years ago woman's activity according to orthodox definitions was in a pretty clearly cut "sphere," including primarily the kitchen and the nursery. . . . The woman of today finds herself in the presence of responsibilities which ramify through the profoundest and most varied interests of her country and race. . . . No plan for renovating society, no scheme for

purifying politics, no reform in Church or in state, no moral, social, or economic question . . . is lost on her.[12]

Fannie Barrier Williams, active in social welfare work in Chicago and another outspoken leader in the cause of black women, echoes Cooper.

> . . . we are living, in what may be called a woman's age. The old notion that woman [sic] was intended by the Almighty to do only those things that men thought they ought to do, is fast passing away. In our day . . . a woman's sphere is just as large as she can make it and still be true to her finer qualities of soul. Her world is constantly becoming larger . . . by virtue of her wider influence and larger participation in human affairs.[13]

Josephine Washington also speaks up for the progressive woman, though she realizes that some women "have never sought to extend their influence beyond the domestic circle and others who have are being scorned."[14] In her introduction to a book written by a black physician about outstanding black women, she denies that this woman is neglectful of her domestic duties.

> She is modest and womanly, with a reverence for the high and holy duties of wife and mother. She does not advocate the abandonment of any real duties at hand for fancied ones afar off. She would not have women neglect home and husband and children to enter professional life, or to further any public cause, however worthy.[15]

She goes on to applaud the movement of women into the public sphere which she feels will enhance their effectiveness in the domestic sphere because "contact with the outer world, a little rubbing against other minds . . . refreshes and invigorates the tired wife and mother and enables her to give her best to the dear ones at home."[16] Furthermore, Washington continues, black women have a special role to play in the uplift of the race, which cannot be achieved if they restrict their work to the home, important though it is in the struggle for the regeneration of the race.

Similarly, in a chapter on "The Colored Woman Today" in their book about "the remarkable advancement of the Afro-American," H. F. Kletzing and William Crogman, two black male college professors, remind black women of the dual role they must play in struggling for the race at home and beyond.

> Although the work of the woman is largely in the homes, yet it is not confined entirely to the homes. Woman's sphere is anywhere where she may

do good. Negro women are needed in the school room. . . . Be up and doing. . . . Why should not women of the race . . . prepare to fill the professions of medicine, law, etc. . . . The women of the race . . . in whatever sphere their lot is cast, follow the plain path of duty.[17]

There was not universal agreement, however, about the efficacy of black women assuming a greater role in public affairs. In an editorial entitled "How to Keep Women at Home," written by Fred Moore of the *Colored American Magazine* (1900-1909), it is apparent that women's excursions from home are causing among some members of the male population great discomfort (which is reminiscent of complaints made by contemporary husbands).

> The tendency of the modern woman to "gad about" is a problem that mere man finds difficult of solution. . . . They are on the street, in the club . . . in the theatres, in societies, in the lecture rooms . . . everywhere but home.[18]

His solution to this abuse of the freedom that women have been graciously "given" by men is to call a convention so that they can exchange ideas on the subject.

Other black males, whose views conform to the Victorian ideal of womanhood, were also opposed to black women assuming a public role and receiving the kind of education that would deemphasize their most important function in life—motherhood. Thomas Nelson Baker, a Baptist minister writing for a popular magazine in 1905, insisted that black women should cling tenaciously to the values of the cult of True Womanhood and that the benefits they receive from a Christian education should accrue to the home rather than outside it.

> The hope of the race is conditioned not upon the woman on the platform, but upon the woman in the home—not upon the women whose highest ambition is to appear in public and pass resolutions about the race, but upon the mothers whose highest ambition is not to show themselves and make public speeches, but whose highest ambition is to give the best there is in them to their children. . . . the hope of the race is conditioned upon that class of women who are too busy with their children to attend conventions. . . . One thing the education of the Negro woman must not do, it must not educate her away from being a mother—it must not be an education that will make her feel that there is a higher sphere for women than that of being a mother.[19]

Anna J. Cooper was especially disturbed by what she perceived to be an unenlightened attitude on the part of black men, such as Baker, about issues relating to women, particularly as they related to women in the public sphere.

> While the women of the white race can with calm assurance enter upon the work they feel by nature appointed to do . . . the colored woman too often finds herself hampered and shamed by a less liberal sentiment and a more conservative attitude on the part of those for whose opinion she cares most. . . . The average man of our race is less frequently ready to admit the actual need among the sturdier forces of the world for woman's help or influence. That great social and economic questions await her interference, that she could throw any light on problems of national import . . . that she has a word worth hearing on mooted questions in political economy . . . I fear the majority of "Americans of the colored variety" are not yet prepared to concede.[20]

It seems reasonable to conclude that *A Voice From the South*, a collection of loosely connected essays, had as one of its primary goals raising the consciousness of black males about the need for them to become more informed about the issues of particular relevance to women, especially the women of their race, during a time when progressive ideas about the role of women were being more seriously considered.

The ensuing discussion of attitudes toward black women in the public sphere will focus on the areas of politics and education. The first concerns specifically attitudes toward suffrage as they relate to black women. An investigation of these attitudes enables us to explore to what extent black men have been free or guilty of the sexist attitudes of their white counterparts with respect to granting votes to women. The most important question to be asked is whether their desire for the emancipation of the race encompassed granting black women full social and political emancipation as well. In addition, such an examination provides a historical perspective on black attitudes toward certain aspects of "the woman question," around which considerable debate ensued during this period. Since previous studies have dealt extensively with the debate at the turn of the century among white suffragists over granting the vote to black women, an extensive analysis of white female attitudes toward suffrage for black women will not be repeated here. Some attention has been paid, however, to those white suffragists who chose to express their ideas in black periodicals.

An exploration of attitudes toward educating black women as well as an analysis of the founding in 1881 of Spelman Seminary, the nation's oldest and best-known separate institution for black women, will provide the second major dimension to the consideration of women and the public sphere. An examination of the kind of education that was designed exclusively for black women who attended Spelman, as well as a consideration of the responses of the black community to this education, provides insights about the ways in which both the cult of True Womanhood and the cult of Anglo-Saxonism combined to produce a unique educational experience for women in late nineteenth-century America. Moreover, a consideration of the responses of the black community to the Spelman experiment reveals their acceptance of the True Womanhood ideology, their sensitivity to the realities of the black female experience in America, and their rejection of white supremacist notions concerning the innate intellectual and moral inferiority of blacks. The final discussion of attitudes toward the higher education of women in general is intended to provide additional insights about an important aspect of "the woman question" and blacks' responses to it. Specifically, it enables us to ascertain where blacks stood on the important debate that was taking place during the latter part of the nineteenth century concerning the purpose and nature of women's education. A related issue involving black women in the educational arena, which was discussed infrequently and involved only a small segment of the black community, was the controversy surrounding the ordination of black female preachers.[21] Though training women to be Sunday school teachers and missionaries was considered to be an appropriate goal of their higher education, training for the ministry continued to be reserved for men.

A discussion of black women and the political arena must begin with a brief history of the woman suffrage movement and the nature of black participation in it; this is followed by a summary of Frederick Douglass's attitudes toward women's rights, especially suffrage. I have chosen to deal with his women's rights posture generally because of the impact he later had on attitudes toward the political emancipation of black women, which he perceived to be inextricably bound up with the emancipation of the race. Second, his lifelong commitment to liberty for all people regardless of race, gender, or class made him favorably disposed to woman suffrage but, more importantly, resulted in his being one of the most outspoken advocates for the full emancipation of women in all areas of their public lives. Fannie

Barrier Williams acknowledges the debt owed to him by lovers of liberty everywhere, especially women.

> He so lived not only that men might be free and equal and exalted, but that women, too, by the same emancipating forces, might come equally into the estate of freedom. . . . His eloquence in behalf of women's rights to the equalities of citizenship is a lasting justification of woman's claims and contentions for perfect liberty. By right of his manly confidence in woman . . . Mr. Douglass was easily the strongest and best friend American women ever had among the great men of the republic. The history of progressive women in this country cannot be written without grateful acknowledgement to the helpful and inspiring influence of the incomparable friend of all humanity, Frederick Douglass.[22]

During the 1830s and 1840s American women began lecturing against slavery and found that in so doing they had to defend their own right to speak in public, which in turn led them to demand their own political and legal emancipation. At the Convention of the American Anti-Slavery Society in 1839, doubt was cast upon women's right to participate in the convention, so a resolution was proposed that hereafter women delegates would have votes like the men. A majority of the male delegates were opposed, but the women present insisted on voting and their votes gave the resolution a majority. In 1840 the American delegates to the World's Anti-Slavery Convention arrived in London to find the women delegates among them again excluded from participation. While seated in the gallery behind a curtain with the rest of the women, Elizabeth Stanton and Lucretia Mott felt the striking similarity between themselves and black slaves. During the ten days of frustration that followed, they became friends and agreed to hold a women's rights convention on their return to America, and eight years later the Seneca Falls Convention was held. The people present were, for the most part, members of the abolition movement.[23]

A second convention was held only two weeks later in Rochester, but a year and a half passed before the third convention was held, in Salem, Ohio. The American Equal Rights Association (previously the National Woman's Rights Convention) was organized in 1866 with the aim of securing suffrage for black men and women, though its emphasis shifted under the leadership of Wendell Phillips and others to the passage of the Fourteenth Amendment which was ratified in 1868. The Fifteenth Amendment, introduced six months later, caused a rift in the women's movement because it failed to include women's right to the vote.

Frederick Douglass (1817-1895), former slave and outspoken abolitionist, was also a women's rights advocate. He delivered a major address at the historic Seneca Falls gathering in 1848, which formally initiated the women's rights movement in the United States. Though Negro suffrage was his major preoccupation, he also campaigned for woman suffrage. On the last day of his life he spoke in Washington, D.C., to the National Council of Women.

101

Although small and divided, the women's rights movement showed considerable vitality on the suffrage issue during the 1870s and 1880s. A variety of techniques were used: organizing state suffrage associations, educating public opinion, conducting campaigns in several states for suffrage referenda, and maintaining pressure on Congress for an amendment to the federal constitution.[24] Whatever gains women were making on other fronts, the years from 1896-1910 came to be known among suffragists as "the doldroms."[25] The "turn in the tide" came between 1916 and 1919 with the organization of the Woman's Party as well as other factors.[26] In 1917 a referendum in New York was held, and over a million women expressed their desire for the vote. Then came the war, which advanced their cause because of the general increase in the economic and social opportunities for women. In 1919, Michigan, Oklahoma, and South Dakota extended suffrage to women. Congress also finally voted to submit to the states for ratification an amendment granting woman suffrage, and on August 26, 1920, the required number of states had ratified the Nineteenth Amendment and its inclusion in the Constitution was announced. Interestingly, the former slave states failed to ratify it. The suffrage lobby, after having used all the techniques available—petition, picketing, parades, and other militant procedures—had finally succeeded.[27]

Black participation in the movement prior to 1890 provides the historical perspective for fully understanding black attitudes toward woman suffrage during the years under consideration. This perspective begins with Frederick Douglass. While Douglass believed that the anti-slavery movement was doing much for the elevation and improvement of women, he understood fully the need for an independent, organized movement to achieve equal rights for women.[28] On July 14, 1848, his *North Star* carried the historic announcement of the Seneca Falls Convention. In addition, a constant reminder to his readers of his commitment to the rights of women was the slogan that appeared on every issue of the *North Star*—"Right is of No Sex." At the 1848 convention, when it appeared that Stanton's resolution that "it was the duty of the women of this country to secure to themselves their sacred right to the elective franchise" was headed for defeat, Douglass at a critical juncture asked for the floor and delivered an eloquent plea in behalf of women's right to the vote.[29] The resolution was then put to a vote and carried by a small margin. In 1888, a few years before his death, Douglass recalled his role at the Seneca Falls Convention and told the International Council of Women:

There were few facts in my humble history to which I look back with more satisfaction than to the fact, recorded in the history of the Woman Suffrage movement, that I was sufficiently enlightened at that early day, when only a few years from slavery, to support your resolution for woman suffrage. I have done very little in this world in which to glory, except this one act—and I certainly glory in that. When I ran away from slavery, it was for my people; but when I stood up for the rights of women, self was out of the question and I found a little nobility in the act.[30]

Similarly, in his autobiography, he explains why he became a "woman's rights" man, which is related to his belief that all persons are created equal and should therefore have the right to participate fully in the affairs of government.

. . . I am glad to say that I have never been ashamed to be thus designated. Recognizing not sex nor physical strength, but moral intelligence and the ability to discern right from wrong, good from evil, and the power to choose between them, as the true basis of republican government, to which all are alike subject and all bound alike to obey, I was not long in reaching the conclusion that there was no foundation in reason or justice for woman's exclusion from the right of choice in the selection of the persons who should frame the laws, and thus shape the destiny of all the people, irrespective of sex.[31]

He adds that the same arguments he used for granting suffrage to blacks were applicable to women.

A second convention, in which Douglass was active, was held only two weeks after the Seneca Falls meeting. The first national woman's rights convention took place in Worchester, Massachusetts, in 1850, at which Douglass and Sojourner Truth, famous black ex-slave, were present. Douglass remained a valuable cohort for the movement throughout its history because of his active participation as well as his coverage of it in his various publications. Few woman's rights conventions were held during the 1850s and later at which Douglass was not a featured speaker and whose proceedings were not fully reported in his paper. Equally as important was his persistent encouragement of black organizations in which he was involved to support the women's cause.[32]

At the 1851 Akron, Ohio, woman's rights convention, Sojourner Truth, well-known abolitionist, delivered her now famous "Ain't I a Woman" speech. Some of the delegates to the convention urged that she be prohibited from speaking, fearing that the abolitionists would harm their cause, but she was invited to the platform. She directed her remarks against the previous speaker, a clergyman who had ridiculed the weakness and helplessness of women and argued that they should not be entrusted with the vote.

> Dat man ober dar say dat womin needs to be helped into carriages and lifted ober ditches, and to hab de best place everywhar. Nobody eber helps me into carriages, or ober mud puddles, or gibs me any best place! And ain't I a woman? . . .
> Den day talks 'bout dis ting in de head; what did dy call it? ("Intellect," whispered some one near.) . . . What dat got to do wid womin's rights or nigger's rights? If my cup won't hold but a pint and yourn holds a quart, wouldn't ye be mean not to let me have my little half-measure full? . . . If de fust woman God ever made was strong enough to turn de world upside down all alone, dese women togedder ought to be able to turn it back, and get it right side up again! And now dey is asking to do it, de men better let 'em.[33]

While their first interest was the anti-slavery struggle, two other black women were active in the woman's rights movement in these early years—Frances E. W. Harper and Sarah Remond, sister of Charles Remond.[34]

In 1866, Douglass and Charles Remond, who joined Garrison in protesting the exclusion of women delegates from the World Anti-Slavery Convention, were among the vice-presidents chosen for the newly formed Equal Rights Association. Later in the year at an Albany meeting, Douglass warned the ERA that it was in danger of becoming a woman's rights association only.[35] At the first annual meeting of the ERA in 1867, Sojourner Truth spoke twice. During one of these talks, she addressed herself to the rights of women, especially black women.

> . . . There is a great stir about colored men getting their rights, but not a word about the colored women; and if colored men get their rights, and not colored women . . . there will be a bad time about it. . . . I want women to have their rights. In the courts women have no right, no voice; nobody speaks for them. . . . I am above 80 years old; it is about time for me to be going. But I suppose I am kept here because something remains for me to do. . . . I suppose I am about the only colored woman that goes about to speak for the rights of the colored woman. . . . Now men have a right to vote; and what I want is to have colored women have the right to vote.[36]

By the fall of 1873, even though the resentment over the failure of the Fifteenth Amendment to enfranchise women was still being felt, the leaders of the woman suffrage movement were anxious to reconcile their differences with Douglass. The actual split in the woman's movement had taken place in 1869, a crucial turning point in its history. At the proceedings of the American Equal Rights Association Convention in New York in 1869, the famous debate between Frederick Douglass and the white feminists present took place. Here he argued for the greater urgency of the race issue and defended the positions of abolitionists that now was the Negro hour and women's rights could wait.[37]

The great danger was that linking woman suffrage with Negro suffrage at this point would seriously lessen the chances of securing the ballot for black men, and for the Negro, he reiterated, the ballot was an urgent necessity.

> . . . I must say that I do not see how anyone can pretend that there is the same urgency in giving the ballot to woman as to the negro. With us, the matter is a question of life and death, at least, in fifteen States of the Union. When women, because they are women, are hunted down through the cities of New York and New Orleans; when they are dragged from their houses and hung upon lamp-posts; when their children are torn from their arms . . . then they will have an urgency to obtain the ballot equal to our own. . . .[38]

When asked whether what he had just said was true about black women, he quickly responded, "Yes, yes, yes . . . but not because she is a woman, but because she is black."[39] Frances E. W. Harper, black poet and anti-slavery lecturer of national repute, supported Douglass. Following this meeting, Stanton and Anthony organized the National Woman Suffrage Association (NSWA) for women only. They did so in the belief that it was largely due to the male leadership of the suffrage movement that women's interest had been betrayed. In November, 1869, in Cleveland, a second organization called the American Woman Suffrage Association (ASWA) was organized with Lucy Stone as chairman. Peace was restored in the 1876 convention of the NWSA during which Douglass was told that his help was needed in the continuing struggle for women's rights. Though he was still somewhat bitter about racist remarks made about black males during the battle over the Fifteenth Amendment, he announced that he was still willing to work for the cause. Once the reconciliation had taken place, he was again a familiar figure at women's rights conventions.[40]

In 1885, Douglass placed woman suffrage second on the list of causes to which he wished to devote the rest of his life—the first, of course, being the struggle for the complete emancipation of his people.[41] In a speech to the

International Council of Women in 1883, Douglass reveals his reasons for supporting woman suffrage for over forty years. First, he firmly believes that women, like blacks, should be granted "all the rights of American citizenship."[42] Furthermore, the achievement of equal rights for women will benefit movements for the emancipation "of mankind everywhere and in all ages."[43] In other words, if the women's rights movement succeeds in destroying "the universality of man's rule over women," it will demonstrate that truth and justice can indeed prevail against "strongly opposing forces, against time-hallowed abuses, against deeply entrenched error, against worldwide usage, and against the settled judgment of mankind."[44] Granting women the vote, which represents a "new revolution in human thought," is only a small part of woman's inherent and inalienable rights.

> When a great truth once gets abroad in the world, no power on earth can imprison it. . . . Such a truth is woman's right to equal liberty with men. She was born with it. It was hers before she comprehended it. It is inscribed upon all the powers and faculties of her soul, and no custom, law or usage can ever destroy it.[45]

Furthermore, the ballot will enable women to protect all of their other rights as citizens of a republican government.

On the afternoon of February 20, 1895, Douglass left home to attend a meeting of the National Council of Women in Washington. He returned home that evening and after dinner, while he was talking to his second wife, Helen Pitts Douglass, herself an active suffragist, about the events of the day, he suddenly collapsed and died.[46] He was certainly the greatest black American of the nineteenth century and the one who had fought the hardest for the rights of women and blacks. Having spent the last day of his life at a woman suffrage meeting was perhaps fitting as one of the many eulogies by women's rights leaders to him indicates. "We have lost the most conspicuous advocate of our rights, by the death of Frederick Douglass."[47] In 1908, at the celebration marking the sixtieth anniversary of the Seneca Falls Convention, Mary Church Terrell was invited to speak in Douglass's behalf. Active in club work among black women, she was elected the first president of the National Association of Colored Women, in which position she actively fought Jim Crow and joined forces with white women in the suffrage cause. In a long and eloquent tribute to Douglass for his role in the struggle for woman suffrage, she had this to say:

. . . The incomparable Frederick Douglass did many things of which I as a member of that race which he served so faithfully and well am proud. But there is nothing he ever did in his long and brilliant career in which I take keener pleasure and greater pride than I do in his ardent advocacy of equal political rights for women and the effective service he rendered the cause of woman suffrage sixty years ago.[48]

A thorough examination of the period under consideration reveals a broad range of attitudes toward woman suffrage within the black community and the development of two major phases in the debate. The first phase included the 1890s and the first decade of the twentieth century and was carried out mainly by black clubwomen. During the 1890s suffrage is seen as a means for black women to assume a broader place within the public sphere, which will in turn assure her equality with men. Equally as important, granting black women the vote will also contribute to the overall emancipation of the race since black women will help black men get elected to public office. The second phase, which begins during the second decade of the twentieth century, is characterized by a broadening of interest in the issue of woman suffrage as it becomes more apparent that the passage of the Nineteenth Amendment is inevitable. Joining the debate during this period are persons from various segments of the black community, conservatives and liberals alike, and a few white suffragists anxious to swell the ranks of those in favor of the Nineteenth Amendment.

In order to ascertain what black women themselves felt about granting the vote to members of their own sex, it is imperative that one peruse the pages of *Woman's Era*, the first periodical ever published by black women in this country and perhaps the best vehicle for the articulation of the political aspirations of black women during the period. In 1895 the first national convention of black women, later named the National Association of Colored Women (NACW), was called in Boston by Josephine St. Pierre Ruffin, who had for many years been associated with Julia Howe, Susan Anthony, Elizabeth Stanton, and other women's rights advocates. The national association was brought about by the consolidation of the Women's League of Washington, D.C., and the Woman's Era Club of Boston. The most conspicuous work of this Boston woman's club was the publication of *Woman's Era*.[49] The periodical, eventually designated the official organ of the NACW, considered itself "as a medium of intercourse and sympathy between the women of all races and conditions," as representing "the best thought and work of the most advanced women of your race," and as keeping women informed about matters of critical concern to them.[50] Since *Woman's Era* was founded, edited, and published by Ruffin, who was active in the Massachusetts woman suffrage movement, and had as editors of its departments such women as Mrs. Booker T. Washington, Ida Wells-Barnett, Mary Church Terrell, Fannie Barrier Williams, and Josephine Silone Yates, who were all pro-suffrage, it is not surprising to find in the publication a strong advocacy of the right of women, including especially black women, to vote, even though this was not its central focus.

The front page of the first issue carried a portrait and feature article on the women's rights leader Lucy Stone, which sets the tone for the publication. "No movement begun in the interest of human progress can start unmindful of the pioneer work projected and carried on by the saints and martyrs who are on the eternal side of right" (March 24, 1894). The first issue also contained an article on the closing meetings of the New England Woman Suffrage Association of which Ruffin was a member. An August, 1894 article written by a member of the Association for the Advancement of Women, an interracial women's organization whose purpose was "to help women forward in every line of progress moral, intellectual, political, social, and industrial," mentions that, though the organization does not exclusively advocate any one reform, there are among its members those who are for and against woman suffrage. Therefore, they frequently hold symposia in which all aspects of the case are presented. The author then comments on the widespread interest in this movement. The issue also contained an editorial that deals with woman suffrage. The author of the editorial, though previously reluctant to respond to the ridiculous arguments against woman suffrage, feels compelled to respond to two articles recently published by the *Virginia Baptist*. She then directs her readers to *The Illustrated American*, which had been publishing a series of prize papers for and against woman suffrage and indicates that they contain the best available arguments for suffrage. The "weak" arguments used against it (especially that through suffrage women will lose their womanliness) will only have the effect of turning the indifferent ones into suffragists, she says. The editorial ends with the assurance that victory will come eventually despite these "small attacks." It is apparent from this early issue that the promoters of *Woman's Era* (which had a wide circulation among black women in various parts of the country) wanted to make their readers aware of the importance of black women's right to vote and to convert those who were either indifferent to the question or opposed to it.

They also felt that black women should enter the public arena in order to solve their unique problems.

An awareness of the dilemma that black women faced as a result of the "double jeopardy" of race and sex is apparent throughout the periodical. Like contemporary black feminists, the women who wrote for this publication saw the necessity for black women to align themselves with organizations that dealt with both racism and sexism. To illustrate, Mary Church Terrell in the November, 1894 issue has this to say:

> . . . The Colored Woman's League has been invited to send delegates to the National Council of Women of the United States. . . . Only national organizations are invited to participate. Such an invitation from such an important body as the Council furnishes another proof of the advantage of a national organization of colored women. If they are to become an important factor in solving the knotty problems of race and sex, they must get a hearing and play a conspicuous part in all deliberations which look toward that end.[51]

In the November 1895 editorial of *Woman's Era*, the argument is made that black women need suffrage more than other women because of the added burden of race.

> There is no class in the United States that suffers under such disadvantages as the colored women. This class has everything to gain and nothing to lose by endorsing the woman suffrage movement. Race prejudice is expressed in many ways, but the exhibition of it is often crushed when a vote is wanted.[52]

At the end of the article, an incident is described concerning a letter written to white suffrage leaders by two residents of the Boston Home for Aged Colored Women, who expressed their desire to vote. This letter is a small indication of the support of woman suffrage among ordinary black women, and the fact that white suffragists find supporters among black women, though they have frequently not seen them as allies.

In her defense of woman suffrage, Fannie Williams, like other suffragists, argues that the enfranchisement of women in general will have a positive impact on American politics because of their commitment to various reforms.

> If our enfranchisement is to contribute nothing to the corrective forces of independence in American politics, there will be much disappointment among those who believed that the cause of temperance, municipal reform and better education would be more surely advanced when the finer virtues of women became a part of the political forces of the country.[53]

In other words, women have a special responsibility as voters to make sure that a better world is created. The black female voter faces a special challenge since "for the first time in our history we are to receive public attention and have our womanly worth tested by the high standards of important public duties."[54] She then urges women's clubs and other organizations in which women participate to take an active role in teaching them "the best lessons of citizenship" so that black women will "exert a wholesome influence in the politics of the future."[55] Finally, she argues that suffrage should be seen as a means of total liberation for blacks so that blacks should be especially mindful of the importance of their vote.

Woman's Era was not a lone voice, however, in the debate surrounding suffrage for black women. Prominent black women also expressed their views on suffrage in articles and speeches in other publications. Adella Hunt Logan,[56] life member of the National Woman Suffrage Association, argues passionately for suffrage in an article written for *Colored American Magazine* in 1905. Echoing Douglass, she reiterates his earlier point that as American citizens, women have certain constitutional rights, and because they are governed by the laws of the land, they should also have a voice in its operations. In other words, "the fundamental principles of republican government" should also apply to women.

> Government of the people, for the people and by the people is but partially realized so long as woman has no vote. . . . The power that coerces, that controls without consent, is unjust. Such is the status of most American women.[57]

Echoing Fannie Williams, she believes that suffrage is even more urgent for blacks.

> If white American women, with all their natural and acquired advantages, need the ballot . . . if Anglo Saxons have been helped by it—and they have—how much more do black Americans, male and female, need the strong defense of a vote to help secure their right to life, liberty and the pursuit of happiness.[58]

For Logan, as was the case with Douglass, the arguments for black suffrage are also relevant for woman suffrage.

> The price of their [blacks'] freedom . . . was too dear a price to be treated lightly. Every morsel of political right and duty should be cherished, and in the opinions of many wise and eminent men, as well as women, these privileges

should be extended even to women. Susan B. Anthony stands today easily among the foremost ranks of the world's greatest women and men. Her message to civilization has been a beautiful plea for political justice to the weaker members of the human family, whether the black man or all women.[59]

Mrs. Margaret Murray Washington expressed her desire for woman suffrage for similar reasons and believes that, despite the continued struggle, its attainment is inevitable.

> . . . Colored women, quite as much as colored men, realize that if there is ever to be equal justice and fair play in the protection in the courts everywhere for all races, then there must be an equal chance for all women as well as men to express their preference through their votes. There are certain things so sure to come our way that time in arguing them is not well spent. It is simply the cause of right which in the end always conquers, no matter how fierce the opposition.[60]

She discusses the purpose of the NACW's Department of Suffrage, whose primary aim is informing women of governmental affairs so that they will be prepared to handle the vote intelligently when it comes. Apparently, their aim was not to fight for woman suffrage though some of the members were active in various parts of the country in the movement to attain the vote for women.[61] Interestingly, however, she admits that woman suffrage is not the most important issue for her, though it must eventually be accepted by the country.

> . . . Personally, woman suffrage has never kept me awake at night, but I am sure before this country is able to take its place amongst the great democratic nations of the earth it has got to come to the place where it is willing to trust its citizens, black as well as white, women as well as men, to be loyal to their government.[62]

For Mary Church Terrell, outspoken feminist, educator, and first president of NACW, the struggle for woman suffrage and the right of black women in particular to vote was something that she probably did lose sleep over since it consumed much of her energy. In her autobiography, she writes in some detail of her participation in the suffrage movement. She admits having attended most of the NAWSA meetings in Washington, which were held every two years. Recalling the large 1898 meeting of NAWSA, she takes pride at having been among the few who stood when the presiding officer requested all those to rise who believed that women should have the vote.

> . . . I forced myself to stand up, although it was hard for me to do so. In the early 1890's it required a great deal of courage for a woman publicly to acknowledge before an audience that she believed in suffrage for her sex when she knew the majority did not. I can not recall a period in my life, since I heard the subject discussed for the first time as a very young girl, that I did not believe in woman suffrage with all my heart. When I was a freshman in college I wrote an essay entitled, "Resolved, There Should Be a Sixteenth Amendment to the Constitution Granting Suffrage to Women." Nevertheless, it was not easy for me publicly to commit myself to woman suffrage in that large meeting.[63]

Though she spoke before this body again on numerous occasions in defense of woman suffrage, an excerpt from the speech in which she pays tribute to Douglass will reveal her belief, which was shared by many blacks during this time, that the race issue was the primary one as long as blacks remained in a subservient position.

> If at any time Mr. Douglass seemed to waver in his allegiance to the cause of political enfranchisement of women, it was because he realized as no white person, no matter how broad and sympathetic he may be, has ever been able to feel or can possibly feel today just what it means to belong to my despised, handicapped and persecuted race. I am a woman and I know what it means to be circumscribed, deprived, handicapped and fettered on account of my sex. But I assure you that nowhere in the United States have my feelings been so lacerated, my spirit so crushed, my heart so wounded, nowhere have I been so humiliated and handicapped on account of my sex as I have been on account of my race. . . .[64]

Around 1910 Ida Wells-Barnett, noted for her crusade against lynching and her clubwoman activities, organized the Alpha Suffrage Club in Chicago after the Illinois legislature granted the vote to women for local elections. This club has the distinction of being the first organization for black women in the nation,[65] and its activities are a perfect example of arguments made by some blacks concerning the advantages of granting the vote to black women as far as the advancement of the race is concerned. A major objective of the Alpha Suffrage Club in the beginning was encouraging black women in the Second Ward to register to vote so that they could help elect a black to the city council. Though black men in the neighborhood discouraged clubmembers by telling them to go home and take care of the children, these women continued to go from house to house in the predominantly black Second Ward and eventually were courted by black male politicians. During

Mary Church Terrell (1863-1954), teacher and civil rights leader, was also an activist in the women's rights struggle. A tireless clubwoman, she was elected first president of the historic National Association of Colored Women in 1896. In the early 1920s, she was second vice-president of the International Council of Women of the Darker Races of the World. She was also an active member of the National American Woman Suffrage Association and an important figure in the international women's movement. In 1904, she represented black women in the American delegation to the International Council of Women in Berlin, and was the only American to give her speech in German, French, and English.

the second year of their struggle, a black alderman was elected from the Second Ward, and they were at least partially responsible for his victory.[66] A chapter in Barnett's autobiography discusses her efforts to block, through the Alpha Suffrage Club, the efforts of white women ·in Illinois in 1914 to effect a restricted suffrage for women, whose purpose was to prohibit black women from attaining the vote. Though she had been a member of the predominantly white Woman's Suffrage Association since moving to Chicago in 1895, it now became clear to her that black women were going to have to fight separately for their right to vote in the state.[67] She had been unable to arouse widespread interest in woman suffrage on the part of the black clubwomen of her state, but she seized this opportunity to convey to them the danger of remaining indifferent to this crucial issue.

The other side of the race argument is voiced in a pamphlet entitled "The Responsibility and Opportunity of the 20th Century Woman," written prior to 1920 by Mrs. A. W. Blackwell, corresponding secretary of the W. H. and F. M. Society. She gives an interesting reason for her failure to support woman suffrage:

> . . . I am not a suffragist or a suffragette, but if I were certain that there would not be a "grandmothers clause" introduced after the franchise was secured, to prevent the more than 3,000,000 Negro women from voting, then I would not raise a note of protest against the suffrage movement. But when we observe closely the trend of legislation as it is directed against equal opportunities for the Negroes in this country and realize the influence that women exert without the ballot—what would it be with the ballot?[68]

In other words, granting only white women the vote (since she assumes that black women will be disenfranchised, as was the case with black men after the passage of the Fifteenth Amendment) will make matters worse for black people since an increase in the numbers of enfranchised whites will result in a further erosion of the rights of blacks and the subsequent reinforcement of inequality between blacks and whites. Du Bois, on the other hand, argued in a *Crisis* editorial on "Votes for Women" that it was going to be more difficult to disfranchise black women because of social sanctions against the violent treatment of women in public places and the likelihood that black women are less vulnerable to bribes.

> Even southern "gentlemen," as used as they are to the mistreatment of colored women, cannot in the blaze of present publicity physically beat them away from the polls. Their economic power over them [black women] will be

Ida B. Wells-Barnett (1862-1931), civil rights leader, journalist and anti-lynching crusader, organized in 1893 the Alpha Suffrage Club in Chicago, and was an active member in the early years of the National Association of Colored Women. She marched in the famous woman suffrage parade in Washington, D.C., in 1913 and wrote an autobiography which was edited by her daughter, Alfreda Duster, as *Crusade for Justice* (1970). The period under consideration could be more appropriately be called the Age of Washington and Wells-Barnett.

smaller than their power over the men and while you can still bribe some pauperized Negro laborers with a few dollars at election time, you cannot bribe Negro women.[69]

Blackwell goes on to say that white women are not ready for the franchise at this point anyway since they still harbor prejudices against women of color.

If the women of the dominant race had a broader and clearer vision of the Fatherhood of God and the brotherhood of man, and would exert that influence now in the legislative halls and criminal courts to correct some of the pernicious laws that discriminate so outrageously against a part of the citizens of this country because of their color, then I would say, God speed the day when all women might be thrown in the balance that justice, a fair chance, and equal opportunity might be given to every man regardless of color or race. Not until the Anglo-Saxon mother will teach her sons and daughters to respect and protect every honorable woman, will she be ready for the franchise. . . .[70]

As the debate over woman suffrage continued and expanded, an even wider range of perspectives became apparent. As one might have expected, the compatibility between the overall goals of black and woman suffrage continued to be a major theme. At opposite ends of the pole, however, were those who believed that suffrage would strengthen women in their roles as wife and mother and those who viewed suffrage as an "unwomanly" activity.

The black periodical that contained the most extensive coverage of the woman suffrage question during this phase was the *Crisis*, the official organ of the NAACP, which can be attributed to the intense interest and commitment on the part of Du Bois, its editor from 1910-1934, to the women's rights struggle. An editorial in the October 1911 issue contains Du Bois' first statement of his position on woman suffrage. Here he argues that racism within the women's movement was a deterrent to its progress, though he was in agreement with its goals.[71] In one of his frequent editorials on woman suffrage, he reiterated his sensitivity to the oppression of women.

The meaning of the twentieth century is the freeing of the individual soul; the soul longest in slavery and still in the most disgusting and indefensible slavery is the soul of womanhood.[72]

The *Crisis* is the best source of black attitudes on the issue of granting the vote to black women during this period; it also contains a few short statements by white suffragists on the general issue of woman suffrage. While exploring many other aspects of the woman question from 1910 to 1920, Du Bois focused on the issue of woman suffrage in the September 1912 issue (the first special issue on the subject), the August 1915 issue, and the November 1917 issue. At the 1912 convention of the National Woman Suffrage Association, Du Bois argued that disenfranchised women and blacks shared similar problems, which he was to continue discussing in subsequent issues of the *Crisis*. In his speech, Du Bois reveals his strong belief that both blacks and women should have the vote for similar reasons. As he was to continue to do throughout his career, he reminded white suffragists of their often narrow point of view and urged them to base their arguments for woman suffrage on a broad demand of justice for all human beings.

> . . . The advocates of woman suffrage have continually been in great danger of asking for the ballot not because they are citizens, but because they occupy a certain social position, are of a certain grade of intelligence, or are "white." Continually it has been said in America, "If paupers and Negroes vote why not college-bred women of wealth and position?" The assumption is that such a woman has superior right to have her interests represented in the nation and that Negroes and paupers have few rights which society leaders are bound to respect. . . .[73]

Like some blacks today, Du Bois realized the difficulty of being a black supporter of woman suffrage because of the racism within the suffrage movement and the racism of American white women generally.[74] This was also discussed in an editorial that appeared in the August 1914 issue of the *Crisis*. Du Bois maintained an interest in the views of white suffragists with respect to blacks and may have invited them to participate in the debate on woman suffrage in which the *Crisis* was involved for nearly a decade. Their views on the relationship between woman and black suffrage are an indication of a change in attitude among white suffragists over the issue of granting black women the vote. This shift in attitude occurred between the 1890s and the years immediately preceding the passage of the Nineteenth Amendment, or the second phase of the woman suffrage struggle.

The last special issue of the *Crisis* (November 1917) contained statements by three prominent white feminists—Anna Shaw (she succeeded Carrie Chapman Catt as president of NAWSA in 1902 and retired in 1915; Catt, president of NAWSA (she succeeded Anthony in 1900, withdrew in 1902, and resumed the presidency again in 1915); and Mary Hay, chair of the New York Woman Suffrage Party, a NAWSA affiliate. Shaw simply states that all American citizens, regardless of race or sex, should be granted the right to vote. Catt also argues that *all* women, irrespective of their national origin or race, should be enfranchised. It is apparent here that her attitudes have shifted since her earlier days as president of NAWSA, when southern suffragists were being wooed. In her presidential address to the 1901 and 1904 NAWSA conventions, Catt had expressed views that revealed her capitulation to southern suffragists whose main argument during the 1890s in support of woman suffrage was that it would ensure white supremacy by increasing the majority in the white electorate. In these speeches she questioned the wisdom of the enfranchisement of blacks in 1868, and her solution to the problem of the influx of irresponsible voters into the electorate was a proposal for literacy tests and property requirements.[75] Mary Hay spoke specifically about the need for black men, recently enfranchised in the state of New York, to support woman suffrage.

> The colored race is a progressing race. Woman constitutes a progressing sex. This similarity should make colored men sympathetic toward woman's struggle for political freedom. . . . The women of New York City, colored and white alike, appeal to men to be just and democratic and to make them voting citizens.[76]

Each of these women seeks support for woman suffrage because she believes in the ideals of a democratic government; however, they fail to address themselves directly to the benefits to be gained for the black community when suffrage is extended to all women. Only Catt addresses the issue of black women and the vote in a direct manner, even though the audience is primarily black. Their major concern seems to be getting the vote for themselves, which would of course also benefit women of other groups. In addition, Catt and Hay seem to harbor mild resentment about black men being enfranchised before white women. Catt reminds readers that black men had failed to support woman suffrage after the Civil War because of their sexism. "He had his chance then to stand by the woman's rights cause that stood by him. . . . Like the white men around him, he could not . . . recognize that women were people. . . . he wanted democracy applied for himself, but not for woman."[77]

Though Du Bois was aware of the bitterness in the black community over the racist attitudes of many white suffragists, he still urged his readers to support woman suffrage (especially the 75,000 black voters in New York who would be voting within a few weeks on the issue of woman suffrage in their state). First, blacks must remember

> that the day when women can be considered as the mere appendages of men, dependent upon their bounty and educated chiefly for their pleasure, has gone by; that as an intelligent, self-supporting human being a woman has just as good a right to a voice in her own government as has any man, and that the denial of the right is as unjust as is the denial of the right to vote to American Negroes.[78]

He also argues that two wrongs do not make a right. "We cannot punish the insolence of certain classes of American white women or correct their ridiculous fears by denying them their undoubted rights."[79] When the triumph of woman suffrage appeared imminent, Du Bois repeatedly addressed himself to black women, urging them to prepare themselves for the vote.

In the September 1912 issue of *Crisis*, Du Bois links the struggle for women's rights with the struggle for the liberation of blacks. His central theme is suggested by the cover, which contains a portrait of Frederick Douglass and the title "Woman's Suffrage Number." In his lead editorial, entitled "Votes for Women," he asks rhetorically why black voters should concern themselves with woman suffrage and answers:

> First, it is a great human question. Nothing human must be foreign, uninteresting or unimportant to colored citizens of the world. Whatever concerns half mankind concerns us. Secondly, any agitation, discussion or reopening of the problem of voting must inevitably be a discussion of the right of black folk to vote in America and Africa. . . .
>
> Finally, votes for women mean votes for black women. . . . The enfranchisement of these women will not be a mere doubling of our vote and voice in the nation; it will tend to stronger and more normal political life . . . and the making of politics a method of broadest philanthropic race betterment. . . .[80]

The overall message of the symposium on suffrage that follows, which includes the remarks of black and white women and black men, is that the nineteenth-century bond between suffragists and blacks must be continued in the twentieth century. What follows is a summary of the contents made by the various participants.

Mary Church Terrell, a strong advocate of woman suffrage in her piece entitled "The Justice of Woman Suffrage," alludes to the absurdity of any black person opposing woman suffrage, especially the men.

It is difficult to believe that any individual in the United States with one drop of African blood in his veins can oppose woman suffrage. It is queer and curious enough to hear an intelligent colored woman argue against granting suffrage to her sex, but for an intelligent colored man to oppose woman suffrage is the most preposterous and ridiculous thing in the world. What could be more absurd than to see one group of human beings who are denied rights which they are trying to secure for themselves working to prevent another group from obtaining the same rights. For the very arguments which are advanced against granting the right of suffrage to women are offered by those who have disfranchised colored men.[81]

She goes on to add, however, that on a recent lecture tour, she frequently discussed woman suffrage with the leading citizens in the communities (presumably black) where she spoke and only a few black males were opposed to woman suffrage. "It was very gratifying, indeed, to see that in the majority of instances these men stood right on the question of woman suffrage."[82] Adella Logan, an outspoken suffragist and the final participant in the symposium, alludes to the increased political consciousness of black women and discusses the relevance of the women's rights movement to black women in "Colored Women as Voters."

More and more colored women are studying public questions and civics. As they gain information and have experience in their daily vocations and in their efforts for human betterment they are convinced, as many other women have long ago been convinced, that their efforts would be more telling if women had the vote.

The fashion of saying "I do not care to meddle with politics" is disappearing among the colored woman faster than most people think, for this same woman has learned that politics meddle constantly with her and hers.[83]

She goes on to argue that if women were allowed to vote they could better protect their families and therefore become better wives and mothers.

Building inspectors, sanitary inspectors and food inspectors owe their position to politics. Who then is so well informed as to how these inspectors perform their duties as the women who live in inspected districts. . . . Adequate school facilities in city, village and plantation districts greatly concern the black mother. But without a vote, she has no voice in educational legislation, and no power to see that her children secure their share of public-school funds. . . .[84]

This view conflicts with those opposed to women entering the public sphere. A recent historian comments on the desire to confine women to the home during this period.

> The political extension of women's role, more than education or employment, was seen as a threat to both the family and society. It questioned the role of women as wives and mothers. The magnitude of the antagonism to the campaign for the vote reflects the fear of this challenge. . . . There was an active campaign to persuade middle-class women that the most important (and perhaps only) contribution which they could make to social progress was in their role as mothers. If women fulfilled their duty as mothers they would be prevented from full social and political participation. The question of women's rights would be in practice solved. Hence the campaign for motherhood was a powerful and persuasive tool against political and social rights.[85]

The August 1915 issue of *Crisis*, also devoted to woman suffrage, carried on its cover a picture of Sojourner Truth and Abraham Lincoln, which reminded readers of Du Bois' earlier efforts to point out the historic alliance between women and blacks. Introduced by Du Bois as "one of the strongest cumulative attacks on sex and race discrimination in politics ever written"(p. 177), the second symposium includes statements by twenty black men and women who have varying reasons for supporting woman suffrage. Commentators include John Hurst, bishop of the A.M.E. Church; Benjamin Brawley, dean of Morehouse College; Judge Robert Terrell, husband of Mary C. Terrell; Mary Talbert, vice president of the NACW; Nannie Burroughs; Josephine Ruffin; and Mary C. Terrell, honorary president of NACW. While a detailed discussion of their various arguments will not be presented, it is important to note in the summaries that follow the wide range of reasons for their support of woman suffrage. In general, the arguments fall under two main categories and are traceable to the participants' acceptance of traditional definitions of women and their desire to see the black female vote used in a practical manner for the welfare of the black community. Their views have also been shaped by their knowledge of the realities of the black female experience in America. For example, Miss M. E. Jackson, president of the Rhode Island Association of Colored Women's Clubs and a civil servant of the same state, states that many of the arguments against woman suffrage, especially those made by advocates for the cult of True Womanhood, do not apply to black women or working women who must leave the confines of home daily out of economic necessity and join the work force with other women.[86] The conventional argument that a woman's place is in the home is irrelevant, in other words, in the debate over granting suffrage to black women.

The symposium, in which twenty-six "leading thinkers of colored America"[87] participated, contains the greatest amount of information on black attitudes toward woman suffrage, especially for black women, assembled in one place. Rev. Francis Grimke, pastor of a Presbyterian church in Washington, admits in the lead article having been opposed to woman suffrage before he began to give it serious consideration. His reasons for supporting woman suffrage now are three-fold. First, "the interests of women are just as much involved in the enactment of laws . . . as are the interests of men."[88] Moreover, laws involving the liquor traffic, the social evil, and other demoralizing influences have a special interest for women because these issues directly affect the peace and happiness of the home. Second, the average woman is as qualified as the average man to assess the qualifications of those entrusted with the power to run government. In fact, since the average woman is superior in character to the average man, she is better fitted to share in the selection of public officials. These two arguments illustrate Grimke's acceptance of prevailing nineteenth-century notions about women, which emphasized their moral superiority and their domestic interests. Third, to deny women the vote is "to govern her without her consent which is contrary to the fundamental principle of democracy."[89] This last point is reminiscent of Adella Logan's reason for supporting woman suffrage.

Other participants also base part of their support of woman suffrage on their Victorian belief in the special traits and concerns of women that will cause them to vote for social reforms. Echoing Fannie Williams, Charles Chesnutt, well-known novelist, says that "their sympathies are apt to be in support of those things which are clean and honest and just and therefore desirable."[90] Mrs. Coralie Cook, member of the Washington, D.C., Board of Education, echoes the same theme in her piece entitled "Votes for Mothers," which underscores the significance of motherhood during this period.

> . . . Mothers *are* different, or ought to be different, from other folk. . . . Who should be more competent to control the presence of barrooms and "red-light districts" than mothers whose sons they are meant to lure to degradation and death? Who knows better than the girls' mother at what age the girl may legally barter her own body? Surely not the men who have put upon our statute books, 16, 14, 12, aye, be it to their eternal shame, even 10 and 8 years, as "the age of consent!"[91]

Similarly, votes by mothers will mean votes *for* children, according to Carrie Clifford, honorary president of the Federation of Colored Women's Clubs of Ohio.

> That the child's food may be pure, that his environment shall be wholesome and his surroundings sanitary—these are the things which engage her thought. That his mind shall be properly developed and his education wisely directed; that his occupation shall be clean and his ideals high—all these things are of supreme importance to her, who began to plan for the little life before it was even dreamed of by the father. . . . Her dream is of a State where war shall cease, where peace and unity be established and where love shall reign. Yes, it is the great mother-heart reaching out to save her children from war, famine, and pestilence. . . .[92]

Again, conventional notions about the special responsibilities of women are being used to advance the progressive idea that women should be granted the vote. Miss Anna Jones, chair of the Department of Education of the NACW, also indicates that women voters, because of their special qualities, will have a different set of priorities than male voters.

> . . . Her work is the prevention of vice with its train of physical and moral evils; the enactment of laws to secure and regulate sanitation, food, prohibition, divorce; the care of the aged, the unfortunate, the orphan. All the questions touch in a very direct way the home—woman's kingdom . . . her close view and sympathetic touch will be of material assistance in the solution of the social problems that confront her as the homemaker. The century awaits the "finer issues" of woman's "finely touched spirit."[93]

Here again the political emancipation of women is not believed to be in conflict with the good of the race and the nation. A persistent anti-suffrage argument had been that granting the vote to women would "undermine marriage, the family, and the structure of society."[94] By emphasizing the importance of maintaining the integrity of the family, the suffrage supporters mentioned above hoped to appeal to a broader range of persons in the black community. Though these kinds of arguments were based on conventional and certainly debatable assumptions about women, they also reveal the extent to which both women and men felt the female sex to be special and more humanitarian than the male sex. While these attitudes would be considered sexist by contemporary feminists, women in the nineteenth century felt that their unique attributes or what made them different from men should be the basis upon which they should be granted the vote.

Still other participants insisted that the attainment of the vote by black women would result in improvements for the race generally. Josephine St. Pierre Ruffin, who had been in suffrage work in Massachusetts for over forty years, believed that "equality of the sexes means more progress toward equality of the races," so that it was counter productive for any black to be opposed to universal suffrage.[95] Additionally, the black woman's moral character will become apparent when she is able to perform in the political arena. In fact, only when *all* American women are granted the vote will the world get "a correct estimate of the Negro woman's moral qualities," according to Nannie Burroughs, secretary of the Women's Auxiliary to the National Baptist Convention.[96] She continues her defense of the morality of black women, which the vote will illustrate.

> It will find her a tower of strength of which poets have never sung, orators have never spoken, and scholars have never written. . . . Had she not been the woman of unusual moral stamina that she is, the black race would have been made a great deal whiter, and the white race a great deal blacker. . . . She has been left a prey for the men of every race, but in spite of this, she has held the enemies of Negro female chastity at bay. The Negro woman is the white woman's as well as the white race's most needed ally in preserving an unmixed race.[97]

Having demonstrated that because of their part in preserving race purity, black women should not be perceived as enemies by whites, she then goes on to discuss the benefits that would accrue to black women themselves as a result of attaining the vote. The argument is again related to the issue of morality, which black women perceived to be the most serious problem (along with poverty) that they as a group faced during this period.

> The ballot, wisely used, will bring to her the respect and protection that she needs. It is her weapon of moral defense. Under present conditions, when she appears in court in defense of her virtue, she is looked upon with amused contempt. She needs the ballot to reckon with men who place no value upon her virtue, and to mould healthy public sentiment in favor of her own protection.[98]

This particular argument—that black women would be better able to defend their morality with the vote—was unique among the arguments presented and reveals the extent to which black women were painfully aware of their sexual vulnerability and their need, by whatever means, to protect themselves.

Racial arguments are also used by the remaining participants for their support of woman suffrage, but their perspectives are more practical. Here the approach is not an appeal to justice emphasizing the human rights argument (as was the case with Douglass), or an evocation of the True Womanhood ideal emphasizing women's moral superiority (as was the case with Chesnutt and Jones). Suffrage for black women is seen as a means to an end. The most obvious results will be both social and individual—overall improvements in the black community as well as an increase in the productivity and self-esteem of black women themselves. Oscar de Priest, alderman of Chicago, alludes to the aldermanic campaign of 1915, in which voting black women rallied behind the black male candidates, resulting in their victory as well as a victory for the race.[99] Nannie Burroughs also refers to the value of the black female voter.

> Because the black man does not know the value of the ballot, and has bartered and sold his most valuable possession, it is no evidence that the Negro woman will do the same. The Negro woman, therefore, needs the ballot to get back, by the wise *use* of it, what the Negro man has lost by the *misuse* of it. She needs it to ransom her race. . . .[100]

Similarly, Mrs. Mary B. Talbert, vice-president of the NACW, refers to the recent reform efforts, both political and educational, of such black women as Nannie Burroughs and Mary Bethune, founder of Bethune-Cookman College in 1904. She argues that black women have much to contribute in the political arena because of skills they have developed in other areas.

> By her peculiar position the colored woman has gained clear powers of observation and judgment—exactly the sort of powers which are today peculiarly necessary to the building of an ideal country.[101]

Many see the absurdity of blacks, who themselves have been denied rights, impeding the progress of women in their struggle for the vote. Judge Robert Terrell, justice of the municipal court of Washington and husband of Mary Church Terrell, asserts emphatically that "the Negro should be most ardently in favor of woman suffrage, for above all others, he knows what a denial of the ballot means to a people."[102] He also feels that blacks owe a debt to white female suffragists who fought during the abolitionist movement for the rights of blacks, even when their own cause was in jeopardy. "Now what our fathers failed to do for these pioneers who did so much for our cause before and after the great war, let us do for these who are now leading the fight for woman suffrage."[103]

The most unconventional argument for granting women the vote was advanced by Mrs. Paul L. Dunbar (Alice), wife of the well-known poet and novelist. She believes that the denial of the vote results in a narrow, incomplete life as well as a limitation upon the mental development of women, preventing them from attaining the kind of experience that makes for great literature or other great work. "No person living a mentally starved existence can do enduring work in any field, and woman without all the possibilities of life is starved, pinched, poverty-stricken."[104] This kind of argument is closer to the attitudes of contemporary feminists who see the denial of certain rights to women as detrimental to their total development as human beings. Furthermore, Mrs. Dunbar argues, such oppression results in a negative self-image on the part of women.

It is difficult to love your home and family if you be outcast and despised by them; perplexing to love humanity, if it gives you nothing but blows; impracticable to love your country, if it denies you all the rights and privileges which as citizens you should enjoy.[105]

This attitude is also more characteristic of contemporary feminists as well as psychiatrists who have attempted to explain some of the negative results of oppression on the psyche of a group.

This panel reveals the wide range of opinions among blacks about the need for woman suffrage. The panel also provides concrete evidence of the extent of interest in the issue among various segments of the black community. At the end of the symposium, there is a note that articles were received too late for publication from John Hope, president of Morehouse College, and other less-well-known persons.

The debate over woman suffrage, which spanned a forty-year period, also resulted in strong views against granting women the vote among certain segments of the black community (mostly male), most of whom advanced arguments that were similar to those made by well-known white males. Three months after the *Crisis* symposium of 1915, Du Bois published a response entitled "The Risk of Woman Suffrage" submitted by Kelly Miller, the well-known Howard University professor. Reacting to the one-sided nature of the symposium, he offers his reasons for opposing woman suffrage.

Sex is the one fixed and unalterable separatrix of mankind. . . . Woman's sphere of activity falls mainly within while man's field of action lies largely without the domestic circle. . . . Woman is physically weaker than man and is incapable of competing with him in the stern and strenuous activities of public and practical life. . . . Suffrage is not a natural right, like life and liberty. . . . It is merely a convenient agency through which to secure life, liberty, and happiness to all. It cannot be maintained that woman is deprived of any of these objects under male suffrage. . . . It is alleged that Negro suffrage and woman suffrage rest on the same basis. But on close analysis it is found there is scarcely any common ground between them.[106]

An avid supporter of the cult of True Womanhood, Prof. Miller subscribes to the Victorian notion that woman's place is in the home and that women are physically incapable of functioning in the public arena because of biological disabilities.[107] Though Du Bois did not indicate whether there were other negative responses to the symposium and the arguments for woman suffrage contained therein, this response does indicate that some black males were as sexist in their attitudes toward women as their white counterparts.

As one might have predicted, given his conservative position on other issues, Booker T. Washington—outspoken advocate of social separation between the races and the value of industrial as opposed to liberal education for blacks—was opposed to woman suffrage. His article "Booker T. Washington Questions the Benefit to Women" appeared in the New York *Times* on December 20, 1909.

I am in favor of every measure that will give to woman, the opportunity to develop to the highest possible extent, her moral, intellectual, and physical nature. . . . I do not . . . see that this involves the privilege or the duty . . . of voting. The influence of woman is already enormous in this country. She exerts, not merely in the homes, but through the schools and in the press, a powerful and helpful influence upon affairs. It is not clear to me that she would exercise any greater or more beneficent influence upon the world than she now does, if the duty of taking an active part in party politics were imposed on her.[108]

Rev. Dickerson, a black male from Oberlin, Ohio, and a strong advocate of the cult of True Womanhood, felt that activity outside the domestic sphere would contaminate women.

. . . nothing which disturbs the family is beneficial to the State or society. . . this would be the inevitable should women go into public life. . . . "Politics is more likely to contaminate woman than woman to disinfect politics." Her gentle nature would soon deteriorate under such a corrosive influence. They would then become more schemy than men. . . . The Republic could not be visited with a greater plague than female politicians. . . . It [woman suffrage] revolutionizes society . . . and it revolutionizes the opinions of those so old-fashioned among us as to believe that the legitimate and proper sphere of woman is the family circle, as wife and mother, and not politician and voter. . . .[109]

Joining the debate over woman suffrage in the final years were two black periodicals whose perspectives on the issue reflect their liberal or conservative philosophies. Moreover, their radically different positions on the issues are an illustration of the broad range of attitudes in the black community over the controversial issue of woman suffrage during the long debate. The first publication is the *Messenger*, published in New York from 1917 to 1920 by A. Philip Randolph and Chandler Owen. One is not surprised at its pro-suffrage stance given its reputation as the only radical Negro magazine in America because of its socialist leanings. In an editorial in the November 1917 issue, blacks are urged to vote yes in the upcoming election on the question of woman suffrage so that black women, like white women, will be allowed "to express their sentiments as regards the school system, sanitation, the high cost of living, war, and everything else which affects the general public."[110] In addition, the author of the editorial argues that "the artificial standards of sex or race" should not stand against the great sweep of democracy. In an editorial contained in the January 18 issue, the magazine takes credit for being the "only publication by Negroes in New York which supported woman suffrage."[111] In addition, they claim that the Political Council led by the *Messenger* editors was the only largely black political organization that supported woman suffrage. All the other Negro publications either opposed it or ignored it, thinking that the question of woman suffrage was a minor consideration. In addition to congratulating themselves for having supported woman suffrage "by voice and pen for the last eight years," the editors commend the magazine for "being in the vanguard of progress and not of reaction with the other Negro publications who fail to grasp the national and international movements and currents sweeping through the world." Editorials on woman suffrage continue through 1920. In the Who's Who section of the publication, Carrie Catt is applauded for her role in the woman suffrage movement (January, 1919, p. 30) while Kelly Miller is criticized for his opposition to woman suffrage (March, 1919, p. 23).

The *Competitor*, published in Pittsburgh in 1920 and 1921 and edited by Robert Vann, is at the opposite end of the pole on the question of what woman suffrage will mean to black women now that it has been attained. In the March, 1920 issue, George White is opposed to black women having the right to vote because of what he believes will be their negative treatment at the polls in the South. "Can you even tolerate the thought of your mother, wife or sister going to the polls and being insulted and otherwise maligned by unscrupulous, unprincipled crackers?"[112] As far as he is concerned the disadvantages will outweigh the advantages of black females having the vote. He ends with an essentially sexist argument for his opposition to the vote for black women that reveals his acceptance of the major components of the cult of True Womanhood.

> What man, after a vexing day in his office, or at his labor, does not look forward hungrily to meeting his mate, in all her natural womanly sweetness, that wonderful quality which God has bestowed on her. . . . She is here to be the mother of man, to be loved, petted and cared for. Her natural habitat is in the home. . . .[113]

In the June 1920 issue of the *Competitor*, Willie Mae King responds to White. She discusses what suffrage will mean to black women and points out the weaknesses in White's argument that black women should not have the vote. "Woman suffrage will mean enlightenment, progress, and political freedom not for our women alone, but for the race as well."[114]

It seems fair to say that only a few blacks were committed to the woman's rights struggle to the same extent that they were committed to the struggle to emancipate their race from the oppressive conditions under which they lived, though most who were in favor of woman suffrage acknowledged the similarities in the plights of women and blacks. In the black publications examined, woman suffrage, if treated at all, was, with a few exceptions, not a major source of concern. It also seems clear that many prominent members of the black community (males and females alike) most of whom were middle- to upper-class and educated, were in favor of granting women, especially black women, the vote. There was a smaller number among this group who were opposed to woman suffrage. What is not as apparent from this investigation is the degree to which the masses of blacks were concerned about woman suffrage or the nature of their attitudes toward it. It is safe to assume that given the problems they faced during this period—lynching, unemployment, segregation, the convict-lease system—the issue of whether women, even black women, should be given the vote on a national basis had a low priority.

Just as the vote was perceived by reformers to be a solution to sex inequality and a means of gaining entry into the man's world, higher education for women was seen as having the potential for achieving the same end. Though higher education for white women had increased dramatically during the decades following the Civil War, ex-slave women—prohibited from learning to read and write during slavery—were in need of the most basic literacy skills. In the post-Reconstruction era, arguments about the education of black women began to surface and were part of the larger debate surrounding education for blacks, which focused primarily on industrial vs. classical education. Unlike the suffrage question, however, this issue was considered to be more critical to the solution of "the Negro problem." Despite the urgency of the problem of educating a previously enslaved people, opinions varied widely concerning the efficacy of providing liberal arts as opposed to domestic training for black women. Very few, however, were opposed to providing grammar school level or normal education for black women.

Southern whites tended to be less sympathetic toward the entire issue of black women's education, and some perceived the increased attempts at educating black women to be futile or, worse still, counterproductive. Not only is the black woman incapable of learning very much, one southern white woman argued, but what is more detrimental is that education will turn her against her proper role, which is to serve whites.

> . . . education has done but little for the great mass of negro women. . . . As yet the only visible result has been to teach the girl a scorn of the work she is fitted to do, and to implant in her breast an insatiable ambition to be a school teacher—an ambition that must be futile unless the supply of scholars can be miraculously increased or the Government subsidizes every kinky-headed little coon and farms him out among the several million negro girls in the South who are looking forward to the glorious career of being schoolma'ams.[115]

Apparently aware of increased educational opportunities for black women, she goes on to say that these "imperfectly educated women" with their "half-awakened intelligence" are actually "one of the menaces of our time."[116] Both sets of comments reflect conventional racist attitudes.

Equally hostile and racist in her remarks about educated black women, an unidentified white woman, who admits that she only knows the Negro as a servant, claims that the "educated negro" is an artificial creature; she argues that education does not change the basic character traits of blacks. To illustrate her point, she alludes to having hired two black female college graduates "to vary from the monotony of stupidity in my servants."[117] Not only were they immoral and deceitful, but they also aroused her hatred because of their attempts to defy "our national order."

> In illiterate negroes these vices seem so natural they fail to shock the sensibilities or to excite aversion, but I conceived a horror of these yellow Jezebels, who had come to me from schools that have million-dollar endowments for the education of negro girls.[118]

The endowment figure is certainly inaccurate, as are many of her remarks in this article, but she is probably referring to Spelman, which will be discussed later. Similarly, her earlier remarks about black women being incapable of learning more than the equivalent of a second- or third-grade education and the futility of their aspirations to become school teachers also reveal her ignorance of the facts, since several hundred black women had already earned college degrees and an even greater number were common school teachers (over 10,000) by the time this article was published.[119]

Radical differences are apparent in the attitudes of Yankee teachers about the value of educating black women. They disagreed with southern whites who believed that nothing, including education, could alter the innate mental and moral deficiencies of blacks. These northerners felt that environmental factors were crucial variables and that education could in fact mold character. In her study of northern white teachers who came South to Georgia after the Civil War to teach the freedmen, a contemporary historian defines their philosophy of education, which emphasized the building of character and the eradication of vices learned during slavery. In other words, "education" involved not only teaching of basic skills but also imparting moral values.

> The twin goals of morality and literacy became inextricably entwined. . . . A rigid emphasis on classroom decorum was intended to encourage respect for authority and personal self-control. . . . The problems of punctuality and discipline preoccupied the teachers. . . . Traditional school books reinforced the teachers' attempts to impress upon the freedmen the Yankee virtues of industry, thrift, temperance, patriotism, and piety.[120]

Most of these New England schoolmarms, whom Du Bois attempted to immortalize in *The Souls of Black Folk*,[121] were white, female, middle class, single, and products of female seminaries or academies. Jones's analysis of their educational goals reveals much about their attitudes toward blacks in general and black women in particular. First, most subscribed to the notion that blacks were different from whites, especially in the area of moral development. Strong believers in the importance of the family, these teachers were particularly concerned about improving the quality of home life in the black community so that much of their focus was on the women.

> Special classes for women . . . provided instruction in the responsibilities of motherhood for adults and girls. . . . Denied suffrage and lacking a formal education, she [the black woman] wielded a potentially dangerous influence over the future of the black race. While her husband led the way in the political sphere, she must assume the central position in the moral and religious regeneration of the family.[122]

Within this general framework of educational reform carried out by northern missionaries, the majority of whom were representatives of the American Missionary Association,[123] an analysis of the specific case of Spelman Seminary is illuminating. While there have been a few studies that deal with northern teachers, especially missionaries, who came South after the war (see Chapter One, Note nine), none of them focuses specifically on the attitudes of these white women toward the education of black women. The archival material at Spelman College, which contains the most extensive collection of primary sources dealing with the motivations of its two New England founders, provides an excellent source for the examination of one set of white female attitudes toward the higher education of black women during the period under consideration.

Sophia Packard and Harriet Giles were perhaps the finest examples of the long line of missionaries who came South to improve the lives of ex-slaves, especially the women. They were firm believers in the philosophy that higher education for black women should be separate and in the liberal arts tradition. They also felt, however, that considerable attention should be devoted to moral training and the imparting of practical skills, especially domestic training so that black women would make good wives and mothers. Their views on the nature of women's education place them in the category of "separatists" according to Sara Delamont in her analysis of the controversy surrounding women's education at the turn of the century.[124]

In 1883, the future of this separate school for young women was in doubt as a result of a proposal by Dr. Henry Morehouse, field secretary of the

American Baptist Home Missionary Society, that it be combined with Atlanta Baptist Seminary, which had moved from Augusta to Atlanta in 1879. The seeds of the problem were sown even before the arrival of Packard and Giles in 1881 because of the desire of the ABHMS and local black Atlantans (including Father Quarles, who was a trustee of Atlanta Baptist Seminary) to make provisions for the education of both sexes in their city. While plans were in progress to get the newly acquired property, known as the "Barracks" because it had been occupied by Union soldiers during the Civil War, ready to accommodate both men and women, the board of the ABHMS was strongly urged by Packard and Giles to devote the property exclusively to a school for girls. They disagreed with the proposed coeducational scheme because it was their experience that in coeducational schools the courses were planned primarily for men, and training for women received only secondary consideration; they also believed that the special education women required could best be accomplished apart from the distractions caused by constant companionship with men. This confrontation over the need for a separate educational institution for black women resulted in perhaps the most heated debate ever to occur over the issue of coeducational vs. single sex institutions in the black community.[125]

A close examination of the numerous diaries Packard and Giles[126] kept religiously during these early years, as well as the letters they sent to solicit funds, provides valuable insights into how two white women, who were typical in many ways of northern missionaries, felt about black women's education. First, the preoccupation with industrial and practical education at Spelman in the early years set it apart from the white female seminary tradition that concentrated, for the most part, on academic subjects. Like Booker T. Washington, Packard and Giles were sensitive to the temper of the times. Unlike their white counterparts in the North, the birthplace of higher education for American white women, Spelman's founders never agonized over the need to offer black female students the classical education that white male and, to some extent, female students were being offered elsewhere. Whether women's education should be the same as men's was one of the major issues in the debate about women's education during the nineteenth century. Ever mindful of the peculiar history of black women in America and the realities of their everyday lives, Packard and Giles' primary aim was to provide training for teachers, nurses, missionaries, and church workers—areas of employment open to black women. Training for mission and church service would enable students to organize Sunday schools, mothers' and children's meetings, sewing classes, temperance bands, and Bible meetings. In other words, they would provide assistance to pastors and others in all branches of Christian work. In this regard, Spelman would find her true counterpart not in the Mount Holyokes, but in other black schools influenced by the industrial or practical educational philosophy that Washington and others propagated with such vigor.

Equally important was the imparting of those practical skills that would make black women good homemakers and mothers, since Packard and Giles were also in favor of those aspects of the cult of True Womanhood, which stressed domesticity and piety. "We would like to extend our course in cooking and domestic science, since we consider this the most important branch of a woman's education," Giles wrote in a fund-raising letter sent North on January 24, 1901. Their philosophy of education for black women was clearly articulated by Giles in the same letter to Rev. Morgan, officer of the ABHMS and board member of Morehouse College, written in response to his letter of January 3 regarding industrial education for blacks.

> I consider industrial training more important in Negro schools than in white schools, inasmuch as there is a lack of intelligent training in labor among Negroes in their homes. A large portion of our students . . . have been engaged in manual labor before entering school here. They have been engaged in house work at home, in domestic service, laundry work, farming and cotton-picking. They are like white students in expecting that their education will prepare them for some more remunerative employment. . . . We have regular classes in sewing, dress-making, domestic science and nurse training. . . . We expect all our students to be good housekeepers and homemakers. . . .[127]

It is clear Packard and Giles perceived their mission to be educating black women to function in a world that had greatly restricted their opportunities rather than providing them with skills they would be unable to use.[128] At the end of the letter, however, Giles insisted that both blacks and whites were in favor of the industrial training Spelman was providing, but added that the literary work they were undertaking to build teachers and *"leaders of the race"* (emphasis mine) was also necessary.

> It seems to me that in connection with missionary schools whose primary purpose is to educate teachers and preachers, industrial training should be insisted upon, but that it should hold a secondary place.[129]

This clear acknowledgement of the dual function of education at Spelman is reflected in the curriculum and in extra-curricular activities in which students were compelled to participate.

In an article appearing in *Home Mission Monthly* (the official publication of the ABHMS) commemorating Spelman's twentieth anniversary Cornelia Denslow, another white female, comments on the school's mission to train "future race-leaders" as well as to produce students "equally proud of their ability to interpret a poem or to keep a floor clean."[130] However, she also stresses the importance of the vocational training available to students—courses in housekeeping, cooking, printing, and dressmaking, for example. Denslow also alludes to nurse training, which will reinforce "the natural talent for nursing common to Negro women."[131] This idea of black women as nurturers was common among southern whites whose primary experience of black women was in their role as mammy. Dr. J. Elmer Dellinger, a practicing white male physician in the South, also stresses vocational training for black women and indicates that black women are especially suited for nursing.

> I am persuaded that the Negro woman could have no superior in its execution. She is as intelligent, when she is intelligent, perhaps more obedient to orders and directions than even the white nurse could be. . . . As is characteristic of the sex, she is light of hand and foot. . . . She is vigilant and wakeful; patient and faithful; subordinate to authority, obedient under orders, not asking why. . . . Her larger sympathy with the suffering and sorrowing is her most distinguishing trait of character.[132]

The practical and industrial nature of the curriculum starkly contrasted with the mostly classical curriculum offered at several colleges for white women during the same era. At Spelman there was a definite emphasis on training for jobs, mainly teaching and missionary work, as well as the building of Christian character, which was reflected in the school's motto, "Our Whole School for Christ." This emphasis on developing strong moral character must be seen as a reflection of prevailing societal attitudes about black women that have been discussed in detail in the previous chapter. According to Professor Jeanne Noble in her pioneering study of the historical development of collegiate education for black women, the emphasis on moral education was directly related to perceptions about black women that persisted during slavery and lingered afterwards.

. . . the one role of her past that did come up in discussions concerning the Negro woman's education related her to her foremother's role as concubine. The Negro woman's new role carried not only the stigma of being a Negro but also a new sense of inferiority in being a woman. . . . Authorities prescribed a rigid moralistic curriculum. . . . Many of the Negro women's rules and regulations may possibly have been predicated on reasons relating to her foremother's sex role as slave. Overnight she was to so live that by her ideal behavior, the sins of her foremothers might be blotted out. Her education in many instances appears to have been based on a philosophy which implied that she was weak and immoral and that at best she should be made fit to rear her children and keep house for her husband.[133]

The extent to which Packard and Giles had also internalized prevailing stereotypes about blacks, including women, is revealed by a close reading of their numerous diary entries. Temperance is constantly stressed, and near Christmas Spelman students are especially urged not to partake of alcohol. Giles' December 25, 1882, diary entry, the year during which the most extensive coverage of the school's first year can be found, reads as follows: "Most of these things occur among the colored people. Surely something must be done for them and to prevent whiskey drinking if we would save our country." It is clear from this and other references to moral and religious concerns, especially the careful recording of each student's being baptized and embracing the Christian faith, that Packard and Giles perceived a critical component of education for black women should be the molding of Christian character and the eradication of those traits that were a carry-over from slavery—dishonesty, tardiness, drunkenness, idleness, immorality, and irresponsibility. This same diary entry also records a letter written by Anna Cohill, a white teacher at Fisk University to the AMS, and it reveals her preoccupation with providing moral guidance to black female students and training them to run a household since their home life was in dire need of improvement.

It is my mission to carry help and counsel to the lowly homes of our city. I might tell you such tales of the wretchedness and discomfort of many of these homes as would fill your hearts with pity—a wretchedness growing out of an utter lack of comprehension of the meaning of home and showing the need of instruction in the simplest facts of household cleaning.[134]

Her materialistic posture (even arrogance) and racist notions about black women are also apparent as the letter continues.

Speaking of the future of the colored women these days; what choices she will make is [sic] a question of breathless interest. How to help her make the choice wisely and in time is the problem upon which we are at work. The door to greater evil is wide open at her feet. The tempter can no longer command but he can allure with deadly certainty because *inherited tendencies* [emphasis added] and customs of the past aid in gaining easy victory. . . . The fountain of a strong moral nature must be laid first of all as the basis of *true womanhood* (emphasis mine). Let me not question the power of God's grace to illuminate the heart and change the will; but until she [black women] better understands the force of Bible truth and has a nature more sensitive to reflect it than is the case with many who come to us, religion, as she comprehends it, will do her no good. So divorced is it from morality, so satisfied as to the future, and so reckless as to the present are many who suppose they possess it, that I dare not present this last great motive of Christian principle until I see the moral sense working under direct and pointed Bible teaching, so that the Christian life may be grasped in its true meaning.[135]

This statement is perhaps the clearest illustration of the fact that the education of black women could not be separated in the minds of white women from the imparting of moral instruction so that black women could transcend their alleged genetic make-up and bad habits. This letter also reveals that white women felt they had a special responsibility to work for the uplift of their "sisters" through the educational process, during which a major focus would be the teaching of Christian ethics through Bible study. And, finally, educating black women would also involve instructing them in such a way that they would become followers of the cult of True Womanhood. Any evidence of self-indulgence (which violated the principles of True Womanhood), such as the consumption of alcohol, promiscuity, or excessive emotionalism during worship, was perceived to be correlated with racial degeneracy, and every effort was made to eliminate it.

Packard and Giles also meticulously recorded comments from their students, many of whom were adult women with children, which revealed the impact that their education at Spelman was having on their personal lives. The founders were especially proud of the impact of their religious instruction and the fact that they were bringing enlightenment to a downtrodden race. On December 6, 1888, the following entry appears:

Mrs. Humphreys said I thank the Lord he has spared me to read by Bible. This school was planted for me, it *seems just for me*. I am going to stay here to get all the good I can not for *me* but for *my race*. [Emphasis in original.][136]

On September 15, 1888, Giles refers to a pupil who has taken her little bit of knowledge and shared it with others:

> She could hardly read when she first commenced school two years ago. She says, "I told them I could only give them just a little light for I did not know very much myself but what I had learned in school I want to tell to others—one thing hurts me so bad—when I open by Bible and read I think how much precious time I have lost and how much I might have known about it if I had commenced school before. O why, didn't you come two years ago!" She found her scholars in one of the worst places in the city and has been teaching them texts of scripture and how to be honest.[137]

Imagery associated with moving from darkness to light persists throughout the diary and suggests that the students had internalized conventional Western notions with respect to blackness being associated with things negative and whiteness being associated with things positive. Quotes from another married student reveal the theme of rebirth.

> I feel like the lame man at the beautiful gate just beginning to walk. My eyes are just coming open. I cant [sic] sleep nights. I am so thankful. I wake up and ask my husband some questions about my lessons.[138]

A statement from the AMA magazine, written by a white minister regarding the importance of educating black mothers to be good Christians, is recorded under December 31, 1883. One can reasonably assume that such remarks reconfirmed for Giles and Packard the correctness of their mission at Spelman since others agree with their objectives.

> The first need of the colored people is to be Christianized, for this alone lifts them up and gives a desire for better things. How much we owe to the training of Christian mothers. Let us do all we can to teach them what true religion is. We must also teach them how to use it. They must be taught thrift and industry, cleanliness and order. Four million people, half civilized, uneducated, untrained, with the judgment and reason of children hitherto knowing little of the outer world suddenly brought into life's conflicts.[139]

Frequently, Packard and Giles would comment on the success of their work. The following comments in the March 25, 1884, entry reveal that they believed their greatest accomplishment was in moral and religious instruction.

In educational and religious results the past year has been our best. Temperance Society. No field in all the South more important or inviting. Missionary work done by the pupils. It is a pleasure.[140]

Their desire to establish a temperance society on campus is a clear indication of their concern for the moral climate in the black community.[141] They were also aware of the tremendous power they had over the lives of their black students who were extremely appreciative of what was being done for them. In fact, the students perceived Packard and Giles to be their saviors for whom nothing short of worship was in order. The following 1884 entry illustrates this point.

> These pupils are as clay in the hands of the potter. They strive to live as they see us live. Our responsibility is tremendous. Nothing but the best teachers with the best methods can do justice to the work. The hope of the race lies not in their getting knowledge alone but with it a true appreciation of the value of labor and its necessity together with right ideas of Christian living.[142]

Black attitudes toward the education of black women are also revealed in the diaries, especially in the touching accounts of students who attest to the success of their teachers' mission at Spelman. The entry for September 15, 1883, records the contents of a letter that an unidentified husband wrote to his wife concerning the impact of Spelman on their home life.

> My home is so different since you went to school. I want you to go to school every day and learn all you can. There is something in my home so different from what it used to be.[143]

On the same day, an unidentified mother alludes to the impact her experience at Spelman has made on her behavior at home.

> I did not know how to act at home and I tried to act like folks when out but didn't know how. If I could have had this privilege before how differently I could have brought up my children.[144]

Another mother makes a similar comment in the October 12 entry.

> I think my coming to this school is the cause of my children turning to the Lord. What I learn here I go home and tell to my children and I know better how to teach them.[145]

On the same day another entry reveals that black women perceived that the education they would receive at Spelman would help them to become better mothers.

> I came to get my little girl in school not thinking I could come myself but I asked the Lord to help me and He has answered my prayer. I wanted to learn how to train my children.[146]

Clearly, Spelman was a virtual training ground for potential followers of the "cult of True Womanhood," and like the Mothers' Meetings being conducted by black women's clubs throughout the nation, it was producing enlightened mothers for the race.

An examination of the numerous letters Spelman students wrote to the founders once they had joined the work force also reveals the extent to which black women felt indebted to Spelman's teachers for the work they were doing for the race. These students spoke as well about the impact their Spelman education had on their everyday lives and on the development of their character.[147] In a letter dated May 14, 1906, which was written to Giles, a former student teaching in Jackson, Mississippi, reveals her intense feelings about her experiences at Spelman at the turn of the century.

> My dear teachers, again my mind has wandered back to my dear Alma Mater; who has devoted time and talent for the purpose of raising me to a higher standard of Christian civilization. To think of you seems to me as I have thought of a friend, yea a parent. I hope that at some time I will be able to view the faces and campuses of that dear school that seem so dear to me. So often do I refer to the teachings received there within your walls and to the dear teachers that imparted this instruction to myself and others.[148]

In a letter dated March 20, 1922, to Miss Kendall, a white member of the faculty, an African student who attended Spelman in the early 1900s and returned to her native country to do missionary work and found a mission school wrote of her indebtedness to Spelman.

> I received the Spelman Messenger last Friday and I laid down all my work until it was read thru; it was just like enjoying a square meal that I had not eaten for a long time. . . . My training and experiences and long stay at Spelman have aided me greatly to endure great hardships in my missionary career. I can never love my "Alma Mater" hard enough; her name ever rings in my native land, and every one with whom I come in contact and for whom I work seem to put great confidence in me.[149]

In her June 30, 1924, letter to Kendall, she reiterates her appreciation of the kind of training she received at Spelman.

> . . . I must praise myself that I really know how to economize; all these teachings I own to dear Old Spelman. . . . I find sincere happiness and joy in teaching our children and students the beautiful lessons I received at Spelman. May God continue to bless the dear Teachers in their strenuous efforts in moulding those young lives into beautiful women. And may the girls likewise appreciate and grasp every opportunity they are receiving in this "Golden Age." . . . Ora Horton [another Spelman alumnae] and I are indeed trying to up "Spelman" by the lives we live among our students and in the communities in which we live and work.[150]

It seems clear that in spite of the materialistic posture of the white faculty and administration at Spelman (or maybe because of it!) and their rigid attitudes about what constituted "proper" behavior for blacks, especially women, the students were not inclined to question their motives or their educational philosophy. Getting an education, however it was defined, was so important to blacks that they were willing to put themselves totally in the hands of those benevolent whites who were making their schooling possible. Another explanation has been advanced for this phenomenon in a study of the development of black colleges in Georgia.

> The observance of this multitude of rules was not difficult for the majority of those ignorant folk who went to the schools in the earliest days. With those freedmen, accustomed to generations of slave discipline, good conduct was still a matter of submission to the white man. They knew no other way. White teachers marveled at their pupils' openness to suggestion, their willingness to work for moral development, and their submissiveness to authority under kindness and confidence.[151]

The extent to which the Spelman model was perceived to be the ideal education for black women is revealed in the comments of pioneering black educators. On the twenty-fifth anniversary of the founding of the college, John Hope, professor and first black president of Morehouse College, expressed his approval of the educational venture carried out at Spelman by Packard and Giles in a speech that appeared in the college's first major publication, a report on the school's progress.

> The purpose of the founders was to give colored woman an education that would enable them to earn a living in domestic pursuits, that is, to make them efficient homemakers; then to prepare women who could teach; but over and

141

above all it was to make colored women intelligent Christians, full of the knowledge as well as the power of righteousness. How well this program has been followed is to be seen from the fact that some of the best domestic servants, trained nurses for the sick, school teachers, and missionaries on the home and foreign fields are the women that have been educated at Spelman Seminary.[152]

Similar praise was heaped on Spelman by Claudia White, class of 1902, who referred to her alma mater as "our virgin queen" and a "glorious achievement in the uplift of the character of our womanhood."[153] As she continues her eloquent defense of Spelman and the part it plays in the uplift of black womanhood, it is apparent that she is aware of the scorn that had been heaped on her sisters.

Once upon a time it was shamefully asked in the tone of bitter incredulity, "Can a black woman be pure?" "Can the black woman be elevated to culture and piety?" I call for an answer to these cynical, heartless, unchristian and pagan questions: My answer is Ask Spelman Seminary! . . . Spelman Seminary stands for a trained hand in domestic science, for a cultured brain in liberal education, for a pure heart in biblical morality and for a consecrated life in the battle of life for the womanhood of the race. She stands for a redeemed and elevated womanhood for the Negro race in all the lines that have made for the best things among the best women of any other race. She has proved to the world that Negro womanhood when properly treated and educated will burst forth into gems of pure brilliancy unsurpassed by any other gems among any other race.[154]

Here Claudia White espouses the philosophy of True Womanhood as it relates to black women and credits Spelman for imparting these values to its students. For Hope, White, Packard, and Giles, the Spelman experience has demonstrated that racial traits are not innate or permanent and that if black women are exposed to the appropriate environment they can match or even surpass the Victorian ideal of womanhood.

According to Sara Delamont, the debates on women's education that took place in the nineteenth century were integrally related to the widely accepted belief that men and women should occupy separate spheres. She goes on to say that while women's education advocates and feminists in general challenged the notion that women's sphere was exclusively the home, "most of them never challenged the domestic ideology itself."[155] They simply tried to broaden the definition of women's sphere to include certain activities in the public sphere—public service, teaching, and nursing. Though they rejected many of the arguments of their opponents—that education would impair women's health and ultimately result in "race suicide" and that it would make women masculine, unmarriageable, and unfit for motherhood—they were as concerned about the future of the family and argued that education would actually make women better wives and mothers and more feminine.[156]

Many blacks were in favor of the kind of education that was stressed at Spelman during the early years because it took into consideration the reality of the black female experience, which always included work outside the home. However, the Spelman model, like women's education in general, was characterized by a strong adherence to the domestic ideology and stressed the importance of training its students to be good wives and mothers. It also included a strong moral development component that distinguished it in many ways from those white women's institutions where the greater emphasis was on refinement and propriety. White women were not presumed to be immoral, in other words; they simply needed to be taught how to become more ladylike. The middle-class values of Spelman's founders, which resulted in an emphasis on ladylike behavior, were acceptable to blacks because of their desire to remove the stigma of immorality from black women. As was the case in the dominant culture, however, there were some blacks who were skeptical about educating women at all, though this group was the exception. There were also a few "radical" proponents of women's education who would have considered the Spelman model limiting because it did not fundamentally challenge the status quo or attempt to develop the full potential of black women. The discussion that follows focuses on the broader debate within the black community concerning the critical issue of the higher education of black women and helps to explain why the Spelman model was acceptable to most blacks. A consideration of black attitudes toward the higher education of women in general is instructive because it sheds additional light on the heated debate surrounding women's education, which persisted during most of the nineteenth century.

In the appendix of his history of blacks, William Alexander expresses conventional views about the nature of higher education for black women, the primary purpose of which is to transform them into True Women. Women's education should stress morality, spirituality, and the importance of self-sacrifice, all important components of the cult of True Womanhood. The most important function of education for black women is to make them better mothers and wives, which will in turn ensure a more noble race.

> . . . it is the glory of a woman, that for this end she was sent into the world, to live for others rather than for herself. . . . Surely this is woman's calling—to teach man to temper his fiercer, coarser, more self-assertive nature by the contact of her gentleness, purity, self-sacrifice. . . . Let the higher education of women be undertaken with such ends in view. . . . "Good teachers make good scholars, but it is only mothers that form men."[157]

In a passionate plea for equality of opportunity for higher education for both sexes, Reverend R. E. Wall, a black minister, also evokes the cult of True Womanhood as a defense for his argument.

> If we elevate the future mothers of the race to a higher level, we shall thus erect a platform upon which to elevate the race itself. . . . Women are the mothers of mankind, and on them devolves the duty of training mankind.[158]

He argues that women are the equals of men socially, morally, and intellectually, though not politically, but he also says that education should be practical, which echoes Spelman's founders.

> I do not mean a mere theoretical knowledge of books . . . transforming an otherwise lovely and loveable woman into a bluestocking, but train them in domestic economy as well as the choice literature of the day and thus fit and prepare her for fully discharging the higher duties and responsibilities of life.[159]

Mary McLeod Bethune, one of the most prominent educators during this period and a pioneer in the cause for black women's education, felt strongly that the education of Negro girls should be different from that of Negro boys. She expressed her views in a statement entitled "A Philosophy of Education for Negro Girls." Delamont would categorize her as a "separatist" because of her belief that women's education should be different from men's. This group argued that the curriculum should reflect women's traditional activities and responsibilities, the major ones of which are carried out in their role as wife and mother. Bethune's philosophy, which emphasizes the black woman's domestic obligations, does not depart in any significant degree from statements made by Packard, Giles, Hope, and others.

> The challenge to the Negro home is one which dares the Negro to develop initiative to solve his own problems. . . . This is the moral responsibility of the education of the Negro girl; her activities must lead her into endeavors in her educational life; this training must be inculcated into the school curricula so that the result may be a natural expression, born into her children. . . . Early emancipation did not concern itself with giving advantage to Negro girls. The

Mary McLeod Bethune (1875-1955), educator and civil rights leader, founded the Daytona Normal and Industrial School (now Bethune-Cookman College) in 1904. In 1935 she founded the National Council of Negro Women. She was particularly concerned about the education of black girls and women.

domestic realm was her field and no one sought to remove her. Even here, she was not given special training for her tasks. . . . The education of the Negro girl must embrace a larger appreciation for good citizenship in the home. Our girls must be taught cleanliness, beauty and thoughtfulness and their application in making home life possible, For proper home life provides the proper atmosphere for life everywhere else.[160]

While Bethune does not mention the immorality of black women as a rationale for the type of education she envisions for black women, as was the case with many whites mentioned earlier, she does agree that an improved home life should be one of the major goals of black women's education.

Others stressed professional training (preparation for the labor force) as the primary purpose of education for black women. Some argued that training for domestic service was the most important and useful kind of education for black women since the majority of them were already engaged in household service. Even liberal whites, such as Oswald Villard, stressed the importance of household training for housewives and servants alike in a speech before black businessmen in 1905.

. . . the crying economic need of the hour is the skilled cook, the skilled waitress, and the skilled matron. . . . Could we but place in every southern home a well-trained and respectful colored servant the relations of the race would be changed overnight.[161]

It is interesting to point out here that southern whites were suspicious of Spelman in the early years because they believed that the white female missionaries from the North were "foolish sentimentalists" who "do not understand Negro character" and who will, therefore, "spoil our good Negro cook and make instead an impossible, ridiculous creature composed of vanity and half a dozen Latin words, abhorrent to Nature because absolutely useless to our own race or any other."[162] Many whites did not realize that much of the training at Spelman and other black institutions was practical rather than classical and designed to make women better household workers, though not necessarily domestics.

Some black males also agreed with Villard and others, who stressed vocational training and felt that every city with a large black population should have a school to train domestics. These black men also felt that leaders of the race needed to assume a more favorable attitude toward the "remunerative field of domestic service," since over half of black working women were domestic servants.[163] In fact, these women should be praised rather than ridiculed or discouraged from bettering their condition and the lot of their children.

> The old-fashioned, homely Negro mother who washed and ironed till her fingers bled and burned, in order that her children might improve their status, exhibited a spirit that should elicit the highest admiration. The Negro woman is handicapped by such an unfavorable environment that it seems almost inhuman to make her the butt of witticism and ridicule. . . .[164]

Booker T. Washington, the most outspoken advocate of industrial education for blacks, argued in a speech to the theology faculty of Vanderbilt University in 1907 that whites in particular should support these local training schools for domestic servants.

> In the average white family of the South . . . the white child spends a large proportion of his life in the arms . . . of a Negro woman. . . . It is mighty important . . . for the civilization, for the happiness, for the health of the Southern white people that the colored nurse shall be intelligent, that she shall be clean, that she shall be morally fit to come in contact with that pure and innocent child.[165]

This statement is a clear indication that Washington's major concern is the welfare of the white family rather than the black home, which distinguishes him from most other blacks during the period. Washington also felt that southern black women (and poor white women) needed institutions in which industrial training was available so that they could find suitable employment in the South in various industries—dairying, fruit growing, fruit canning, poultry raising, and floriculture, for example. He goes on to say that female students at Tuskegee, in addition to literary courses and courses in sewing, cooking, general household science, and laundering, are being trained in the industries mentioned above. Not only is such training rewarding from an economic standpoint, but it also imparts discipline and provides the masses with a constructive way to spend free time. The greatest advantage, however, of such training is its practical nature and its compatibility with conditions as they exist for blacks in the South where, in Washington's opinion, their greatest need is "bread and butter." And, finally, this approach to the problems of the South will help to dissipate the racial prejudice that plagues the region.

> Production and commerce are two of the great destroyers of race prejudice. In proportion as the black woman is able to produce something that the white

or other races want, in the same proportion does prejudice disappear. Butter is going to be purchased from the individual who can produce the best butter and at the lowest price, and the purchaser care not whether it was made by a black, white, yellow or brown woman.[166]

Similarly, his wife, Margaret Murray Washington, director of Industries for Girls, describes the industrial training that was a crucial part of the curriculum for women at Tuskegee. In fact, it was Tuskegee's practical approach to education that made parents sacrifice to send their children away from home where their help was desperately needed, argued Mrs. Washington.[167] Along with their academic training, female students took courses in dress making, millinery, horticulture, printing, broom making, mattress making, upholstery, cooking (required), and basketry. Like girls at Spelman, they were taught housekeeping and other aspects of domestic science, such as shopping and the planning of meals. Not only were they being trained for the world of work but also for an improved home life, which, according to Mrs. Washington and others, is a critical need in the black community.

> In all of our schools this questions of home life is receiving special attention because those of us who are teachers realize that our civilization depends upon the training we receive for the making of homes and for the carrying out of high home ideals.[168]

Many blacks were in favor of industrial education for women and felt that domestic service should be dignified because it provided a means for black women to ease the financial burden that plagued their families since their husbands had menial jobs. Booker T. Washington even indicated that black women were particularly suited for this kind of work because of their "natural human sympathy," a notion reminiscent of those held by some white males.

> Whatever may be said about the thought and the failings of Negro women, no one . . . has ever denied to them this gift of sympathy. Most people have recognized this quality but nowhere is the kindness and helpfulness of Negro women better known and appreciated than among white people of the Southern states.[169]

Though Washington was one of the most outspoken proponents of the domestic ideology where black women's education is concerned, his position with respect to the need for them to perform well in the public arena

Booker T. Washington (1856-1915), former slave, educator, and the most prominent black leader at the turn of the century, became in 1881 the first principal of Tuskegee Institute. His address at the opening of the Cotton States and International Exposition in Atlanta in 1895, in which he articulated his conciliatory racial philosophy, thrust him into the national limelight.

149

illustrates his sensitivity to their special burdens and responsibilities. His belief that black women's education should be practical and responsive to the needs of the race places him in the separatist category. In fact, it was the black woman's willingness to work outside her home, as well as her "thrift and industry," that Washington saw as the greatest contribution she could make to the improvement of the race. He complimented black women for contributing to the race's wealth (which amounted to twenty-five million among free blacks before the war) and to the accumulation of property since the Civil War.

> In the struggle for homes and for a substantial family life, the women of no race have shown a greater devotion and more constant self-denial than have the Negro women. . . . They have engaged in all forms of personal and domestic service, to supplement the small wages of their husbands, in order that their children might be fed. . . . The statistics show that colored women, as wage earners, do more than their full share of the work of the race.[170]

He also praises black women for their work as teachers, social workers (especially for their work in the care of orphans), freedom fighters (most notably, Sojourner Truth and Harriet Tubman), evangelists, clubwomen, and crusaders for the advancement of black women. In the last category he singles out Frances E. W. Harper, Mary Church Terrell, and Josephine Ruffin for special attention. Washington's lengthy and positive discussion of the club activities of black women (his wife, Margaret, was president of the Tuskegee Women's Club) would seem to indicate his approval of the involvement of black women in the public sphere if they were struggling for a worthy cause, many of which he enumerated. He especially liked those activities in which clubwomen engaged to "develop that character and moral sense in the members of the race in which it is sometimes said that Negro women are lacking."[171] This last statement reveals his own feelings about the need for moral development in the education of black women, which are again reminiscent of notions held by whites, especially southerners.

An issue about which there was less discussion concerned the education of black women for another profession—the ministry. In a series of articles in *A.M.E. Church Review*, a debate ensued surrounding the ordination of women preachers. Most black male preachers were opposed to women delivering sermons in the pulpit, interpreting the Scriptures, and administering the Lord's Supper—though they supported them in their role as deaconess, which included such traditional women's work as visiting the sick and imprisoned.[172] In a lengthy article, Rev. James Johnson, a proponent of the cult of True Womanhood, enumerates the reasons for his opposition to female preachers though he is aware that black women desire to be "occupants of the pulpit."[173] First, he argues that the differences in the intellectual capabilities of women make them unsuitable for ministerial training, which requires "stern, intellectual, masculine qualities."[174] Second, because she is the "weaker" sex, she is physically unsuited for the hard work the profession requires. This allusion to the biological inferiority of women is reminiscent of arguments made by other opponents of women's education who believed that "females lack the energy required to participate in society; their energy, such as it is, is entirely required for reproduction."[175] And, finally, she was intended to occupy the domestic sphere as helpmate for men. Alternatively, she can go out into the world and visit the sick or offer prayers and serve as a helpmate for men ordained to preach the Gospel. A bishop of the Fourth Episcopal District of the A.M.E. Church in Washington D.C., was more favorably disposed to women preachers and indicated that the church should be proud that it had allowed women in its pulpits as early as 1835. His argument in favor of women preachers was that they should be allowed "the largest liberty to exercise their gifts in the Church of God."[176]

Most of the women's education advocates, no matter how diverse their perspectives, stressed the benefits that would accrue to society and ignored the benefits for the individual. Anna J. Cooper, an 1884 Oberlin graduate and a crusader for liberal arts education for women and blacks, advanced a different argument for her support of the liberal education of women, regardless of their race.[177] While she agreed that such an education would make women better mothers and housekeepers, her primary concern was not education for True Womanhood. Cooper felt strongly that there were personal benefits to be gained from the pursuit of liberal education. First, it would make women less dependent economically on men and their own intellectual development would be enhanced. An educated woman does not have to "look to sexual love as the one sensation capable of giving tone and relish, movement and vim to the life she leads."[178] Furthermore,

Her horizon is extended. Her sympathies are broadened and deepened and multiplied. She is in closer touch with nature. Not a bud that opens . . . but adds to the expansiveness and zest of her soul. . . . She can commune with Socrates about the *daimon* he knew and to which she too can bear witness;

151

she can revel in the majesty of Dante, the sweetness of Virgil, the simplicity of Homer. . . .[179]

For the first time, higher education for women is seen not simply as a means for them to help others but, as a vehicle for self-improvement, which is an end in itself. Having spoken about the need for higher education for women in general, she then moves on to her major concern, "the higher education of colored women" (p. 73). First, she indicates that black men are hopelessly conservative on the issue of the need for liberal arts education for black women.

> . . . while our men seem thoroughly abreast of the times on almost every other subject, when they strike the woman question they drop back into sixteenth century logic. They leave nothing to be desired generally in regard to gallantry and chivalry, but they actually do not seem sometimes to have outgrown that old contemporary of chivalry—the idea that women may stand on pedestals or live in doll houses . . . but they must not furrow their brows with thought or attempt to help men tug at the great questions of the world. I fear the majority of colored men do not yet think it worthwhile that women aspire to higher education. . . . . The three R's . . . a first rate dressmaker and a bottle of magnolia balm, are quite enough generally to render charming any woman possessed of tact and the capacity for worshipping masculinity.[180]

Many of the remarks alluded to earlier by black men concerning the purpose of education for black women would seem to support her observations. She describes her personal experiences at St. Augustine Normal School in Raleigh, North Carolina (whose purpose was the training of teachers and ministers), where she began as a pupil at age seven and later taught. There she observed discrimination against women where curriculum matters were concerned and where there was little encouragement for women to pursue collegiate training. At the end of her discussion, she pleads with male and female teachers "to give the girls a chance," so that the "highest interests of the race" will be served.

> Let us insist then on special encouragement for the education of our women and special care in their training. . . . Teach them that there is a race with special needs which they and only they can help; that the world needs and is already asking for their trained, efficient forces. Finally, if there is an ambitious girl with pluck and brain to take the higher education, encourage her to make the most of it.[181]

For Cooper, education for black women has both a social and a personal function. It will help to improve the race, but it will also contribute to their individual growth and development.

The particular case of Blanche Armwood Perkins, who graduated from Spelman in 1906, illustrates the paradoxical nature of black women's education at the turn of the century. She also epitomizes the primary purpose for which black women were educated—to be useful, both to the community at large and to the race. Perkins, referred to as the "feminine Booker T. Washington," founded the first School of Household Arts during World War I in Tampa, Florida.[182] While in Tampa on other business, she learned that its gas company was looking to hire a black woman to train cooks, who were mainly working as domestics in white homes, to operate their new gas stoves. Perkins liked the idea but was unable to convince gas company executives that what was needed was not a mere training course but a well-equipped training school for black cooks and housewives. The Tampa school board had for many years provided domestic science departments for white schools, but not for black ones. During the first term, ironically, the Tampa School of Household Arts was besieged by housewives and only a few cooks. The course consisted of twenty practical lessons in marketing, food values, cooking, home decorating, and similar subjects. Though the gas company had anticipated providing training for primarily for domestics, it continued to support the school. Later, after an agreement with the city schools was worked out, the school was expanded to accommodate black girls above the seventh grade who came for a few hours in the morning. The curriculum was also strengthened when a well-equipped model home was established so that students (cooks, housewives, and young girls from the public schools) could be trained in all aspects of homemaking. The three-year course in cooking was fashioned after the one Perkins had taken from Professor Shellenberger at Spelman.

The school was so successful that other gas companies in Athens, Georgia, Rock Hill, South Carolina, and even as far away as Honduras requested that similar schools be established for them. The most interesting aspect of this venture, however, was that Perkins seized a rare opportunity to do something significant for the black community, and black women in particular, rather than simply providing whites with more efficient domestic help. That is, she exploited a scheme she knew southern whites would support and proceeded to carry out her own agenda, which was to provide educational opportunities for black women in the city of Tampa.[183] In time, she convinced the gas company to support a night school designed to provide older students with an opportunity to receive a common school education. Her major argument was that educated domestics were more efficient. She also used the school as a springboard for other services to the black community. She organized the City Beautiful League and encouraged high school students enrolled in her household arts classes to become junior sanitary inspectors for the clean-up campaign initiated in the black community in 1916. When working girls came to the city, she also made sure, through her associations with the Florida Federation of Colored Women's Clubs, that they found respectable housing and came in contact with the right people.

As a spokesperson for domestic training schools, Perkins manifests the emphasis on practical training for both the private and the public spheres of activity in which most black women were engaged—the home and workplace. Ironically, training for domestic work, which had come to be defined as black women's work during this period, illustrates the way in which both race and gender force black women into particular roles. Domestic service is considered women's work because it occurs within the household; such work is also menial and low-paying and relegated, therefore, to certain racial or ethnic groups. In her role as domestic servant, the black woman is, paradoxically, confined to both the domestic and the public sphere at the same time; she is a paid worker at the same time that she carries out the work of a wife and a mother, though she functions in someone else's home.

Perkins' domestic training at Spelman, which aligns her with Washington and Bethune, and her career after graduation are also paradoxical. Though the cooking courses students took at Spelman were meant to benefit their own homes, Perkins used her skills to train other black women to work in the homes of whites. Her need for a job as well as her desire to provide jobs for other black women place her in this paradoxical situation. More ironically, while black women are socialized and trained to value their roles as wife and mother, they are forced in their role as household servant to carry out their domestic responsibilities in the households of others for much of the day. This dilemma represented for Du Bois and others a major burden for black women. The Perkins case also demonstrates in a dramatic way the dual and perhaps contradictory nature of the educational experience at Spelman. Not only was she trained to function effectively in the domestic sphere by being a good wife and mother, she also received an education that prepared her for a career in the public sphere as a competent educator and administrator.

Finally, her example fulfills the more progressive educational ideal put forward by Anna Cooper. Perkins' community organizing efforts are an indication of her serious commitment to the race. Her courage, aggressiveness, cleverness, and vision are indicators of her own personal development. She is a wife and a mother and presumably able to function well in the home also. Having received both a liberal and practical education at Spelman, she is ideally suited for the burdens and challenges that confront black women in the domestic and public arenas.

Where blacks stood on the issue of women extending their sphere of activity beyond the domestic circle was, almost without exception, a function of whether they adhered to the tenets of the cult of True Womanhood, were lukewarm toward them, or rejected them entirely. At one extreme are men like Reverend James Johnson, who felt that God had intended for men and women to occupy different spheres. As the weaker sex, she is to be "an indoor agent" and concentrate her efforts on the affairs of the home. By contrast, man is "the outdoor agent, made for sterner work," according to the well-known poet James Weldon Johnson.[184] A True Woman should not intrude herself on a man's world or do man's work—such as making laws or preaching.

> Woman never was intended to be as man. . . . There are certain avocations in life which cannot be followed by her with any degree of comeliness. . . . She never looks so well upon a bicycle as she does upon a throne. . . . She was not made to show the brawny arms of Vulcan, nor the ponderous proportions of the Atlantis. . . . She holds undisputed sway in the gentler walks of life. . . . They struggle now for callings which belong to man, nor do they fall into a dilemma by a perversion of their nature. . . . A *true woman* [emphasis mine] . . . thinks she is as great in the pew as man is in the pulpit; and hence she strives to satisfy the Lord and not the bubbling ambition of her soul. . . . The woman who claims admission to every position occupied by man . . . is a monstrous outgrowth of the coarser elements of female nature.[185]

Assuming a middle-of-the-road position in the debate was a group of black women, primarily, who felt that the True Woman was man's equal, though they did not reject entirely certain aspects of the cult of True Womanhood. They felt, for example, that women were certainly different from men, but they rejected the notion that women should confine themselves exclusively to the domestic sphere. Their concern was that woman "retain her womanly dignity and sweetness, which is at once her strength and shield" whether she is a housewife and mother at home "or struggling in the ranks of business and professional life."[186] In other words, women should not suppress their innate femininity and become like men. In their estimation, the progressive woman, though she enters the professional world, still takes seriously her duties as wife and mother. In other words, there is no incompatibility between her professional and domestic roles.

> This widening of woman's sphere of thought and action is a thing to be encouraged rather than denounced, even in those who reverence most highly the home-life and believe that woman finds there her true element and highest usefulness.[187]

This approach has been referred to as domestic feminism, which espouses the notion that women should work in the domestic sphere to "upgrade the morality of home and family" and work in the public sphere to bring about needed reforms."[188]

In *The National Association Notes*, the official organ of the National Association of Colored Women, numerous articles appeared acknowledging "the awakening of woman" as "the great social phenomenon of our times."[189] Many of these black clubwomen, feminists if you will, were at the opposite end of the argument from the more fervent upholders of the cult of True Womanhood and were less rigid in their beliefs than the middle-of-the-roaders. Though they valued motherhood, they also realized that the realities of black women's lives were in conflict with the major tenets of the cult of True Womanhood.

> Two Negro women out of every five are bread winners. Our women are engaged in almost all the occupations in which our men are engaged.[190]

Unlike the middle-of-the-roaders, these women tended to under-emphasize women's differences from men. They argued that a woman's influence should be exerted in the public arena and that her community work was as important as her family duties.

> I am not one of those who believe that woman's sphere should be confined to the home. Woman must become familiar with social and economic conditions; she must be a working force in the larger influences that affect her trade as homekeeper. Her highest duty to her family is to exert an influence in the making of laws governing unsanitary meat markets, filthy bakeries and dirty groceries. . . . She should be allowed the privilege of the ballot. . . .[191]

Furthermore, black women must be recognized as principal actors in the movement for the emancipation of women as well as the uplift of the race. They are more than the helpmates of their men.

> The Colored woman has awakened to her responsibility and realizes that she is a factor in the world's civilization and in the race's progress. Her ability to discuss logically and philosophically the most complex questions of the day and to fully grasp their bearing upon church and state is no longer in doubt.[192]

It is interesting to note that whites, especially men, were less vocal about the roles of black women in the public sphere, especially the political arena, than they had been about their roles in the domestic sphere (both in their own households and in those of the whites for whom they worked). Their views on the education of black women—about which white women, for the most part, expressed a variety of opinions—were influenced, to a great degree, by their racial views. At one end of the pole were southern white women who felt that educating black women was a waste of time since their intellectual capabilities were limited. Furthermore, education would distract them from their proper roles—taking care of whites' children and homes. Though northern white women were not free of negative racial attitudes, they were more likely to support the education of black women and to believe that proper training, especially where moral development was concerned, would result in the eradication of negative traits *acquired* during slavery. The missionaries who came south for the purpose of helping to educate black women (and men) felt that they were contributing to the development of the race by helping to produce better wives and mothers for the black community. They also felt that black women should enter the public arena, where their knowledge and skills could be used for the improvement of society in general.

It is fair to say that the majority of those who engaged in discussions about the proper roles for black women recognized that they must be both indoor and outdoor agents. It was imperative, in other words, that black women have a reverence for home and hearth, but also a commitment to the important work needed to be carried out in the public arena. Moreover, most black women could not afford the luxury of staying at home and devoting their lives to wifehood and motherhood given the pressing economic needs of their families. An examination of the lives of such women as Mary Church Terrell, Ida Wells-Barnett, Lugenia Burns Hope, and Margaret Murray Washington, to name only a few, reveals the extent to which black women juggled the demands of their private and public lives through most of their adulthood. In her autobiography (which was edited by her daughter), Ida Wells-Barnett, who married in 1895 and gave birth to a son a year later, describes the life of the activist/mother as she joins a national political campaign.

> I started out with a six-month-old nursing baby and made trips to Decatur, Quincy, Springfield, Bloomington, and many other towns. . . . I honestly believe I am the only woman in the United States who ever traveled throughout the country with a nursing baby to make political speeches.[193]

After the birth of her second son, however, she retired from public life, believing, like a True Womanhood advocate, that "motherhood was a profession by itself."[194] However, her self-imposed confinement to the home was shortlived because "the needs of the work [anti-lynching] were so great that again I had to venture forth."[195] Her concerns for the race appear to outweigh the constraints imposed on her by gender. So, again, she took her five-month-old nursing baby with her as she launched the most ambitious anti-lynching campaign ever mounted. For progressive black women like Ida Wells-Barnett, a woman's proper place was wherever there was important work to be done. And, despite the obstacles, not the least of which was a barrage of attitudes about the greater importance of the home, black women knew that there was much to be done and responded in large numbers to the challenge.

> With all the wrongs and neglects of her past, with all the weakness, the debasement, the moral thralldom of her present, the black woman of today stands mute and wondering at the Herculean task devolving upon her. No other hand can move the lever. She must be loosed from her bands and set to work.[196]

FIVE

Conclusion

The most intriguing aspects of woman's place in nineteenth-century American society have only begun to be explored. . . . Perhaps we might profit in the future from an entirely new set of questions.

Regina Morantz, 1974

. . . revaluations are needed—new definitions, conceptions, and methodologies which encompass the reality of Black women's experiences.

Gloria T. Hull and Barbara Smith, 1979

Because black women embody the tension between race and gender, the two most important categories used to assign people to a particular status and role in America, their historical experiences can illustrate the cultural connections between race and gender in perhaps the most direct way. It is for this reason that an examination of attitudes toward black women from 1880-1920 (when racial and sexual attitudes were extremely rigid) provides an excellent case study for the cultural connections between race and gender within the American context.

As this study has indicated, while black and white males had similar ideas about the nature of womanhood, especially the importance of motherhood, in general their attitudes toward black women were dissimilar, as one would expect given their drastically different vantage points from 1880-1920. This period represented a high point for the native-born white and the nadir for blacks, as historian Rayford Logan observed. That black and white men had similar conceptions of womanhood is indicative of the extent to which members of a given culture, despite their ethnic identity, accept, at least to some degree, the sex-role stereotypes foisted upon them by virtually every institution. This means that black women must confront the sexist attitudes of black and white men alike.

Another revealing aspect of this examination is the discovery that many of the attitudes that black men were later to harbor about black women are absent from their pronouncements during this period. There is no indication that black women are perceived to be castrators or overly aggressive. The "black matriarchy" thesis (which E. Franklin Frazier advanced in 1939 and Daniel P. Moynihan popularized in 1965) emerges later. In fact, one of the most persistent themes in the writings of black males is the black woman as victim. Her powerlessness and vulnerability, especially where white men are concerned, have rendered her incapable of the aggressive posture implicit in the image of black woman as castrator. Because of the legacy of slavery, black women are perceived to be weighted down by heavy burdens, the most painful of which has been sexual exploitation. Daniel Webster Davis's poem "The Black Woman's Burden" is indicative of this attitude.

> Ye daughters of a long down-trodden race,
> Rouse ye to action bold, and do not dread
> To meet they dreary task. Thy burden great
> May well alarm; yet God did give,
> He will no strength withhold from those
> Who bravely bear their load. (1-6)[1]

Here the black woman is seen not as the castrator but as the prey for the men of both races. She is encouraged to develop the strength to throw off her various yokes so that she can "rise to nobler, grander heights" (11. 22-23). Du Bois echoes Davis in a glowing tribute to black women in which he indicates that he "always felt like bowing myself before them in all abasement, searching to bring some tribute to these long-suffering victims, these burdened sisters of mine. . . . "[2]

Despite the struggle for women's rights, which persisted throughout the nineteenth century, however, the majority of black men, like their white male counterparts, were reluctant to challenge accepted notions of True Womanhood. Doing so would free black women to develop their full potential. Instead, they wished that black women could climb on the pedestal and take their rightful place beside white women. They also wanted to assume the traditional paternalistic posture toward their women whom they felt needed even more protection than other women given the hostile environment in which blacks operated. As Friedman observed in his discussion of southern male attitudes toward women during the period under consideration, "the effort to fortify racial pride through exaltation of pure womanhood was likely as disastrous for the black race as for the white."[3] Only Du Bois, the most outspoken feminist among the group examined, felt compelled to devote his life's work to the emancipation of blacks *and* women. The egalitarian sexual ideology that Terborg-Penn attributed to the nineteenth-century black male was an ideal not fully realized. Three examples illustrate this point.

Ida Wells was one of the few women to get involved in the predominantly male Afro-American Council, which was founded in 1898 by Monroe Trotter, the "radical" editor of the *New York Age*.[4] She was elected financial secretary at one of the meetings, which caused a stir among some of the conservative Booker T. Washington supporters who were already disturbed by her "radical" bent. What is interesting, however, is their attempt to oust her from office on sexist grounds. They felt that she should not continue in this position because it was not suitable women's work and because the demands of the job would interfere with her domestic duties. Their suggestion was that she form a national auxiliary of women to the Council and vacate the post so it could be filled by a man.[5]

Similarly, when the Niagara Movement was established in 1905, a conflict developed between Trotter and Du Bois over admitting women to the all-male organization.[6] Du Bois organized a women's auxiliary that Trotter opposed, being an avowed chauvinist, but he eventually capitulated to Du Bois and women were admitted to the auxiliary. A contemporary manifestation of the same problem is the situation black female SNCC workers found themselves in during the 1960s when they were relegated to the less important menial and clerical responsibilities of making coffee, typing, and stuffing envelopes. Pauli Murray, noted civil rights attorney and writer, alluded to perhaps the most obvious way in which black women were excluded from major roles in the Civil Rights Movement by indicating that the main speakers at the now famous March on Washington in 1963 were men. The choice was deliberate, for when the organizers were confronted with their "oversight," they indicated that black women would have had a problem deciding on a representative. Their decision to exclude black women, therefore, kept the women from facing such a dilemma![7]

Last, the American Negro Academy, the first learned society for blacks, was founded in Washington, D.C., in 1897, and though women were not barred from the membership, it remained an all-male organization during its thirty-one-year existence. At the first organizational meeting, a member argued that women should be admitted and was assured by the other founding members that women could join, but no efforts were made to recruit black women. In 1898, Alexander Crummell invited a black woman to present a paper at the second annual meeting, and though she was unable to attend, the Academy invited another woman to read the paper. This was the only occasion at which a female presented a paper. Despite the outstanding contributions of many black women during this era, among them Mary Church Terrell, Anna J. Cooper, and Nannie Burroughs, none was ever invited to join the Academy.[8] Though black women assumed in each of these cases that there existed a natural alliance between them and black men, they were rejected, ironically, on the basis of their sex.

Though many black men were unable to accept black women as their equals, however, or to reject the True Womanhood philosophy, it is important to realize the commitment on the part of some black males to the struggle of women for full equality, not just for their right to vote. There was almost total agreement among them, despite their views on other aspects of "the woman question," that black women should have equal access to education, which was seen as the major vehicle for uplifting the race. On this particular issue, the achievement of racial equality was more important than concerns about black women deviating from the True Woman ideal, which emphasized traditional roles for women. The most enlightening aspect of the examination of attitudes toward woman suffrage, which was seen as another vehicle for the improvement of the race, is the revelation that some black men and many black women saw as early as a century ago no contradiction in associating themselves with struggles for women's rights (despite the opposition of many whites) at the same time that they were fighting for the emancipation of the race. They saw themselves as fighting for the liberation of all people. At a time when there is controversy among academics and activists alike over whether blacks should be fighting for the liberation of women *or* the liberation of the race, one can look at the lives of Frederick Douglass, Sojourner Truth, Du Bois, and Mary Church Terrell, to name a few, and resolve this seeming dilemma rather easily.

Of the groups examined, black women were more outspoken about the diversity of roles they needed to assume in order to lead a useful life. Not only did they consider their roles as wives and mothers important, but they also felt that they had equally as important duties outside the home, the most significant of which was their duty to work for the general improvement of society and especially the uplifting of the race. Black women felt that they must work for improvements in the status of black women also. In other words, black women were more painfully aware than any other segment of the population of the peculiar burden of race and sex under which they struggled. They were aware of the necessity of their being "at least an assistant bread winner if the finances of the race are to be improved," so that they could never be looked upon as only housewives, despite the appeal of the cult of True Womanhood.[9] Kindergartens (even free ones) and day nurseries were encouraged by black women's clubs so that mothers could be assured that their children were receiving proper care while they were at work or pursuing other activities.

The feeling that a woman's place was not necessarily the home was expressed more often by black women, though they certainly recognized the home as a real source of strength for any group, especially an oppressed one. Rejecting the prevailing ideology that women have a prescribed place, they felt that "it is according to law, gospel, history, and common sense that woman's place is where she is needed and where she fits in and to say that place will affect her womanliness is bosh; womanliness is an attribute not a condition; it is not supplied or withdrawn by surroundings."[10] There was even the direct (even radical) remark made in the March 1894 issue of *Woman's Era* that a woman's staying at home too much can be detrimental and that all women are not suited for marriage and motherhood.

> A great deal of the advice given to women about their staying at home is wrong altogether, for if a woman stays at home too much she will forget how to manage that home. At the club she will get new ideas from other women of how to live and manage her home, and great help in training her children, and to gain experiences in various domestic traits. Women's clubs are educators of mothers and women who have no homes. Not all women are intended for mothers. Some of us have not the temperament for family life. . . . Clubs will make women think seriously of their future lives and not make girls think their only alternative is to marry.[11]

Black women were also more vocal about the problems they faced as a result of their race and sex. Progressive black women urged their sisters to align themselves with organizations that dealt with racial as well as with women-related issues. They also felt that white women should accept some responsibility for the "wrongs and outrages done to the black race."[12] That is, white men were not totally at fault. They reminded white women that, in addition to fighting for votes for women, they needed to be more sensitive to the problems of race. Contemporary black feminists have also felt the need to remind white feminists that they need to be more sensitive to racism as they struggle for the liberation of women. In fact, black women felt that the solution to the race problem was in the hands of women.

. . . We thoroughly believe that it is the women of America—black and white—who are to solve this race problem, and we do not ignore the duty of the black woman in the matter. They must arouse, educate and advance themselves; they are to exert that influence through the homes, the schools and the churches that will build upon intelligent, industrious and moral people. . . . But the white woman has a duty in the matter also; she must see to it that no obstructions are placed in the way of a weak, struggling people, she must no longer consent to be passive. We call upon her to take her stand.[13]

It is important to point out here that progressive black women did not feel that white women must assume the major responsibility for saving the race, but rather that they should assist black women by not placing obstacles in their path.

In her opening address at the National Conference of Colored Women held in Boston in July 1895, Josephine Ruffin explains clearly what the concerns of black women should be:

. . . we need to talk over not only those things which are of vital importance to us as women, but also the things that are of especial interest to us as *colored* women, the training of our children, openings for our boys and girls, how they can be prepared for occupations . . . what *we* especially can do in the moral education of the race . . . our mental elevation and physical development, the home training it is necessary to give our children in order to prepare them to meet the peculiar conditions in which they shall find themselves, how to make the most of our own, to some extent, limited opportunities, these are some of our own peculiar questions. . . . Besides these are the general questions of the day, which we cannot afford to be indifferent to: temperance, morality, the higher education, hygienic and domestic questions. . . .[14]

This conception of the role of the "ideal" black woman differs radically from the majority culture's notions of the ideal woman whose responsibilities seem to end at her own front door. Black women felt that they could not afford the luxury of being concerned only about their own households when the race as well as society in general suffered from a vast array of problems.

In general, black men and women felt compelled to affirm the worth and dignity of black womanhood during a time when they were being scorned because of their alleged immorality and ignorance. Frequent references are made to the activities and accomplishments of prominent black women as well as to the activities of ordinary black women whose work is also seen as

Josephine St. Pierre Ruffin (1842-1924), pioneering club woman and civil rights leader, organized the Woman's Era Club in Boston in 1894. She was responsible for convening in 1895 a convention of black women which would provide the catalyst for the birth of the black clubwoman's movement and the founding of the National Association of Colored Women (NACW). She also edited *Woman's Era*, the first monthly periodical for black women in the United States.

valuable. Ruffin is only one of many who pay a special tribute to those large numbers of black women who lead meaningful lives because they advance the cause of the race.

> All over America there is to be found a large and growing class of earnest, intelligent, progressive colored women, women who, if not leading useful lives, are only waiting for the opportunity to do so, many of them warped and cramped for lack of opportunity. . . . Now for the sake of the thousands of self-sacrificing young women teaching and preaching in lonely southern backwoods, for the noble army of mothers who have given birth to these girls . . . for the sake of the fine cultured women who have carved off the honors in school here and often abroad, for the sake of our own dignity, the dignity of our race, and the future good name of our children, it is "mete, right and our bounden duty" to teach an ignorant and suspicious world that our aims and interests are identical with those of all good aspiring women.[15]

In fact, in *Woman's Era* the black woman who is involved in meaningful work outside the home is consistently singled out for praise and admiration. The "ideal" woman in the black woman's mind seems to be the woman who also assumes responsibility for the problems of the larger society, not the isolated housewife who is only concerned about the needs of her own family, though certainly black women consider the needs of the family to be important as well. Nearly a century later, it appears that the "ideal" role model for women in general more closely conforms to the model that black women admired during this period.

This study is important for a number of reasons. First, it provides an opportunity to test the theory that one's racial identity, as opposed to one's gender classification, is the most important determinant of attitudes about a particular segment of the American population, in this case black women, at any given point in history. During the period under consideration, race appears to be more important than any other variable in determining how black women are perceived. In fact, whites, male and female, see black women as black first and as women only secondarily. This is not surprising given the wide acceptance of white supremacy at the turn of the century. Because of the racial caste system that lumped black men and women together, blacks were also sensitive first to the racial identity of black women. It seems safe to assume, I might add, that black women will continue to be perceived in this manner as long as race continues to be the most important determinant of a person's status within the American context.

Second, it provides additional knowledge about an aspect of black women's history that is seldom the subject of scholarly inquiry—the intellectual thought *about* black women during a given historical period. Since scholarship undertaken about the history of black women in America has focused on reconstructing their experiences during particular eras or on describing the lives of prominent, forgotten, or ordinary black women (both difficult undertakings), this study is unique because of its focus on the relationship between currents in the intellectual thought of the time and particular attitudes toward black women. Such an examination is critical, I would argue, if one is to fully understand black women's history—both what happened to black women as a group and the particular life histories of individual black women. To illustrate, the founding of schools near the turn of the century to train black domestics occurred because of a particular set of attitudes about black women that were peculiar to that time period.

Third, this study is important because it provides insights into how black women viewed themselves. Sub-groups are not passive onlookers, as traditional history would have us believe, but active participants in the formulation and transmission of cultural attitudes. Anna J. Cooper—feminist, educator, and spokesperson for the cause of black women at the turn of the century—has spoken eloquently not about the silence of the black woman but about society's refusal to hear the "muffled chord" of her voice, "crying in the night."

> One important witness has not yet been heard from. . . . The "other side" has not been represented by one who "lives there." And not many can more sensibly realize and more accurately tell the weight and the fret of the "long dull pain" than the open-eyed but hitherto voiceless Black Woman of America.[16]

Fourth, the study underscores the ambivalent nature of attitudes toward women generally during the period.

> Woman's image was riddled with contradictions: guardian of the race, but wholly subject to male authority; preserver of civilization, religion, and culture, yet considered the intellectual inferior of man; the primary socializer of her children, but given no more real responsibility and dignity than a child herself.[17]

Black women also experienced these ambiguities as well as others. They were considered the guardians of the race but were subject to both male and white authority. They were considered the preservers of civilization within the context of their own race, but were perceived to be the intellectual inferiors of black men and white men and women and the moral inferiors of white women. They were the primary socializers of their own children and, in the South, had major responsibility for their mistress's children as well, but at the same time they were considered to be morally depraved and childlike. In other words, the Victorian ambivalence toward women, "symbolized by its obsession with two polar images—the angel and the prostitute,"[18] is most apparent in conceptions of white and black womanhood at the turn of the century. The study also suggests that many present-day attitudes about black women, especially the black woman as whore, are prominent during this period.

Finally, and perhaps most importantly, this study provides insights into some of the theoretical problems involved in doing Black Women's Studies, a new field that has emerged during the past few years because of the failure of both Black Studies and Women's Studies to deal adequately with the experiences of black women in America and throughout the world. Proponents of Black Women's Studies have advanced the following argument for its existence:

> Women's studies courses . . . focused almost exclusively upon the lives of white women. Black studies, which was much too often male-dominated, also ignored Black women. . . . Because of white women's racism and Black men's sexism, there was no room in either area for a serious consideration of the lives of Black women. And even when they have considered Black women, white women usually have not had the capacity to analyze racial politics and Black culture, and Black men have remained blind or resistant to the implications of sexual politics in Black women's lives.[19]

The most noteworthy developments in the area of Black Women's Studies have come from a small but growing group of women scholars who have been teaching and doing research on black women for the past two decades. The pioneering work of educator Anna J. Cooper, who wrote *A Voice from the South by a Black Woman of the South* in 1892, has the distinction of being the first scholarly publication in the area of Black Women's Studies, though the concept had certainly not yet emerged. Eighty years later, the publication of Gerda Lerner's documentary history *Black Women in White America* underscored the importance of treating the experiences of American black women as distinct from those of white women and black men. More recently, the publication of the first interdisciplinary anthology in Black

Women's Studies (. . . *But Some Of Us Are Brave*) provides concrete evidence of the wealth of material available to the teacher and scholar in Black Women's Studies.

The most valuable theoretical work in the area of Black Women's Studies is Bell Hooks' ground-breaking monograph, *Ain't I A Woman: Black Women and Feminism*, which is a long-overdue examination of the complexity of black womanhood from the perspective of black women themselves. The major strengths of the book are its delineation of the impact of sexism on the lives of black women; its analysis of the devaluation of black womanhood, both historically and contemporaneously; its discussion of the persistent racism of the women's movement, and its careful treatment of the involvement of black women in struggles to achieve equality for women even when they were discouraged from doing so by various segments of the white and black communities. Hooks' major contribution to both Black Studies and Women's Studies, however, is the theoretical framework she provides for analyzing what it has meant to be a black woman in America. In her chapter "Sexism and the Black Female Slave Experience," for example, she advances the thesis that slavery, a reflection of a patriarchal and racist social order, not only oppressed black men, but also defeminized the slave woman. Though scholars have emphasized the impact of slavery on black men, which focuses in large part on the theory of the emasculation of the slave male, Hooks and other black feminist scholars argue that it is imperative that historians and other researchers begin to pay more attention to the impact of sexual exploitation on slave women. Furthermore, it is important to point out that black women were not permitted to conform to the dominant culture's model of True Womanhood, just as the black male was unable to act out the majority culture's definition of "true manhood."

Until the emergence of Black Women's Studies, most of the research on black women focused on their roles within the black family, especially the role of the black matriarch.[20] A second area of research has focused on the public lives of such notable black women as Sojourner Truth, Harriet Tubman, Mary Church Terrell, and Mary Bethune. Part of the motivation for this "great black women" in history approach is simply to record the fact that black women were indeed present. In her analysis of research priorities in Black Women's Studies, Scott has argued that "there is a wealth of unexplored areas which must be investigated during the next century." High on her list would be "more examinations of the black and female experience that are sensitive to the ways in which racism and sexism bear upon black women."[21] While such approaches to the study of black women are appropriate, a major problem that continues to confront the Black Women's Studies scholar, whose primary challenge remains exploring the intersection of race and gender, is the difficulty of arriving at theoretical frameworks that will enable one to understand the black female experience.

According to Gerda Lerner, the major conceptual framework for studying American women has been provided by feminist scholars who, using the women as minority group model,[22] see women mainly in terms of their oppression and their struggles to overcome it. As a consequence, the history of American women has unduly focused on how they got the vote. To counter this tendency, Mary Beard denied that women were oppressed and asserted that what was important about women was their impressive contributions to society throughout history.[23] This examination of attitudes toward black women suggests that the history of American women is more complex than what can be learned from an analysis of the suffrage struggle or the contributions of women to society. First, the history of women cannot be fully understood in isolation. One cannot, for example, understand the history of black women during the period under consideration without considering the impact of the cult of True Womanhood *and* the doctrine of white supremacy on their lives. A contemporary historian has commented on the value of studies, such as this one, which take an integrationist approach to women's history:

> . . . it is precisely the complex nature of women's position that historians ought to illuminate. Moreover, the best "women's history" is not confined to the study of women alone, but deals with the social, intellectual, and cultural context within which women lived out their lives. Therefore, the sooner we can integrate the study of women into investigations of that larger framework, the more valuable its pursuit will become.[24]

Second, this study avoids the pitfall of the "either/or" approach to women's history (which focuses either on the oppression of women *or* on their contributions) by approaching the study of black women from the perspective of their multi-faceted existence. As a consequence, it deals with the black woman as victim, but also acknowledges that this is only one aspect of her condition. The study also deviates to some extent from an entirely elitist approach to the history of nineteenth-century black women (which focuses on the contributions of outstanding black women) by considering attitudes about the masses of black women and taking into account class differences among black women. There is still, however, greater reliance on the writings of middle-class, educated black women in assessments of how black women perceived themselves.

The shortcomings of the more widely used minority group model to explain the history of American women have been analyzed by William Chafe and others. His major points concerning the problematic nature of the analogy between race and sex are that the collective oppression of blacks, especially the physical abuse they have suffered, is substantially greater than that of white women; that there is physical distance between whites and blacks, whereas white women live in close contact with white men giving them greater access to the sources of power than is the case with black women; and that white women are not as conscious of their oppression as a group as are blacks.[25] The major weakness in this analogy between women and blacks, which Chafe also recognizes, is that it obscures the critical differences between black and white women, the major one being that black women suffer the double burden of racism and sexism, which makes them a unique group in American society. Moreover, black women have not had the so-called "benefits" of being female; they have not been sheltered, protected, or idealized by their men to the extent that was possible for white women. More importantly, because of the thoroughly entrenched and therefore persistent racial caste system that defines relations between blacks and whites (and relegates blacks to a subordinate position), the oppression of black women links them to black men rather than to white women. Finally, the economic realities of the black community have forced black women to participate in the labor force to a greater extent than white women.

This brief summary of the weaknesses of the blacks/women parallel (which Chafe and others have discussed) points to a major problem that confronts the Black Women's Studies scholar. If women do form a distinct social group, how does one formulate a conceptual framework that takes into consideration race and its interaction with gender in the case of the black woman's experience? A number of conceptual issues arise when one considers the race/gender nexus in this context. Is it possible given the rigidity of the racial caste system to perceive American women as a distinct social group? Since black women belong to a minority group, can one completely reject the minority group model when conceptualizing them as a group? What happens to the minority group model when one considers that, despite their subordination to whites, including women, black men are in a position to exercise power over black women because of the benefits that accrue to them because of their gender? Are the bonds of womanhood sufficiently strong to counteract the racial barriers that separate black and white women, or does race override gender in most interactions between these two groups?

While this study has not solved all of the theoretical problems inherent in Black Women's Studies, it can provide some answers to these difficult conceptual issues. First, this study demonstrates that it is not possible to conceive of American women as a distinct social group. Since attitudes about black women were different from attitudes about white women during the period under consideration, it is clear that the racial identity of black women places them in a different category from other women. The problem of being black and female in a culture that has assigned a "place" for both groups is perhaps most apparent when black women attempt to ally themselves with white women on an issue related to their womanhood, in one case woman suffrage, and are rejected on the basis of their race. Less well known but indicative of the same problem was the struggle of black women to be represented at the Chicago World's Fair in 1893. Since the Board of Lady Managers had the responsibility for making decisions about the nature of black female participation at the exhibition, one might have assumed that conflicts between the women would have been minimal. However, this was not the case. The major point of controversy centered upon the appointment of a black women to the board. It was indeed prophetic that the white board members used the same argument initially that black male organizers of the 1963 March on Washington were to later use when they decided to exclude black women: "Our Board was entirely willing to appoint a national representative from the Negro women, and only refrained from doing so because they were quarrelling so among themselves and could not decide on a leader."[26] After numerous appeals, meetings, and petitions, Fannie Barrier Williams was finally appointed by the board "to help supervise the installation of all exhibits in the Woman's Building."[27] In the case of the woman suffrage campaign and the World's Fair, the "bonds of womanhood" were not sufficiently strong to counteract the racial barriers that separated black and white women at the turn of the century.

Ironically, the racial minority group model is also inadequate when examining black women because it suggests that gender is insignificant where minorities are concerned. This study indicates, however, that black men also internalize at least some of the culture's notions about sex roles. Because they are male, for example, black men believe that they should protect their women from the evils of the world and that black women, because of their sex, should assume the major responsibility for the moral stature of the race.

Furthermore, this study confirms Lerner's thesis that women should not be perceived as *a* sub-group and, more importantly, that "no single methodology and conceptual framework can fit the complexities of the historical experience of all women."[28] Chafe echoes this same point when he asserts that "the differential experience of women in material conditions of life, and in group orientation according to class, race, and ethnicity, tends to undercut the definition of women as a homogeneous . . . group within the larger society."[29] Lerner suggests that at various stages in the rewriting of history so that women's experiences can be included, special attention needs to be given to race, class, and ethnicity; new questions need to be asked; new subjects need to be explored, and ultimately a synthesis needs to be forged between male and female cultures. This study has certainly demonstrated the significance of race in its examination of a critical era in women's history. It has also exploited new subjects and asked new questions, the most important ones of which have been: Can one differentiate between attitudes toward members of the same minority group and toward members of the same gender group at a given point in time, and, if so, what is the significance of these differences? What can be learned about a given point in history as a result of this kind of examination? What does the study of black women reveal about women's history in general or the intellectual history of the period in general? In her discussion of the black mammy figure, Barbara Christian analyzes the significance of such an examination because it sheds light on an important aspect of black women's history and, equally important, because it provides insights about women's history and American intellectual history in general.

> Even as the planters praised the black woman as the "contented mammy," they also insisted that black slave women neglected their own children. Above and beyond these factors stands a major contradiction: that the planters could relegate the duties of motherhood, a revered and honored state, to a being supposedly lower than human, reveals their own confusion about the value of motherhood. That they could separate spiritual aspects of motherhood, which they acknowledged in their religion, from the physical aspects and give the duties of childrearing to a "subhuman" gives us some indication about the value they placed on women's work.[30]

Black Women's Studies scholars are in a unique position because of their ability to explore the intersection of race, sex, and class as experienced by black women in ways that are impossible for other segments of the population. The study of black women also renders invalid many of the generalizations that abound in the historiography of American women and are considered "universal." An example from the introduction to *Root of Bitterness*, a documentary social history of American women, will illustrate this point. Here Nancy Cott states that most of the late-nineteenth-century women who initiated significant social welfare activities in cities did their work while unmarried or widowed, and one thinks immediately of Jane Addams and nods in agreement. Cott then speculates that these educated women were unable to reconcile the demands of the nuclear family with their newly defined roles, so they evaded the problem by remaining single. When one recalls the history of black women during this same period, however, one thinks of Lugenia Burns Hope, Ida Wells-Barnett, and other middle-class, educated, married black women who performed pioneering social welfare activities when racial uplift preoccupied the black elite. A critical question for the Black Women's Studies scholar is why these women were better able to juggle the roles of wife, mother, and career than their white female counterparts. For example, Ida Wells-Barnett, determined not to give up her public life, carried her baby Charles (and nurse) along with her to women's conventions and political campaigns. He became such a fixture at the National Association of Colored Women's meetings that on one occasion he was elected Baby of the Association.[31] In order to explain why black women's lives diverged from white women's lives in this respect, it would be helpful to consider the special historical experiences of blacks, the particulars of the women's lives,[32] and the sociology of sex roles. What I am suggesting is the necessity of employing the perspectives of those outside the discipline of traditional history (especially sociology and social psychology) in the writing of women's history.

Another generalization in women's history is that women can be compared to other minority groups because their physical characteristics make them easily identifiable and therefore they can be "singled out from the others in the society in which they live for differential and unequal treatment."[33] The case of Lucy Parsons renders invalid even this seemingly indisputable fact. Lucy is the relatively obscure "invisible" black woman who was married to Albert Parsons, one of the anarchists accused of the Haymarket bombing in 1886 and later executed.[34] Because Lucy refused to acknowledge her racial identity (she pretended she was of mixed ancestry, mainly Indian) after her marriage, she becomes "invisible" as a black person. That is, her name is mentioned on numerous occasions in histories of working women (because of her life-long struggle to alleviate their plight) and in histories of radical movements, but her race is ignored, as Lucy would have preferred. She is therefore missing from black history. She is missing from "general" histories because of her sex, for it is presumed that her only significance was that she was the wife of Albert Parsons. She is even frequently missing from women's histories because her anarchist activity was out of the mainstream of nineteenth-century women's activities, such as suffrage, settlement, and club work, which have attracted more of the historian's attention. So, despite her persistent and dedicated struggle to improve the lives of the working class (before and after her husband's untimely death), which can be documented because of her many publications and because her activities were followed in newspapers throughout the country, she mainly appeared in footnotes before the publication of Carolyn Ashbaugh's study. That very little about her life prior to her marriage (except that she was an ex-slave born in Texas) was uncovered by Ashbaugh is indicative of the "invisibility" of blacks during slavery, one of the most difficult periods to study for the Black Women's Studies scholar. Though Lucy is certainly easily identifiable as a woman, she avoids the "differential and unequal treatment" she would have experienced as a *black* by passing and denying her minority group status. She, therefore, escapes the indignities members of her own race suffer even though she is female because, in effect, she becomes white. As a member of the dominant race, despite her gender, she does not suffer the differential and unequal treatment that proponents of the race/sex analogy argue is universal among blacks and women.

Finally, this study also confirms the validity of arguments advanced by Gerda Lerner and others concerning the challenges confronting the student of black women's history.

> . . . there is a rich and accessible history of black women. Those wishing to write and interpret that history share with those writing women's history the conceptual problems of interpreting known materials from a new point of view, a different angle of vision. But first they must do the job which the early compilers and collectors of women's history . . . did for their field—they must unearth, compile, and organize the raw materials on which interpretations can be based.[35]

The ultimate challenge, from my perspective, however, is for women's studies scholars, such as Lerner, to recognize that black women's history is in fact

175

women's history, and that "the black female experience, by the very nature of its extremity, illuminates the subjugation of all women."[36] Such a perspective would render Black Women's Studies unnecessary, or at the very least redundant, over the long run.

Notes

CHAPTER ONE

1. George Frederickson, *The Black Image in the White Mind* (New York, 1971), p. xi.
2. The most important studies of racial thought in America include Alexis de Tocqueville, *Democracy in America* (London, 1835-1840); Gunnar Myrdal, *An American Dilemma* (New York, 1944); Winthrop Jordan, *White Over Black: American Attitudes Toward the Negro, 1550-1812* (Chapel Hill, 1968); George Frederickson, *The Black Image in the White Mind: The Debate on Afro-American Character and Destiny, 1817-1914* (New York, 1971); George Stocking, *Race, Culture and Evolution* (New York, 1968); Oscar Handlin, *Race and Nationality in American Life* (Boston, 1957); Thomas Gossett, *Race: The History of an Idea in America* (Dallas, 1963); Louis Ruchames, ed., *Racial Thought in America: From the Puritans to Abraham Lincoln* (Amherst, 1969); Lawrence Friedman, *The White Savage: Racial Fantasies in the Post-Bellum South* (Englewood Cliffs, N.J., 1970); Claude Zolen, *The Negro's Image in the South: The Anatomy of White Supremacy* (Lexington, Ky., 1967); I. A. Newby, *Jim Crow's Defense: Anti-Negro Thought in America, 1900-1930* (Baton Rouge, 1965); Forrest Wood, *Black Scare: The Racist Response to Emancipation and Reconstruction* (Berkeley, 1968); William Stanton, *The Leopard's Spots: Scientific Attitudes Toward Race in America, 1815-1859* (Chicago, 1960); Naomi Goldstein, *The Roots of Prejudice Against the Negro in the United States* (Boston, 1948); Rayford Logan, *The Negro in American Life and Thought, The Nadir, 1877-1901* (New York, 1954). A collection of essays edited by Gary Nash and Richard Weiss, *The Great Fear: Race in the Mind of America* (New York, 1970), is also useful.

    The following articles are equally significant: Guion Griffis Johnson, "The Ideology of White Supremacy, 1876-1910," in *Essays in Southern History* (Chapel Hill, 1949); George Frederickson, "Toward a Social Interpretation of the Development of American Racism," in *Key Issues in the Afro-American Experience* (New York, 1971); Lawrence Friedman, "The Search for Docility: Racial Thought in the White South, 1861-1917," *Phylon* 31 (Fall 1970), 313-323; Charles Wesley, "The Concept of Negro Inferiority in American Thought," *Journal of Negro History* 25 (October 1940), 540-560; Earl W. Count, "The Evolution of the Race Idea in Modern Western Culture During the Period of the Pre-Darwinian 19th Century," *Transactions of the New York Academy of Sciences* 8 (1946), 139-165; Guion Griffis Johnson,

"Southern Paternalism toward Negroes after Emancipation," *Journal of Southern History* 23 (1957), 483-509.

3. Fannie Barrier Williams, "The Club Movement Among Colored Women of America," in *A New Negro for a New Century*, ed. John E. MacBrady (Chicago, 1900), pp. 381-382.

4. In her biography of Jessie Daniel Ames, founder of the Association of Southern Women for the Prevention of Lynching (1930), Jacquelyn Dowd Hall, in the chapter entitled "A Bond of Common Womanhood," discusses the involvement of white women in interracial cooperation with black women during the early decades of the twentieth century. The assumption was that women's mutual experience of motherhood would enable them to transcend their racial differences. The phrase "Thine in the bonds of womanhood" had been used by Sarah Grimble when she ended her correspondence, and according to Hall this idea (which the early women's rights movement espoused) implied that "Women's oppression combined with their common experience of domesticity to create a bond of sisterhood that transcended class and racial lines." *Revolt Against Chivalry* (New York, 1974), p. 105.

5. Noel A. Cazenave, " 'A Woman's Place': The Attitudes of Middle Class Black Men," *Phylon* XLIV (March 1983), p. 13.

6. See G. Q. Barker-Benfield, *The Horrors of the Half-Known Life: Male Attitudes Toward Women and Sexuality in 19th Century America* (New York, 1976); Verne Bullough and Bonnie Bullough, *The Subordinate Sex: A History of Attitudes Toward Women* (Urbana, Illinois, 1973), which includes a discussion of black women and makes comparisons between them and white women; Charles Z. Ferguson, *The Male Attitude* (Boston, 1966); H. Carleton Marlow and Harrison Davis, *The American Search for Woman* (Santa Barbara, 1976); Robert Riegel, *American Women: A Story of Social Change* (Rutherford, 1970); Barbara Welter, *Dimity Convictions: The American Woman in the 19th Century* (Athens, 1976).

7. These include Bernard Braxton, *Women, Sex and Race: A Realistic View of Sexism and Racism* (Washington, 1973); Beth Day, *Sexual Life Between Blacks and Whites* (New York, 1972); Grace Halsell, *Black/White Sex* (New York, 1972); Calvin Hernton, *Sex and Racism and America* (New York, 1965); Charles Stember, *Sexual Racism* (New York, 1976).

8. Friedman, *The White Savage* (Englewood Cliffs, N.J., 1970), pp. 142-143.

9. Rosalyn Terborg-Penn, "Black Male Perspectives on the 19th-Century Woman," in *The Afro-American Woman, Struggles and Images*, eds. Sharon Harley and Rosalyn Terborg-Penn (Port Washington, New York, 1978), pp. 28-42.

10. For a discussion of racism in the women's movement, see Aileen S. Kraditor, *The Ideas of the Woman Suffrage Movement, 1890-1920* (New York, 1965); Rosalyn Terborg-Penn, "Discrimination Against Afro-American Women in the Women's Movement, 1830-1920," in *The Afro-American Woman*, edited by Sharon Harley and Rosalyn Terborg-Penn (New York, 1978); Rosalyn Terborg-Penn, "Historical Treatment of Afro-Americans in the Women's Movement, 1900-1920: A Bibliographical Essay," *A Current Bibliography on*

African Affairs, 7 (Summer 1974), 254-59; Kenneth R. Johnson, "White Racial Attitudes as a Factor in the Arguments Against the Nineteenth Amendment," *Phylon* 31 (Spring 1970), 31-37; Bell Hooks, *Ain't I A Woman: Black Women and Feminism* (Boston, 1982); Angela Y. Davis, *Women, Race and Class* (New York, 1982); Robert L. Allen and Pamela P. Allen, *Reluctant Reformers: Racism and Social Reform Movements in the United States* (Washington, D.C., 1974). There are no published studies of the racial attitudes of southern suffragists at the state or local level.

For a discussion of the experiences of white teachers with freedmen and a discussion of their racial attitudes, see Henry Lee Swint, *The Northern Teacher in the South, 1862-1870* (Nashville, 1941); James M. McPherson, *The Abolitionist Legacy: From Reconstruction to the NAACP* (Princeton, 1975); Joseph A. Mills, "Motives and Behaviors of Northern Teachers in the South During Reconstruction," *Negro History Bulletin* 42 (Jan.-March 1979), 7-17; Jacqueline Jones, *Soldiers of Light and Love: Northern Teachers and Georgia Blacks, 1865-1873* (Chapel Hill, 1980); Elizabeth Jacoway, *Yankee Missionaries in the South: The Penn School Experiment* (Baton Rouge, 1980).

11. See Jacquelyn Dowd Hall's *Revolt Against Chivalry: Jessie Daniel Ames and the Women's Campaign Against Lynching* (New York, 1974).

12. Hooks, pp. 130-131.

13. Though secondary sources are few, several primary sources dealing with the experiences of white women in the South after the Civil War are useful. See Myrta Lockett Avary, *Dixie After the War: An Exposition of Social Conditions Existing in the South, During the Twelve Years Succeeding the Fall of Richmond* (Boston, 1906); Lura Beam, *He Called Them by the Lightning: A Teacher's Odyssey in the Negro South, 1908-1919* (New York, 1969); Elizabeth Bothume, *First Days Amongst the Contrabands* (Boston, 1893); Laura S. Haviland, *A Woman's Life-Work: Labors and Experiences of Laura S. Haviland* (Chicago, 1897); Mary Helm, *From Darkness to Light* (New York, 1909) and *The Upward Path: The Evolution of a Race* (New York, 1909); Lily H. Hammond, *In Black and White: An Interpretation of Southern Life* (New York, 1914); Laura M. Towne, *Letters and Diary of Laura M. Towne, Written from the Sea Islands of South Carolina, 1862-84*, ed. Rupert Sargent Holland (Cambridge, 1912).

14. A major primary source for white female attitudes toward black women during the ante-bellum period are the diaries of mistresses of plantations, such as Mary Boykin Chesnut, *A Diary From Dixie*, ed. Ben Williams (Boston, 1949); Belle Kearney, *A Slaveholder's Daughter* (New York, 1900); Frances Anne Kemble, *Journal of a Residence on a Georgia Plantation in 1828-1839*, ed. John Scott (New York, 1961); Anne Firor Scott's *The Southern Lady: From Pedestal to Politics, 1830-1930* (Chicago, 1970) discusses the bitterness of southern white women over the sexual relationships between black women and their husbands. The most recent publication on plantation mistresses is Catherine Clinton's *The Plantation Mistress: Woman's World in the Old South* (Westminster, Md.: Pantheon, 1983).

15. Beth Day, *Sexual Life Between Blacks and Whites* (New York, 1972), p. 114. David Katzman's *Seven Days a Week* also discusses relationships between white women and their household servants.

16. Ibid., pp. 105-106.

17. See Angela Davis, *Women, Race, and Class*, especially the chapters " The Meaning of Emancipation According to Black Women," "Education and Liberation: Black Women's Perspective," and "Black Women and the Club Movement"; Bell Hooks, *Ain't I A Woman*, especially the chapter on "Black Women and Feminism." Sharon Harley and Rosalyn Terborg-Penn, *The Afro-American Woman* (New York, 1978); Wilson Jeremiah Moses, "Domestic Feminism, Conservatism, Sex Roles, and Black Women's Clubs, 1893-1896," *Journal of Social and Behavioral Sciences* 24 (Fall, 1978), 166-177.

  Also useful are the numerous personal narratives of black women (some detail their experiences as slaves and others describe their war experiences) that were published during the period. These include Virginia W. Broughton, *Twenty Year's Experience of a Missionary* (Chicago, 1907); Fanny Jackson Coppin, *Reminiscences of School Life and Hints on Teaching* (Philadelphia, 1913); Lucy Berry Delaney, *From Darkness Cometh the Light* (St. Louis, 1891); Frances J. Guadet, *"He Leadeth Me"* (New Orleans, 1913); Sarah A. Mix, *In Memory of Departed Worth* (Torrington, Conn., 1884); Amanda Smith, *An Autobiography, of Mrs. Amanda Smith, the Colored Evangelist* (Chicago, 1893); Susie King Taylor, *Reminiscences of My Life in Camp* (Boston, 1902); Marva P. Williams, *My Work and Public Sentiment* (Kansas City, Mo., 1916); Octavia Victoria Rogers Albert, *The House of Bondage: Or, Charlotte Brooks and Other Slaves* (New York, 1890); Jane Blake, *Memoirs of Margaret Jane Blake . . .* (Philadelphia, 1897); Annie L. Burton, *Memories of Childhood Slavery Days* (Boston, 1909); Julia Foote, *A Brand Plucked from the Fire: An Autobiographical Sketch* (Cleveland, 1879); Sojourner Truth, *Narrative of Sojourner Truth* (Battle Creek, Michigan, 1878); Bethany Veney, *A Narrative of Bethany Veney: A Slave Woman* (Worcester, Mass., 1890).

18. One can explore attitudes in ways other than looking at what has been written about a group. August Meier, in *Negro Thought in America, 1880-1915* (Ann Arbor, 1963), also analyzed institutional developments in the black community as a means of uncovering the attitudes of the non-vocal majority.

19. A complete listing of these sources can be found in a pamphlet issued by the U.S. government in 1906: *Select List of References on the Negro Question*, compiled by Appleton Griffin, Government Printing Office. The long list includes such works as Henry Grady, *The Race Problem* (Chicago, 1889); George Cable, *The Negro Question* (New York, 1890); W. Cabell Bruce, *The Negro Problem* (Baltimore, 1891); Frank Gage, *The Negro Problem in the United States, Its Rise, Development and Solution* (New York, 1892); Enoch Spencer Simmons, *A Solution to the Race Problem in the South* (Raleigh, 1898); R.W. Shufeldt, *The Negro: A Menace to American Civilization* (Boston, 1907); Alfred Stone, *Studies in the American Race*

Problem (New York, 1908); Charles Adams, *The Solid South and the Afro-American Race Problem* (Boston, 1908); William Brown, *The Crucial Race Question of Where and How Shall the Color Line Be Drawn* (Little Rock, 1907).

20. Albert Albrecht, "The Relationship of Literature and Society," *American Journal of Sociology* 59 (March 1954), 425-36. See also Albert Albrecht, "Does Literature Reflect Common Values?", *American Sociological Review* 21 (December 1956), 723-29; Ruth Inglis, "An Objective Approach to the Relationship between Fiction and Society," *American Sociological Review* 2 (August 1938), 526-31.

21. Thomas Pearce Bailey, *Race Orthodoxy in the South and Other Aspects of the Negro Question* (New York, 1914), p. 93.

22. Frederickson, *The Black Image in the White Mind* (New York, 1971), p. 321.

23. Richard Weiss, "Racism in the Era of Industrialization," in *The Great Fear: Race in the Mind of America*, eds. Gary Nash and Richard Weiss (New York, 1970), p. 122.

24. Ibid., pp. 137 and 139.

25. For a discussion of nineteenth-century attitudes toward women, see Robert Riegel, *American Women: A Story of Social Change*; Barbara Welter, *Dimity Convictions* (Athens, 1976); Walter Buehr, *Home Sweet Home in the Nineteenth Century* (New York, 1965); Sara Delamont and Lorna Duffin, eds., *The Nineteenth-Century Woman: Her Cultural and Physical World* (New York, 1978); Mary P. Ryan, *Womanhood in America: From Colonial Times to the Present* (New York, 1975).

26. Barbara Welter, "The Cult of True Womanhood, 1820-1860," *American Quarterly* 18 (Summer 1966), p. 151. She indicates that writers who addressed the subject of women in the mid-nineteenth century used this phrase without defining it and simply assumed that readers would intuitively understand what they meant, which attests to a general understanding of the concept.

27. Barbara J. Harris, *Beyond Her Sphere, Women and the Professions in American History* (Westport, Conn., 1978), pp. 33-34.

28. Bullough and Bullough, *The Subordinate Sex*, pp. 309-12. Like Ryan, the authors attribute this change in attitude toward women to their decreased economic importance as a result of industrialization and the growth of factories, which resulted in the home losing out as an economic unit. "The 19th century in America, as in Europe, perhaps as sort of unconscious compensation for lack of economic importance emphasized the finer nature of women, the special qualities that it took to be wife and mother" (p. 310).

29. Riegel, p. 57.

30. Ryan, p. 158.

31. Harris, pp. 33-34.

32. Nancy F. Cott, ed., *Root of Bitterness: Documents of the Social History of American Women* (New York, 1972), p. 12.

33. William E. B. Du Bois, *Darkwater: Voices from Within the Veil* (New York, 1969), p. 172.

34. Explicit references to the twin handicaps of sexism and racism experienced by black women appear as early as the 1920s. See Elise Johnson McDougald's "The Double Task: The Struggle of Negro Women in Sex and Race Emancipation," *Survey Graphic* 6 (March 1925), 689-91. Discussions of the same concept appear in the writings of contemporary black and white women. See Frances Beale's "Double Jeopardy: To Be Black and Female," *New Generation* 51 (Fall 1969), 23-28; Cynthia Fuchs Epstein, "Black and Female: The Double Whammy," *Psychology Today* 7 (July 1973), 57-61; Elizabeth Almquist, "Untangling the Effects of Race and Sex: The Disadvantaged Status of Black Women," *Social Science Quarterly* 56 (June 1975), 129-42.

CHAPTER TWO

1. The most extensive research recently on the cult of domesticity has been done by Mary Ryan, who has compiled a special issue of *Women and History* on "The Empire of the Mother, American Writing About Domesticity, 1839-1869" (Summer-Fall 1982). Barbara Harris's *Beyond Her Sphere, Women and the Professions in American History*, also contains an excellent discussion of the cult of domesticity which she argues "became such an integral part of American social ideology that its definition of women's role long survived the passing of the nineteenth century" (p. 32).
2. Barbara J. Harris, pp. 32-33.
3. See also her "Early Community Work of Black Club Women," *Journal of Negro History* 59 (April 1974), 158-67, in which she discusses the black women's club movement and the Neighborhood Union, which was founded in 1908 in Atlanta by Lugenia Hope, wife of Morehouse College president John Hope.
4. Rayford W. Logan, *The Negro in American Life and Thought, The Nadir, 1877-1901* (New York, 1954), p. 62.
5. Jacqueline Jones, *A Bridge of "Bent Backs and Laboring Muscles": Black Working Women in the Rural South, 1880-1915* (Wellesley, 1981), p. 1.
6. Ibid., pp. 2-3.
7. David Katzman, pp. 81-82.
8. Jacqueline Jones, p. 3.
9. Ibid., p. 19.
10. Ibid., pp. 21-22.
11. Ibid., pp. 22-24.
12. Ibid., p. 25.
13. "A Washerwoman," *The Independent* LVII (November 10, 1904), pp. 1073-76.
14. David Katzman, *Seven Days a Week*, p. 72.
15. Du Bois' *The Philadelphia Negro: A Social Study* (Philadelphia, 1899) contains the results of a study of black domestics in Philadelphia that was conducted by Isabel Eaton. See also Elizabeth Ross Haynes, *Negroes in Domestic Service*

in the United States, Master's thesis, Columbia University, 1923; Julian Roebuck, *Domestic Service: With Particular Attention to the Negro Female Servant in the South*, Master's Thesis, Duke University, 1944.

16. Anna J. Cooper, *A Voice from the South* (Xenia, Ohio, 1892), p. 108. Cooper's book is a collection of her speeches and essays and is the first book-length black feminist analysis of the black woman's situation in America.

17. Ibid., pp. 143-44.

18. Flexner, p. 231.

19. Rothman, *Woman's Proper Place*, p. 18.

20. Ibid., p. 23.

21. The Women's Christian Temperance Union (WCTU), founded in 1874 in Cleveland, came to be, under Frances Willard's leadership, the largest women's organization in America, reaching over 200,000 women in every state, according to Eleanor Flexner, *Century of Struggle*, p. 184.

22. Flexner, pp, 323-33. See Bettina Aptheker, "Quest for Dignity: Black Women in the Professions" in *Woman's Legacy* (Amherst, 1982) for a discussion of professional black women.

23. Ryan, "The Empire of the Mother," p. 38.

24. Ibid., p. 40.

25. Anna J. Cooper, pp. 144-45.

26. Ibid., p. 142-43.

27. Josephine Ruffin, *The Woman's Era* 2 (September 1895), p. 14. A detailed discussion of the development of the historically significant black women's club movement will not be attempted here. See Elizabeth L. Davis, *Lifting As They Climb: The National Association of Colored Women* (n.p.: National Association of Colored Women, 1933) for primary source material.

28. Ida Wells-Barnett, journalist and clubwoman, is perhaps best known for her national and international crusade against lynching during the 1890s. As a result of her lecture tours in Great Britain in 1893 and 1894, an anti-lynching committee was founded. In 1895 she published *A Red Record*, the result of her research on three years of lynchings in the South. In 1893 she organized a club for black women in Chicago, which was later called the Ida B. Wells Club, and later founded the Alpha Suffrage Club in the same city. It was the first woman suffrage club for black women in the nation. For a more detailed account of her life see her autobiography, *Crusade for Justice*, ed. Alfreda M. Duster (Chicago, 1910).

29. A detailed account of this historic convention was written by Richard T. Greener, first black graduate of Harvard College (1870) and a prominent black lawyer, and is located in the Rare Book Room of the Boston Public Library in the manuscript box concerning *The Woman's Era*.

30. Ibid., p. 8.

31. Ibid., p. 1.

32. Ibid., p. 11.

33. Rothman, p. 57.

34. Gerda Lerner, ed. *Black Women in White America: A Documentary History* (New York, 1973), pp. 120-21.

35. *The Souls of Black Folk*, p. 59.
36. Evelyn Brooks Barnett, "Nannie Burroughs and the Education of Black Women," in *The Afro-American Woman*, eds. Sharon Harley and Rosalyn Terborg-Penn (Port Washington, N.Y., 1978), p. 98.
37. Ibid., p. 97.
38. Mary McLeod Bethune, "Faith That Moved a Dump Heap," *Who, The Magazine About People* I (June 1941), pp. 31-35.
39. The Woman's American Baptist Home Mission Society was organized in 1877 by a group of New England women as an auxiliary to the American Baptist Home Mission Society (ABHMS), which had been supporting and building mission schools since 1832. Sophia Packard was a founding member of WABHMS and wrote the legal document applying for incorporation.
40. The Spelman College Archives, located on the campus, is the repository for the numerous diaries of Packard and Giles that contain detailed accounts of the founding of the college.
41. Spelman College Archives, Atlanta, Georgia.
42. *Opportunity*, May 1931, p. 134. This periodical was published monthly by the National Urban League.
43. Frelinghuysen, an evening school for black adults, similar in concept to the community college, began in 1919. Cooper was its second president and served for ten years. When she received her doctorate, Cooper became only the fourth black woman in America to be so honored.
44. *A Voice From the South*, p. 28.
45. *Darkwater*, p. 165.
46. Ibid., pp. 185-86.

CHAPTER THREE

1. Michelle Rosaldo and Louisel Amphere, eds. *Woman, Culture and Society* (Stanford, 1974), p. 19.
2. Ibid., p. 24.
3. Fannie Barrier Williams, "The Club Movement Among Colored Women of America," *A New Negro for a New Century*, ed. John E. MacBrady, (Chicago, 1900), p. 379.
4. Sara Delamont and Lorna Duffin, "Introduction," *The Nineteenth-Century Woman: Her Cultural and Physical World* (New York, 1978), p. 21.
5. An exalted notion of womanhood was especially common in the upper-class South. For comments on this peculiar southern conception of white womanhood, see W. J. Cash, *The Mind of the South* (New York, 1941), which refers to this phenomenon as "gyneolatry"; Laurence Alan Baughman, *Southern Rape Complex: Hundred Year Psychosis* (Atlanta, 1966); Irving Bartlett and C. Glenn Cambor, "The History and Psycho-dynamics of Southern Womanhood," *Women's Studies* 2 (1974), 9-24; John Dillard, *Caste and Class in a Southern Town* (New Haven, 1937); Kathryn Seidel, "The Southern Belle as an Ante-bellum Ideal," *Southern Quarterly* 25 (July 1977);

Lillian Smith, *Killers of the Dream* (New York, 1961); Frank Tannenbaum, *Darker Phases of the South* (New York, 1924).

6. Bell Hooks, *Ain't I A Woman: Black Women and Feminism* (Boston, 1982), p. 31.

7. Ryan, pp. 142-43.

8. Hooks, p. 53.

9. Many writers, commenting on the effects of slavery on the black woman, viewed the destruction of black womanhood as one of the most terrible injustices of slavery. See Hernton, *Sex and Racism in America*, pp. 123-127; Cash, *The Mind of the South*, p. 87; Smith, *Killers of the Dream*; John Blassingame, *The Slave Community*, pp. 80-8; Arthur Calhoun, *A Social History of the American Family*, Vol. 2, Chapters 11 and 12; Eleanor Flexner, *Century of Struggle*, pp. 18-23; Eugene Genovese, *Roll, Jordan, Roll*, pp. 413-431; David Marchal, *The Americans at Home*, pp. 319-320; Page Smith, *Daughters of the Promised Land: Women in American History*, pp. 216-21; and Bell Hooks, *Ain't I a Woman*, pp. 15-49.

10. A.H. Shannon, *Racial Integrity and Other Features of the Negro Problem* (Nashville, 1907), p. 246.

11. William P. Pickett, *The Negro Problem: Abraham Lincoln's Solution* (New York, 1909), p. 14.

12. William B. Smith, *The Color Line: A Brief in Behalf of the Unborn* (New York, 1905), p. 10.

13. Ibid., p. 15.

14. Howard Odum, *Social and Mental Traits of the Negro: Research into the Conditions of the Negro Race in Southern Towns* (New York, 1910), p. 165. He makes some distinction here between the women of various classes.

15. Philip A. Bruce, *The Plantation Negro as a Freeman* (New York and London, 1889), p. 5.

16. Ibid., pp. 11-12.

17. Ibid., pp. 18-19.

18. Ibid., pp. 19-20.

19. Ibid., p. 20.

20. Ibid., pp. 84-85.

21. Eleanor Tayleur, "The Negro Woman: Social and Moral Decadence," *The Outlook* LXXVI (January 30, 1904), p. 266.

22. Ibid., pp. 267-68.

23. Ibid., p. 268.

24. Ibid., p. 270. It is curious that since black women came to dominate midwifery in the South, attending both black and white births, they would be accused of infanticide. According to Richard W. Kertz and Dorothy C. Wertz, *Lying-In: A History of Childbirth in America* (New York, 1979), by 1941, two-thirds of black births in the South were attended by midwives.

25. Ibid., p. 270.

26. Ibid., pp. 270-72.

27. Ibid., p. 269.

28. "The Race Problem—An Autobiography," *The Independent* LVI (March 17, 1904), p 593.
29. Mrs. L. H. Harris, "A Southern Woman's View," *The Independent* LI (May 18, 1899), p. 1355.
30. "The Negro Problem," *The Independent* LIX (September 18, 1902), pp. 2224-28.
31. Ibid., p. 593.
32. "Observations of the Southern Race Feeling," *The Independent* LVI (March 17, 1904), p. 599.
33. Ibid., p. 597.
34. Much of the fiction of white women during the period, like the fiction of white men, was in the Plantation Tradition, and black female characters were usually in stereotyped roles—the faithful servant being the most prevalent. Southern women writers, in particular, weeping over the past glory of the old plantation, peopled their fiction with perfect masters and slaves who lived in harmony. This group would include Ruth Stuart, Mary Louise Gaines (whose *I Heah de Voices Callin*, published in 1916, includes illustrations and stories on "de ole black Mammy"), Mrs. Atwood Martin (pen name George Madden Martin), Martha Gielow Harrison, Mary Johnston, and Emma Speed Sampson. Northern white women, to a lesser degree, wrote about blacks, including women, and this group included Sarah Orne Jewett, Constance Woolson, and the neo-abolitionists—Mary White Ovington and Dorothy Canfield. Ellen Glasgow, a southern liberal who fits neither of the above groupings, also wrote about black women.
35. According to Janet Hobhouse, one of Stein's biographers, the portraits in "Melanctha," one of three stories in the collection, were influenced by her knowledge of the black population in Baltimore where she was enrolled at the Johns Hopkins School of Medicine in 1897. *Everybody Who Was Anybody: A Biography of Gertrude Stein* (New York, 1975), p. 71.
36. Gertrude Stein, *Three Lives* (New York, 1909), pp. 85 and 211.
37. Addison Gayle, *The Way of the New World: The Black Novel in America* (New York, 1976), p. 32.
38. Paule Marshall, "The Negro Woman in American Literature," *Freedomways* 9 (Winter 1966), p. 21.
39. Ibid.
40. The sterotypic tragic mulatto character had its beginnings in the nineteenth century. Myth held that the mulatto possessed a mixture of the blood of both races. The black blood produced certain traits—criminality, savagery, deception, and stupidity—while the white blood produced the superior traits—intelligence, refinement, purity, and beauty. Usually the tragic mulatto suffers because of the inability to resolve these conflicts in her character. See Penelope Bullock, "The Treatment of the Mulatto in American Fiction From 1826-1902," Master's Thesis, Atlanta University, 1944.
41. Ibid., p. 104.
42. Thomas P. Bailey, *Race Orthodoxy in the South and Other Aspects of the Negro Question* (New York, 1914), p. 43.

43. Odum, pp. 243-44.
44. William Dean Howells, *The Shadow of a Dream and An Imperative Duty* (New Haven, 1972), p. 196. Subsequent references are to this edition, which was edited by Edwin Cady. McPherson refers to Howells as a "romantic racialist" (borrowing George Fredrickson's terminology) who, like other "neo-abolitionists," believed that blacks possessed special artistic skills and temperamental traits. This group was opposed to the idea of mental inferiority among blacks and perceived racial differences to be cultural in origin or related to differences in temperament. *The Abolitionist Legacy*, pp. 342-42. Howells reveals the racist attitudes of whites as the story unfolds and something of his own racial attitudes, as is the case with his description of Mrs. Johnson, his family's black domestic, in *Suburban Sketches*, published in 1811. See also Thomas Ford, "Howells and the American Negro," *Texas Studies in Literature and Language* 5 (Winter 1964), 530-37; Anne Ward Smacher, "The Genteel Primitivist and the Semi-Tragic Octoroon," *New England Quarterly* 29 (1956), 216-27.
45. Ray Stannard Baker, *Following the Color Line: American Negro Citizenship in the Progressive Era* (New York, 1908), pp. 169-70.
46. W. D. Weatherford, *Negro Life in the South: Present Conditions and Needs* (New York, 1915). The author, a graduate of Vanderbilt University and past student secretary of the International Committee of the YMCA of the South, met in 1908 with an interracial group of men in Atlanta (four black and three white) to discuss the race question and especially what college-educated southern men might do to better the condition of blacks. After this six hour conference, the agreement was to prepare a textbook on the Negro in the South that could be used in the home mission classes of the college YMCAs.
47. Weatherford, pp. 80-81.
48. Ibid., p. 166.
49. Ibid.
50. Ibid., pp. 167-68.
51. Mary White Ovington, "The White Brute," reprinted in *The Walls Came Tumbling Down* (New York, 1947), p. 95. The story was written upon her return to New York in response to an actual incident told to her during her travels to the South in 1906-1907. Ovington was a social worker and a founder of the NAACP. Her concern about the plight of urban blacks is revealed in her study of the status of blacks in New York, in which she analyzed the black woman as breadwinner. See *Half A Man: The Status of the Negro in New York* (New York, 1911).
52. John James Holm, *Holm's Race Assimilation or the Fading of the Leopard's Spots* (Atlanta, 1910), p. 183.
53. Ibid., p. 355.
54. "Studies in the South," *Atlantic Monthly* XLIV (January 1882), p. 81.
55. Tayleur, p. 267.
56. Lily H. Hammond, "Southern Women and Racial Adjustment," (Charlottesville, Va., 1917), p. 219. She was the first director of the Methodist Women's Bureau of Social Service. Later she married the white

president of Paine College and returned to the South. See Jacquelyn Dowd Hall's *Revolt Against Chivalry* (New York, 1919), Chapter 3, for a discussion of the interracial work of moderate to liberal southern white women, especially Methodist women, during the first three decades of the twentieth century.

57. Ibid., pp. 5-6.
58. Ibid., pp. 29-30.
59. Ibid., p. 30.
60. L.H. Hammond, *In Black and White: An Interpretation of Southern Life* (Nashville, 1914), pp. 217 and 227-28.
61. McPherson, p. 341.
62. William Hannibal Thomas provides extensive autobiographical details in the introduction to his book *The American Negro, What He Was, What He Is, and What He May Become* (New York, 1901). He was born in 1843 in Ohio to freedmen, and his ancestors were mainly white. In 1871 he came South to teach freedmen, and in 1873 he received a license to practice law in South Carolina, where he later became a trial justice and a member of the state legislature. He was attacked by such prominent black males as Charles Chesnutt, Booker T. Washington, W.E.B. Du Bois, and Kelly Miller. William Zoll's "Free Men, Freedmen, and Race: Black Social Theory in the Gilded Age," *Journal of Southern History* XLIV (November 1978), 571-96, discusses the views of free northern (primarily) black intellectuals toward southern freedmen during the Gilded Age. He argues that this group perceived the newly freed slaves as a primitive social class in need of rehabilitation. This article may shed some light on William Thomas's attitudes toward the freedmen with whom he came in contact as a school teacher in the South. James McPherson (mentioned earlier) also provides insights into the racist attitudes of Thomas, which he attributes to his mixed blood and hatred of blacks. He refers to *The American Negro* as "one of the most extreme racist polemics of its time" and the "product of a sick mind" because of Thomas's identification with "the most virulent white stereotypes of Negroes." *The Abolitionist Legacy*, p. 341.
63. Thomas, pp. 195-97.
64. Ibid., pp. 183-84.
65. Ibid., p. 184.
66. Ibid., pp. 184-89.
67. Ibid., p. 200.
68. Ibid., pp. 206-07. In his extensive review of Thomas's book, Professor Kelly Miller of Howard University reveals his indignation at Thomas's persistent attacks on black women, from which group Thomas has, ironically, taken a wife. Instead of wasting his time offering a rebuttal to Thomas's charge that black women are immoral, Miller simply asserts that "he who makes an insidious assault upon the virtue of the womanhood of the race is more of the coward and dastard, and thereby sinks beneath the level of respectful consideration of good men and pure women." *Hampton Negro Conference* V (July 1901), p. 70.

69. Mrs. Addie Hunton, "Negro Womanhood Defended," *Voice of the Negro* I (July 1904), p. 280.
70. Ibid.
71. Fannie B. Williams, "The Club Movement Among Colored Women of America," p. 418.
72. Ibid., p. 282.
73. Ibid., p. 424.
74. Ibid., pp. 424-27.
75. Founded in New York in 1848 as a Congregational anti-slavery weekly, it reached its greatest influence during Reconstruction with a circulation of 75,000 by 1870. It continued its abolitionist fervor during the period under consideration and was opposed to scientific racism, Jim Crow, lynching, and disenfranchisement. It also urged federal aid to education for blacks, federal election laws, and endorsed the Niagara Movement. James McPherson, *The Abolitionist Legacy*, p. 25.
76. "More Slavery at the South," *The Independent* LXXII (January 25, 1912), p. 197.
77. Ibid., p. 200.
78. "The Race Problem: An Autobiography by a Southern Colored Woman," *The Independent* LVI (March 17, 1904), p. 588.
79. Meier, *Negro Thought in America*, p. 166.
80. Jack Thorne, "A Plea for Social Justice for the Black Woman," Occasional Paper No. 2 (Yonkers, N.Y., 1912), pp. 2, 3, 6, 10-11.
81. W.E.B. Du Bois, "The Damnation of Women," in *Darkwater*, p. 165. Du Bois had more to say about black women and women's issues generally than any other black male during the period, with the possible exception of Frederick Douglass, who died in 1895. For this reason, his attitudes toward women deserve a more thorough analysis than can be done here. A partial listing of his writings that deal specifically with black women, excluding his numerous editorials in *Crisis* from 1910-1934, follows: three Special Woman Suffrage Issues of *Crisis*—September 1912, August 1915, November 1917; "The Damnation of Women," in *Darkwater* (New York, 1920); "The Freedom of Womanhood," in *The Gift of Black Folk* (Boston, 1924); "The Work of Negro Women in Society," *Spelman Messenger* 18 (February, 1902), 1-3; *Morals and Manners Among Negro Americans*, Atlanta University Publications, 1914; *The Negro American Family*, Atlanta University Publications, 1908; "The Burden of Black Women" (poem), *Crisis* 6 (November 1914); "The Black Mother," *Crisis* 5 (December 1912). His attitudes toward women have also received more scholarly attention than any other black male except Frederick Douglass. See Jean Fagan Yellin, "DuBois's *Crisis* and Woman's Suffrage." *Massachusetts Review* 14 (Spring 1973), 365-75; Irene Diggs, "Du Bois and Women, A Short Story of Black Women, 1910-1934," *A Current Bibliography on African Affairs* 7 (Summer 1974), 260-303.
82. *Africa and America: Addresses and Discourses* (Miami, 1969), pp. 64-66. In addition to exposing the plight of black women, he had specific solutions to their problems including the establishment of a home for "colored women"

from the money he raised from the sale of over half a million copies of his pamphlet, according to Terborg-Penn (p. 42). Du Bois devotes a chapter of his classic *The Souls of Black Folk* to Crummell, his soul-mate in many ways, whom he eulogizes and in the process immortalizes through his "little tribute." Though Crummell 's work was not widely known, Du Bois says that "in another age he might have sat among elders of the land in purple bordered toga; in another country mothers might have sung him to the cradles" (p. 164).

83. "The Damnation of Women," p. 517.

84. *Crisis* 9 (November 1914), p. 31.

85. *The Voice of the Negro* 1 (July 1904), p. 308.

86. Friedman, p. 142.

87. Du Bois, "The Damnation of Women," p. 517.

88. Ibid., p. 526.

89. Crummell, pp. 70-72.

90. Monroe Majors, ed., *Noted Negro Women: Their Triumphs and Activities* (Chicago, 1893) and Lawson A. Scruggs, *Women of Distinction* (Raleigh, 1893). Additional books by black males that call attention to the accomplishments of black women are G.F. Ritchings, *Evidences of Progress Among Colored People* (Philadelphia, 1909), which contains a chapter on "prominent colored women," photographs of black women, and other scattered references to them; James T. Haley, ed., *Afro-American Encyclopedia* (Nashville, 1895), which includes several articles by prominent black women; H.F. Kletzing and W.H. Crogman, *Progress of a Race or the Remarkable Advancement of the Afro-American* (Atlanta, 1897), which discusses "The Colored Woman of Today" and includes a number of her photos; Daniel W, Culp, *Twentieth Century Negro Literature* (Naperville, Ill., 1902), which includes biographical sketches of twelve black women who respond to the question "What Role Is the Educated Woman to Play in the Uplifting of her Race?"; *The Afro-American Home Manual* (Atlanta, 1910), which contains a chapter on "Noted Afro-American Women and Their Achievements."

91. Griggs, also a Baptist minister and the first black writer to start his own publishing company, solved the problem of distribution by selling his own books to blacks and, as a result, was more widely read among blacks than his contemporaries, Chestnut and Dunbar, according to critic Hugh Gloster in his introduction to Griggs' *Imperium in Imperio*, (p. ii). Griggs also conveys his attitudes toward black women in his five "race-motivated" novels and his nonfiction book, *The Race Question in a New Light* (Nashville, 1909).

92. Repeated references to the black woman's lack of protection are found in the writings of black males. See also Bishop W. J. Gaines, *The Negro and the White Man* (Philadelphia, 1897).

93. *Wisdom's Call* (Nashville, 1911), p. 53.

94. The extent to which black males were disturbed by the home life of the race is revealed in the frequency with which this topic is treated (though not for the same reasons as did whites) in their books and articles on racial problems generally and as the primary focus of one work. William Noel Johnson's

Common Sense in the Home (Cincinnati, 1902), which he dedicated to the memory of his mother, is in this category. Like Adams' manual for the black home, this book was intended for use by black parents and contains advice on all aspects of relationships between mother and father and between parents and children, though special attention is paid to the role of mothers. A chapter on race pride is also included, which reveals his overriding purpose for writing the book.

95. R. A. Adams, *The Negro Girl* (Kansas City, 1914), pp. 80 and 83.
96. Ibid., pp. 84 and 86.
97. There is disagreement among black men with respect to who is to blame for illicit relations between black women and white men. Bishop W.J. Gaines argues that southern black women are not opposed to mixing with white men because they prefer to be mothers of mulattoes because of the premium placed on light skin and straight hair in both the black and the white communities. See *The Negro and The White Man*, p. 155.
98. John Wesley Grant, *Out of the Darkness or Diabolism and Destiny* (Freeport, N.Y., 1972), pp. 45-46.
99. Ibid., p. 155.
100. *Imperium in Imperio: A Study of the Negro Race Problem* (New York, 1969), pp. 82-82. The novel was first published in 1899.
101. *Hindered Hand* (Nashville, 1905), p. 139.
102. Arlene Elder's *The "Hindered Hand": Cultural Implications of Early African-American Fiction* (Westport, Conn., 1978) contains the most comprehensive analysis of the treatment of women in these early novels, though Du Bois is excluded. She views most of their black women characters as mainly "counter-stereotypes."
103. Sterling Brown, *The Negro in American Fiction* (Washington, 1939), p. 102.
104. Ibid., pp. 105-06.
105. Sutton Griggs, *Unfettered* (Nashville, 1902), pp. 10-11.
106. J. McHenry Jones, *Hearts of Gold* (College Park, Md., 1969), p. 14. The novel was originally published in 1896.
107. Elder, p. 17.
108. *Imperium in Imperio*, p. 113.
109. Ibid., p. 97.
110. Ibid., p. 174.
111. Barbara Christian, *Black Women Novelists: The Development of a Tradition, 1892-1976* (Westport, Conn., 1980), p. 5.
112. Ibid., p. 13.
113. Ibid., p. 15.
114. The fact that all members of a given culture learn the sex-role stereotypes appropriate for their social group is the focus of a recent study on the sociology of sex roles. See Janet Saltzman Chafez, *Masculine/Feminine or Human? An Overview of the Sociology of Sex Roles* (Itasca, Ill., 1974).
115. Ruth Bloch, in "American Feminine Ideals in Transition: The Rise of the Moral Mother, 1785-1915," *Feminist Studies* 4 (June 1978), 101-26, traces the development of changing attitudes toward motherhood, which she

attributes to social phenomena, especially the removal of the father from the home as a result of industrialization. Mary Ryan in *Womanhood in America* also devotes a chapter entitled "Mothers of Civilization: The Common Woman, 1830-1860" to the "cult of motherhood" which had emerged by 1860 and continued to be felt throughout the century.

116. Lorna Duffin, "Prisoners of Progress: Women and Evolution," in *The Nineteenth-Century Woman*, p. 78.

117. George Frederickson refers to B. F. Riley's *The White Man's Burden* (Birmingham, 1910) as a "monument of sentimental paternalism and apparent Negrophilia" on p. 28 of his *The Black Image in the White Mind*; he also refers to Riley and other southern liberals as "neopaternalists" and cousins to the romantic racialists of the Northern Christian reformers of the Civil War era.

118. *American Women: A Story of Social Change*, pp. 114-17.

119. B. F. Riley, *The White Man's Burden*, pp. 131-32.

120. Ibid., p. 131.

121. Ibid., p. 133.

122. Du Bois, "The Work of Negro Women in Society," p. 25.

123. "The Risk of Woman Suffrage," *Crisis*, November 1915, p. 37.

124. Rev. James Johnson, "Woman's Exalted Station," *A.M.E. Church Review* 8 (1892), pp. 402-403. See his "Female Preachers," where he explains why he opposes them. *A.M.E. Church Review* 1 (1884), 102-05.

125. "The Higher Education of Women," Appendix, *History of the Colored Race in America* (New Orleans, 1887), pp. 598-99.

126. Crummell, p. 79.

127. Mrs. George Swift King, "Mothers' Meetings," *Social and Physical Condition of Negroes in Cities*, ed. William E. B. Du Bois (Atlanta, 1897), p. 61.

128. Mrs. Booker T. Washington, "The Gain in the Life of Negro Women," *The Outlook* LXXVI (January 30, 1904), p. 271.

129. "The Club Movement Among Colored Women of America," pp. 417-18.

130. Wilson Jeremiah Moses, "Domestic Feminism, Conservatism, Sex Roles, and Black Women's Clubs, 1893-1896," *Journal of Social and Behavioral Sciences* 24 (Fall 1978), p. 175.

131. The proceedings of the conference were published in a book entitled *The United Negro: His Problems and His Progress*, edited by I. Garland Penn and J. W. E. Bowen (Atlanta, 1902).

132. James McCulloch, ed. *Democracy in Earnest* (Washington, D.C., 1918), p. 338.

133. Mrs. E. Azalia Hackley, *The Colored Girl Beautiful* (Kansas City, Mo., 1916), pp. 181-82. In a biography of Mrs. Hackley, an interesting evolution of this book, which discusses in fine detail what black mothers should do in the area of child-rearing, is revealed. During her frequent lecture tours to southern black schools, which began in 1910, Hackley discussed music (especially the value of spirituals) and the art of living. During her first stop at Tuskegee Institute, she was asked by the Dean of the Girls' Department to share with the girls "anything you think they should know." She subsequently talked

about love, beauty, marriage, and happiness, and thought to herself, "If I had a daughter, I would desire that she know these things and more." The talks were so well-received that she decided to give similar talks to girls at other schools. Requests continued to come for her to continue these talks but scheduling conflicts frequently occurred, and finally some one asked her to print her talks and *The Colored Girl Beautiful* was the result. See Marguerite Davenport, *Azalia, The Life of Madame E. Azalia Hackley* (Boston, 1947) for additional details on this remarkable woman's life.

134. "Enlightened Motherhood: An Address Before the Brooklyn Literary Society," November 1892, p. 8.

135. Mary Taylor Blauvelt, "The Race Problem, As Discussed by Negro Women," *American Journal of Sociology* 6 (March 1901), p. 668.

136. Christian, pp. 7-8.

137. Ibid., p. 6.

138. Ibid., pp. 11-12.

139. Thomas Nelson Page, *The Negro: The Southerner's Problem* (New York, 1904), p. 178.

140. Lewis H. Blair, *A Southern Prophecy: The Prosperity of the South Dependent Upon the Elevation of the Negro* (Richmond, Va., 1889), pp. 144-45. Blair was one of the few southerners who opposed segregation for economic reasons and is discussed by George Frederickson in his chapter on "The New South and the New Paternalism, 1877-1890," in *The Black Image in the White Mind*. Frederickson indicates that there were a few white southerners who were foes of racial orthodoxy (an anti-Negro philosophy based on notions of Negro inferiority and white supremacy), the dominant creed of the post-Reconstruction South. These included George Washington Cable, novelist and advocate for the cause of civil and political rights for blacks; John Spencer Bassett, college professor, historian, and founder of the progressive *South Atlantic Quarterly*, which he edited from 1902 to 1915; and Lewis Blair, prominent businessman in Richmond, Virginia, and anti-segregationist. Blair's main argument here, which first appeared as a series of articles in *The Independent*, is that in order to elevate the Negro, the South must stop looking upon him as inferior. He believed the caste system to be the white South's most crippling evil. He was especially opposed to segregation in the public schools and public places, and was in favor of granting the vote to blacks.

141. Osward Garrison Villard, "The Negro and the Domestic Problem," *Alexander's Magazine* 1 (November 15, 1905), p. 9. Villard was editor of the New York *Evening Post* and later *The Nation* and a founding member of the NAACP. He is also the grandson of William Lloyd Garrison, the well-known abolitionist.

142. Ibid., p. 11.

143. Tayleur, p. 268.

144. Lily H. Hammon, *Southern Women and Racial Adjustment* (Lynchburg, Va., 1917), p. 31.

145. Ibid., pp. 31-32.

146. All of the information concerning the Institute comes from June Patton's "Moonlight and Magnolias in Southern Education: The Black Mammy Memorial Institute," *Journal of Negro History* LXV (Spring 1980), 149-55. In addition to describing the evolution of the Institute, the article contains a reprint of its first charter (filed September 19, 1910 in Clark County, Georgia) and excerpts from the pamphlet prepared by the Association, which was used to raise funds for the Institute.

147. *Killers of the Dream*, rev. ed (New York, 1971), p. 27.

148. Ibid., pp. 129 and 128.

149. Ibid., p. 128.

150. Ibid., p. 129.

151. Booker T. Washington, *The Story of the Negro*, Vol. II (New York, 1909), p. 299.

152. Du Bois, "The Black Mother," *Crisis* 5 (December 1912), p. 78.

153. James Weldon Johnson, "The Black Mammy," *Crisis* 10 (August 1915), p. 171.

154. "More Slavery at the South," pp. 197-98.

155. Ibid., p. 200.

156. Sterling Brown, in *The Negro in American Fiction* (Washington, 1937), traces the development of this tradition that perpetuated the stereotype of the happy, loyal plantation Negro and reflected a wish for a happier past. Rayford Logan, in *The Negro in American Life and Thought*, also discusses the writers, black and white, and the magazines that perpetuated this tradition.

157. In general, fiction is not as useful as nonfiction for exploring white male attitudes toward black women during the period under consideration; this is not the case with black authors, however, who frequently used them as major figures, although they sometimes appear as stereotypes also. For a discussion of the tragic mulatto (which will not be dealt with here), see Jules Zanger, "The 'Tragic Octoroon' in Pre-Civil War Fiction," *American Quarterly* 18 (Spring 1966), 63-70; and Penelope Bullock, "The Mulatto in American Fiction," *Phylon* 6 (1945), 78-82.

158. Leslie Fiedler, "The Blackness of Darkness: The Negro and the Development of American Gothic" in *Images of the Negro in American Literature*, eds. Seymour Gross and John Hardy (Chicago, 1966), p. 94. While his comments are generally complimentary, the critical responses to Roxy's character have been far from uniform; they range from unequivocal praise to outright denunciations of Twain's ability to portray blacks. For example, Robert Wiggins, *"Pudd'nhead Wilson*: A Literary Caesarian Operation," *College English* 25 (December 1963), 182-86, refers to her as a "satisfying female character," while Philip Butcher in "Mark Twain Sells Roxy Down the River," *CLA Journal* 8 (1965), 225-33, discusses in detail Twain's "inept representation of Roxana," who is "a footlight figure, a paper cut-out." He ends by saying, "In denying her the stature of a real woman, Mark Twain sold Roxy down the river," a view with which I disagree. I would argue that

Roxy is the most satisfying black female character in the fiction of whites during this period, though she is certainly not perfect.

159. Mark Twain, *Pudd'nhead Wilson and Those Extraordinary Twins* (New York, 1969), p. 58. Subsequent references are to this edition, though the book was first published in 1894. The setting of the novella is Dawson's Landing, a slave-holding town in Missouri before the Civil War. The plot turns on Roxy's switching her child with her master's child in the cradle, thereby altering the fates of both children.

160. Ibid.

161. Ibid., p. 64.

162. Ibid., pp. 114-16.

163. Leslie Fiedler, *Love and Death in the American Novel* (New York, 1960), p. 406. Lillian Smith in *Killers of the Dream* also comments on this southern tradition, which stripped white mothers of their maternal duties and substituted a black surrogate who was often physically and emotionally closer to the child than its natural mother. This phenomenon is also dealt with in Irving Bartlett and C. Glenn Cambor's "The History and Psychodynamics of Southern Womanhood," which relies on history and psychoanalytic theory for their fresh insights into the impact of dual mothers on the personality development of white children.

164. James Cox, "*Pudd'nhead Wilson*: The End of Mark Twain's American Dream," *South Atlantic Quarterly* 58 (Summer 1959), pp. 354-55.

165. Christian, p. 12.

166. Du Bois, *The Crisis*, May 1912, p. 20.

167. Fannie Barrier Williams, "The Colored Girl," *Voice of the Negro* 2 (June 1905), pp. 400-01.

168. Ibid., p. 401.

169. Daniel D. Webster, p. 308.

CHAPTER FOUR

1. Carolyn Forrey, "The New Woman Revisited," *Women's Studies* 2 (1974), 38-39.

2. Ryan, pp. 196-98. As late as 1920, however, nearly 90 percent of the female labor force was unmarried and the bulk of them were less than twenty-five, so that the cult of domesticity had not faded completely.

3. Ibid., pp. 225-26 and 234.

4. William E. B. Du Bois, *Darkwater*, pp. 179-80.

5. Bonnie Thornton Dill, "The Dialectics of Black Womanhood," *Signs* 4 (Spring 1979), 543-55. Similar points are made by Diane K. Lewis, "A Response to Inequality: Black Women, Racism, and Sexism," *Signs* 3 (Winter 1977), 339-61; Joyce A. Ladner, *Tomorrow's Tomorrow*, Introduction (Garden City, New York, 1971); Mae C. King, "Oppression and Power: The Unique Status

of the Black Woman in the American Political System," *Social Science Quarterly* 56 (1975), 116-28.

6. Zora Neale Hurston, *Their Eyes Were Watching God* (Urbana, 1979), pp. 23-31.

7. Ullin N. Leavell, "Trends of Philanthropy in Negro Education: A Survey," *Journal of Negro Education* 2 (January 1933), 41-43. The Peabody Education Fund, founded in 1867, was the first of these philanthropic organizations whose purpose was to provide educational opportunities for black and white children in the South who had suffered from the war; the John Slater Fund, founded in 1882, was established for the specific purpose of aiding southern black education; the General Education Board was established in 1902 by John D. Rockefeller and was designed to promote education without regard to race, sex, or creed; the Anna T. Jeanes Foundation, started in 1907 for the purpose of helping small rural schools for blacks in the South; and finally, the Phelps-Stokes Fund was organized in 1911 to be used for the education of blacks in Africa and the United States and for native Americans as well as needy and deserving white students.

8. The early movement is referred to as the women's rights movement and not the woman suffrage movement because its participants showed little interest in getting the vote until much later. Of more immediate concern during the early years were the control of property and earnings, guardianship of children, opportunities for education and employment, and the concept of female inferiority perpetuated by established religion. Eleanor Flexner, *Century of Struggle* (New York, 1971), p. 82.

9. Ibid., p. 74.

10. Aileen S. Kraditor, *The Ideas of the Woman Suffrage Movement, 1890-1920* (New York, 1971), p. ix.

11. Benjamin Quarles, "Frederick Douglass and the Woman's Rights Movement," *Journal of Negro History* 25 (January 1940), p. 36.

12. *A Voice from the South*, pp. 142-43.

13. Fannie Barrier Williams, "The Woman's Part in a Man's Business," *Voice of the Negro* 1 (November 1904), p. 544.

14. The extent to which there was interest in the public life of black women and pride in their achievements is revealed in the following publications written or compiled by blacks, men and women, during the period. See Monroe Majors, *Noted Negro Women: Their Triumphs and Activities* (Chicago, 1893); Benjamin Brawley, *Women of Achievement* (Chicago, 1919); H. F. Kletzing and W. H. Crogman, *Progress of a Race or the Remarkable Achievement of the Afro-American* (Atlanta, 1897); F. A. Clemmons, *Our Afro-American Women*, n.d.; Irving Penn, *The Afro-American Press and Its Editors* (Springfield, 1891), contains a long chapter on black women in journalism; Gertrude Mossell, *The Work of the Afro-American Woman* (Philadelphia, 1894); Katherine Tillman, "Afro-American Women and Their Work," *A.M.E. Church Review* 11 (1895), 477-99; "Negro Women and Their Work," in *The Story of the Negro*, Vol. II (New York, 1909); "Prominent Colored Women"

in *Evidences of Progress Among Colored People* by G. F. Ritchings (Philadelphia, 1903).

15. Lawson Scruggs, *Women of Distinction*, p. xi.

16. Ibid., pp. xi-xii.

17. H. F. Kletzing and W.H. Crogman, *Progress of a Race*, pp. 213-15.

18. *The Colored American Magazine* 14 (January 1908), pp. 7-8. Referred to as "the first significant Afro-American journal to emerge in the twentieth century," this periodical had an interesting history. It started in 1900 in Boston. Its first editor was Pauline Hopkins, liberal in her views on race and a supporter of Du Bois. New management, under the control of whites, gained control of the magazine in 1904, and its outspoken editor was released. Fred Moore, a supporter of Booker T. Washington, was given the job as new editor. In fact, Washington secretly subsidized the journal and Moore's editorials and the articles included reflected his influence. This probably explains the content of the editorial mentioned above. Abby Johnson and Ronald Johnson, "Away From Accommodation: Radical Editors and Protest Journalism,1900-1920," *Journal of Negro History* LXII (October 1977), 325-38.

19. Thomas Nelson Baker, "The Negro Woman," *Alexander's Magazine* 2 (December 15, 1906), p. 84. This black periodical (1905-1909) was supported financially by Booker T. Washington as was the New York *Age*, the Washington *Colored American*, the Boston *Colored Citizens*, and the *Colored American Magazine*. See Meier, pp. 225-26, in which he analyzes Washington's influence on the black press.

20. *A Voice From the South*, pp. 134-35.

21. See Barbara Welter's "The Feminization of American Religion: 1800-1860," in *Clio's Consciousness Raised*, eds. Mary S. Hartman and Lois Banner (New York, 1974), pp. 137-57, for a detailed analysis of the changing roles of women within the church.

22. Fannie Barrier Williams, *Woman's Era* 2 (April 1895). Page number unavailable.

23. Helen Matthews Lewis, "The Woman Movement and the Negro Movement," Master's thesis, University of Virginia, 1949, pp. 73-74.

24. Flexner, p. 164.

25. Ibid., p. 248.

26. Ibid., pp. 276-77.

27. Lewis, p. 38.

28. Philip S. Foner, ed., *Frederick Douglass on Women's Rights* (Westport, Conn., 1976), p. 12.

29. Ibid., pp. 13-14.

30. Ibid., p. 113.

31. Frederick Douglass, *Life and Times of Frederick Douglass* (New York, 1962), pp. 471-73.

32. Quarles, pp. 37-38.

33. Philip Foner, ed. *Major Speeches by Negroes in the United States, 1797-1971* (New York, 1972), p. 345.

34. Flexner, pp. 95-98.
35. Quarles, p. 39.
36. Foner, *Major Speeches*, p. 345.
37. Flexner, pp. 142-52.
38. Foner, *Frederick Douglass on Women's Rights*, p. 87.
39. Ibid.
40. Ibid., p. 38.
41. Ibid., p. 24. See Benjamin Quarles, "Frederick Douglass and the Woman's Rights Movement," pp. 35-44, and S. Jay Walker, "Frederick Douglass and Woman Suffrage," *Black Scholar* (March-April 1973), 24-31, for further discussion of Douglass' involvement in the women's rights struggle.
42. Philip Foner, ed. *Major Speeches*, p. 519.
43. Ibid.
44. Ibid., pp. 518 and 519.
45. Ibid., p. 519.
46. Ibid., pp. 40-41.
47. Ibid., p. 43.
48. Ibid., p. 176.
49. Fannie Barrier Williams, "The Club Movement Among Colored Women of America," in *A New Negro for a New Century*, ed. J. E. Macbrady (Chicago, 1900), p. 390. The first issue of *Woman's Era* came out March 24, 1894, and twenty-four issues were published through January, 1897. There seem to be no extant issues beyond this date though one source indicates that the publication ran for ten years. Each issue included from sixteen to twenty-four pages, and the subscription price was one dollar per year.
50. *Woman's Era*, I (March 1894). Page numbers did not always appear on the microfilm copy of the original (the only copy of which is located in the Rare Books Room of the Boston Public Library) I used; therefore most quotes appear without page numbers.
51. *Woman's Era*, I (November, 1894) p. 5.
52. "Colored Women and Suffrage," *Woman's Era*, November 1895, p. 11.
53. "Women in Politics," *Woman's Era* 1 (November 1894), p. 12.
54. Ibid., pp. 12-13.
55. Ibid., pp. 13.
56. See Adele Logan Alexander's "How I Discovered My Grandmother . . .," *Ms* (November 1983), 29-37, for a lengthy biographical sketch of Adella Hunt Logan written by her granddaughter who is presently completing the full-length biography.
57. Adella Hunt Logan, "Woman Suffrage," p. 487.
58. Ibid., p. 489.
59. Ibid.
60. Margaret Murray Washington, "Club Work Among Negro Women," in J.L. Nichols and W.H. Crogman, eds., *Progress of a Race*, rev. ed. (Naperville, Ill., 1929), pp. 193-94. Originally published by H.F. Kletzing and W.H. Crogman, eds. *Progress of a Race* (Atlanta, 1987).

61. In order to gain fuller knowledge about the woman suffrage activities of black women's clubs, it would be necessary to look at the notes of specific clubs as well as the notes from the NACW, which were not available for perusal for this paper. *Lifting As They Climb*, published in 1933 by Elizabeth Davis, which gives a history of the black women's club movement, is also helpful. See also Terborg-Penn's unpublished dissertation on the subject.

62. Margaret Murray Washington, "Club Work Among Negro Women," in *New Progress of a Race*, p. 194.

63. Mary Church Terrell, *A Colored Woman in a White World* (Washington, D.C., 1968), p. 144.

64. Foner, *Frederick Douglass on Women's Rights*, p. 179.

65. Dorothy Sterling, *Black Foremothers*, p. 109.

66. Ibid.

67. Alfreda Duster, ed., *Crusade for Justice: The Autobiography of Ida B. Wells* (Chicago, 1970), pp. 345-53.

68. Mrs. A. W. Blackwell, "The Responsibility and Opportunity of the Twentieth Century Woman," p. 3. This pamphlet, located in the Special Collections room of the Atlanta University Library, was written by an unknown black female who was secretary of an organization I have been unable to identify. Unfortunately, the pamphlet contained no date or publication information though it is possible to determine that it was written prior to 1919. William Pickens, field secretary of the NAACP, indicated that what Mrs. Blackwell predicted would happen to black women is precisely what happened in South Carolina after the Nineteenth Amendment passed. When black women, a majority in the state, attempted to register in Columbia, the capital, they were made to stand for hours in line while all the whites were registered ahead of them. The literacy requirement was used as a deterrent by asking black women to explain long passages from the Constitution or other complicated legal questions. Furthermore, if they mispronounced a word they were disqualified. Even teachers were denied the right to vote. *Nation* CXI (October 6, 1920), pp. 372-73.

69. *Crisis*, November 1917, p. 18.

70. Ibid., pp. 3-4.

71. Jean Fagan Yellin, "Du Bois' *Crisis* and Woman's Suffrage," *The Massachusetts Review* 14 (Spring 1973), pp. 365-66.

72. *Crisis*, November 1915, p. 30.

73. Philip S. Foner, ed. *W. E. B. Du Bois Speaks: Speeches and Addresses, 1890-1919* (New York, 1970), p. 237.

74. Yellin, pp. 369-70.

75. Kraditor, pp. 157-58.

76. *Crisis* (November 1917), p. 22.

77. Ibid., p. 19.

78. Ibid., p. 9.

79. Ibid.

80. *Crisis* 4 (September 1912), p. 234.

81. Ibid., p. 244.

82. Ibid.
83. Ibid., p. 243.
84. Ibid.
85. Lorna Duffin, "Prisoners of Progress: Women and Evolution," in *Nineteenth Century Woman*, p. 77.
86. M. E. Jackson, "The Self-Supporting Woman and the Ballot," *Crisis* 10 (August 1915), p. 187.
87. *Crisis* 10 (August 1915), p. 178.
88. Rev. Francis Grimke, "The Logic of Woman Suffrage," Ibid., p. 178.
89. Ibid.
90. Charles Chesnutt, "Women's Rights," Ibid., p. 182.
91. Mrs. Coralie Franklin Cook, "Votes For Mothers," Ibid., pp. 184-85.
92. Mrs. Carrie W. Clifford, "Votes for Children," Ibid., p. 185.
93. Anna Jones, "Woman Suffrage and Social Reform," Ibid., p. 190.
94. Lorna Duffin, "Prisoners of Progress," p. 83.
95. Ruffin, "Trust the Women," *Crisis* 10 (August 1915), p. 188.
96. Nannie Burroughs, "Black Women and Reform," Ibid., p. 187. Burroughs, whose papers are located at the Library of Congress, founded the National Training School for Women and Girls in 1909 in Washington, D.C., which was funded initially by the women's auxillary of the National Baptist Convention.
97. Ibid.
98. Ibid.
99. Oscar de Priest, "Chicago and Woman's Suffrage," Ibid., p. 179.
100. Nannie Burroughs, "Black Women and Reform," Ibid., p. 187. Du Bois also alluded to the black male voter having sold out to whites in an earlier statement.
101. Mary B. Talbert, "Suffrage and Colored Women," Ibid., p. 184.
102. Robert Terrell, "Our Debt to Suffragists," Ibid., p. 181.
103. Ibid., p. 182.
104. Mrs. Paul L. Dunbar, "Votes and Literature," Ibid., p. 184.
105. Ibid.
106. *Crisis* 11 (November 1915), pp. 37-38.
107. For a detailed discussion of the impact of evolutionary theory on the woman question, especially as it relates to biological differences between men and women, see Lorna Duffin's "Prisoners of Progress: Women and Evolution." Her discussion of social theorist Herbert Spencer, to whom she refers as "the supreme ideologue of the Victorian period," is especially relevant here because of his ideas concerning the biological inferiority of women, p. 59. Duffin also discusses the ideas of Patrick Gedder and J. Arthur Thomson, whose *Evolution of Sex* published in 1890 argues that "females lack the energy required to participate actively in society; their energy, such as it is, is entirely required for reproduction" (p. 63). She also discusses the views of Almoth Wright who used biological arguments in his book *The Unexpurgated Case Against Woman Suffrage* (London 1913) for his anti-suffrage position. According to Wright, "the vote . . . is the indirect use of physical force.

Women do not possess this physical force therefore they cannot be given the vote" (p. 64).

108. Louis Harlan, ed., *The Booker T. Washington Papers*, Vol. 9 (Urbana, 1976), pp. 700-01. His wife held a different opinion on this issue as previous remarks from her illustrate.

109. C. Hatfield Dickerson, "Woman Suffrage," *A.M.E. Church Review 4* (October 1887), pp. 197-99.

110. "Woman Suffrage and the Negro," *Messenger* 1 (November 1917), p. 6.

111. "Woman Suffrage and the *Messenger*," *The Messenger*, January 1918, p. 9.

112. George White, *The Competitor*, March 1920, p. 51.

113. Ibid., p. 51.

114. Willie Mae King, "Suffrage and Our Women," pp. 60-61.

115. Tayleur, p. 269.

116. Ibid.

117. "Experiences of the Race Problem By a Southern White Woman," *The Independent* LVI (March 17, 1904), p. 593.

118. Ibid.

119. See Josephine Silone-Yates, "Afro-American Women as Educators," in *Women of Distinction* by Lawson Scruggs, pp. 309-19. Anna J. Cooper's *A Voice from the South* also includes data on black female college graduates. By 1890 there were only thirty black women with college degrees.

120. Jacqueline Jones, *Soldiers of Light and Love* (Chapel Hill, 1980), pp. 122-23 and 126. For a rare discussion of the role of the northern black woman in the education of freedmen, see Linda Perkins, "The Black Female Missionary Educator During and After the Civil War," *Black Women's Educational Policy and Research Network Newsletter* 1 (March/April 1982), 6-9.

121. In his chapter entitled "Of the Training of Black Men," Du Bois speaks reverently of the hordes of white teachers who flocked South to establish a common school system and later colleges. Speaking specifically of the "crusade of the New England school ma'am," which he felt was the Freedmen's Bureau's most valuable legacy to the South, Du Bois heaps the highest praise on those daring women in calico who "did their work well." *The Souls of Black Folk*, p. 31.

122. Jacqueline Jones, p. 150.

123. The American Missionary Association (AMA), the largest freedmen's aid organization, was founded by the abolitionist-congregationalists in 1846, and their first freedmen's schools were founded in the South at the outbreak of the war in 1861. McPherson, p. 153.

124. See Sara Delamont, "The Contradictions in Ladies' Education," in *The Nineteenth Century Woman*, pp. 134-62. She divides supporters of women's education into two groups—the uncompromising and the separatists. The former believed that education for women should be indistinguishable from that of men while the latter group favored a modified curriculum for women which would be in keeping with "their future as teachers, nurses and mothers" (p. 154). Her discussion of several of the founders of women's

institutions does not include Spelman founders Harriet Giles and Sophia Packard, as is the case generally with treatments of women's colleges.

125. The solution to the problem lay in the ability of the WABHMS and Packard and Giles to raise enough money to cover the mortgage since the ABHMS could not afford to purchase separate properties for the girls' and boys' schools. In the meantime, in February 1883, the Atlanta Baptist Female Seminary (Spelman's original name) was moved to the new site and a boarding department was opened which accommodated thirty students. In April 1884, the third anniversary of the school's founding, John D. Rockefeller and his family made a visit to the campus, learned of the serious financial handicap, and donated the remaining balance, thereby insuring the school's continued existence as a separate school for black females.

126. The unpublished, handwritten diaries of Spelman founders Packard and Giles are located in the Spelman College Archives.

127. The correspondence of Packard and Giles is located in the Spelman College Archives.

128. The Industrial Department offered cooking, washing, ironing, sewing, needle work, printing, and telegraphy.

129. Correspondence of Packard and Giles, Spelman College Archives.

130. Cornelia Denslow, "Spelman Seminary," *The Baptist Home Mission Monthly* 24 (January 1902), p. 9. All students received training in the domestic arts, while less than one percent were enrolled in college level courses during this period.

131. Ibid.

132. Dr. J. Elmer Dellinger, "Hospital Work for Negro Women," *The Spelman Messenger* 18 (March 1902), p. 1. A Nurse Training Department was initiated at Spelman in 1886, the first such program for black women in the country.

133. *The Negro Woman's College Education* (New York, 1956), p. 24.

134. Packard and Giles must have been aware of the historical significance of their work at Spelman so they recorded every aspect of their daily activities, the remarks students made to them in class and during visits to their homes, and the contents of important letters sent to them by persons off the campus. The letter from Cohill is only one of the many letters whose contents were also recorded in their diaries.

135. Diaries, Spelman College Archives.

136. Ibid.

137. Ibid.

138. Ibid.

139. Ibid.

140. Ibid.

141. See Frances E. W. Harper's "The Woman's Christian Temperance Union and the Colored Woman," *A.M.E. Church Review* 4 (1888), 314, for a discussion of black female attitudes toward temperance and the WCTU, which was seen as a means of elevating the race. Harper was a black temperance lecturer and head of the Department for Negroes of the National Woman's Christian Temperance Union from 1883 to 1890.

142. Diaries, Spelman College Archives.
143. Ibid.
144. Ibid.
145. Ibid.
146. Ibid.
147. Files on deceased alumnae dating back to the 1880s are housed in Rockefeller Hall on the Spelman campus and they contain, among other items, moving letters written by former students to the various white female presidents at Spelman. It was not until 1954 that a black (Dr. Albert Manley) assumed the presidency of the college.
148. Deceased Alumnae Files, Spelman College.
149. Ibid.
150. Flora Zeto Malekebu was the second Spelman alumna to become a missionary to Africa. She graduated from Spelman high school in 1915, married Morehouse graduate, Dr. Malekebu in 1919, and built a Mission with her husband in Nyasaland in 1926, which included Spelman Hall. She remained a loyal alumna until her death. Deceased Alumnae Files, Spelman College.
151. William Range, *The Rise and Progress of Negro Colleges in Georgia, 1865-1949* (Athens, 1951), p. 141.
152. *The Spelman Messenger* 22 (May 1906), p. 1. The official publication of the college began in 1885, was typeset by students in the printing office on campus, and was published eight times a year. The subscription price was 25 cents a year. Morehouse College president John Hope's wife, Lugenia Burns Hope, also founder of the Neighborhood Union, taught millinery at Spelman in the early 1900s.
153. Claudia White was one of the college's first two students to receive the B.A. degree. She taught at Spelman after graduation and was associated with the college in various capacities until her death in 1952.
154. *The Spelman Messenger* 22 (May 1906), p. 1.
155. Sara Delamont, "The Domestic Ideology and Women's Education," p. 178.
156. Delamont, "The Contradictions in Ladies' Education," p. 149.
157. William Alexander, *History of the Colored Race in America* (Kansas City, 1887), pp. 599-600.
158. Rev. R.E. Wall, "Shall Our Girls Be Educated?", *A.M.E. Church Review* 6 (July 1889), p. 47.
159. Ibid.
160. Mary McLeod Bethune Papers. Amistad Research Center, Dillard University. Photocopy of statement located in Tuskegee Institute Archives.
161. Oswald Villard, "The Negro and the Domestic Problem," p. 9.
162. Dr. J. Elmer Dellinger, "Hospital Work for Negro Women," p. 1.
163. Kelly Miller, *Radicals and Conservatives*, p. 190.
164. Ibid., p. 192.
165. E. Davidson Washington, ed. *Selected Speeches of Booker T. Washington* (New York, 1932), p. 174.
166. "Industrial Training for Southern Women." Pamphlet located in Special Collections, Robert Woodruff Atlanta University Center Library.

167. Mrs. Washington came to Tuskegee in 1889 as dean of the Women's Department and later became superintendent for Girls' Industries, in which capacity she remained for twenty-five years. She explains the program in "What Girls Are Taught and How" in *Tuskegee and Its People*, ed. Booker T. Washington (New York, 1905).

168. Margaret M. Washington, "The Negro Home," address delivered at the Interracial Conference held in Memphis, Tennessee, October 1920, p. 2. Copy of speech available in Tuskegee Institute Archives.

169. Booker T. Washington, "Negro Women and Their Work," *The Story of the Negro*, Vol. 2 (New York, 1909), pp. 298-99.

170. Ibid., p. 303.

171. Ibid., p. 331.

172. "The Ordination of Women: What Is the Authority for It?" *A.M.E. Church Review* 2 (April 1886), p. 453.

173. Rev. James Johnson, "Female Preachers," *A.M.E.Church Review* 1 (1884), p. 102.

174. Ibid.

175. Lorna Duffin, "Prisoners of Progress," p. 63.

176. Rev. John W. Brown, "The Ordination of Women," *A.M.E. Church Review* 2 (April 1886), p. 361.

177. Anna J. Cooper was the second female principal of the famous "M" Street High School for blacks in Washington, D.C., from 1901 to 1906.

178. *A Voice From the South*, p. 69.

179. Ibid.

180. Ibid., p. 75.

181. Ibid., p. 78. See Louise Huchinson's *Anna J. Cooper: A Voice From the South* (Washington, 1981) for a comprehensive discussion of Cooper's life. A biography of Cooper by Leona Gabel is in preparation.

182. This information was culled from a lengthy statement written by Mrs. Perkins on school letterhead and contained in a folder tucked away in the Spelman Archives.

183. It would be instructive to explore whether the Black Mammy Memorial Institute described in the previous chapter had similar covert aims. My suspicion is that the black men who ran it had different motives from Perkins, and it is also possible that its largely white Board kept a closer watch on what went on at the Institute than was the case in Tampa. Further research is necessary, however, before anything definitive can be said about similarities between both institutions.

184. James W. Johnson, "Woman's Exalted Station," p. 403.

185. Ibid., pp. 403-04.

186. Josephine Washington, *Women of Distinction*, p. ix.

187. Ibid., p. xii.

188. Wilson Moses, p. 175.

189. "The Awakening of Women," *The National Notes* 19 (October 1916), p. 3.

190. Ibid., p. 4.

191. Ibid., p. 7.

192. Mary Lynch, "Social Status and Needs of the Colored Woman," in *The United Negro*, eds. Penn and Bowen (Atlanta, 1902), p. 185.
193. Alfreda Duster, ed. *Crusade for Justice* (Chicago, 1970), p. 244.
194. Ibid., p. 250.
195. Ibid., p. 252.
196. Anna J. Cooper, *A Voice From the South*, p. 28.

CHAPTER FIVE

1. *The Voice of the Negro* 1 (July 1904), p. 308.
2. *Darkwater*, p. 186.
3. *The White Savage*, p. 143.
4. The Afro-American League, founded in 1890 as a protest organization, was the forerunner of the Council and provided a forum for the discussion of racial problems. It espoused a philosophy of self-help and solidarity and held its first national convention in Chicago. The League became inactive due to internal problems after a short period and was revived in 1898 as the Afro-American Council. August Meier, *Negro Thought in America, 1880-1915*, p. 71.
5. Sterling, p. 102.
6. Du Bois convened this national organization in 1905 as a means of opposing the conservative race relations policies of Booker T. Washington. Washington was bitterly opposed to the group because it advocated open protest of the denial of civil rights to blacks. Meier, p. 178.
7. "The Negro Woman in the Quest for Equality," in *Black Women in White America*, ed. Gerda Lerner (New York, 1972), p. 598.
8. Alfred A. Moss, *The American Negro Academy, Voice of the Talented Tenth* (Baton Rouge, 1981), p. 78. According to Louise Hutchinson's monograph on Anna J. Cooper, which accompanied an exhibit at the Anacostia Neighborhood Museum of the Smithsonian Institution in 1981, Cooper was the only woman ever to be elected as a member of the Academy. Hutchinson's assertion, for which documentary evidence is unavailable, is in conflict with Moss's findings. In August Meier's discussion of the Academy in *Negro Thought in America, 1880-1915*, he indicates that the membership was limited to forty, and all of the participants whom he mentions are male.
9. Josephine Silone-Yates, "The National Association of Colored Women," *Voice of the Negro* 1 (July 1904), p. 284.
10. *Woman's Era*, Vol. 1, August 1894. Page numbers were generally unavailable in microfilm copy of the original.
11. Quoted material is from report on the Woman's Era Club in Boston. Page number unavailable.
12. *Woman's Era*, Vol. 1. August 1894. Page number unavailable.
13. Ibid. Page number unavailable.
14. *Woman's Era*, July 1895, p. 14.
15. Ibid., p. 15.

16. *A Voice From the South*, Introduction, p. ii.
17. Regina Morantz, "The Lady and Her Physician," in *Clio's Consciousness Raised, New Perspectives on the History of Women*, eds. Mary S. Hartman and Lois Banner (New York, 1974), p. 38.
18. Ibid., p. 44.
19. Gloria T. Hull, Patricia Bell Scott, and Barbara Smith, eds., *All the Women Are White, All the Blacks Are Men, But Some of Us Are Brave* (New York, 1982), pp. xx-xxi.
20. See Du Bois' *The Negro American Family* (Atlanta, 1908); E. Franklin Frazier's *The Negro Family in the United States* (Chicago, 1939); and Daniel Moynihan's *The Negro Family: A Case for National Action* (Washington, D.C., 1965) for a discussion of the black matriarch theory. Critics of this theory include Robert Staples, "The Myth of the Black Matriarchy," *The Black Scholar* 1 (1970), 8-16, and Andrew Billingsley, *Black Families in White America* (Englewood Cliffs, N.J., 1969).
21. Hull, Scott, and Smith, p. 89.
22. The women as minority group analogy was developed in 1951 by Helen Hacker. See "Women as a Minority Group," *Social Forces* 30 (October 1951), 60-69.
23. See *Woman as Force in History* (New York, 1946).
24. Morantz, p. 39.
25. *Women and Equality* (New York, 1977), pp. 45-58.
26. For a well-documented account of the entire scenario see Ann Massa, "Black Women in the 'White City'," *Journal of American Studies* 8, 319-337. This quote appears on p. 329.
27. Ibid., p. 334.
28. Gerda Lerner, "Placing Women in History: A 1975 Perspective," in *Liberating Women's History: Theoretical and Critical Essays*, ed. Berenice A. Carroll (Urbana, 1976), p. 365.
29. *Women and Equality*, p. 174.
30. *Black Women Novelists*, p. 11.
31. Dorothy Sterling, *Black Foremothers* (Westbury, N.Y., 1979), pp. 97-98.
32. Wells' autobiography is an indispensable source of information on her personal and public life and how she was able to manage the two.
33. Louis Wirth, "The Problem of Minority Groups," in *Man in the World Crisis*, ed. Ralph Linton (New York, 1945), quoted by William Chafe, *Women and Equality*, p. 4.
34. See Carolyn Ashbaugh's *Lucy Parsons: American Revolutionary* (Chicago, 1976), for the most comprehensive account of Parsons' life.
35. *The Majority Finds Its Past*, p. 65.
36. Bettina Aptheker, *Woman's Legacy: Essays on Race, Sex, and Class* (Amherst, 1982), p. 2.

Bibliography

BOOKS AND ARTICLES

Adams, R. A. *The Negro Girl*. Kansas City: Independent Press, 1914.

Albrecht, Albert. "The Relationship of Literature and Society." *American Journal of Sociology* 59 (March 1954), 425-36.

Alexander, Adele Logan. "How I Discovered My Grandmother . . ."*Ms.* 12 (November 1983), 29-37.

Alexander, Williams. *History of the Colored Race in America*. New Orleans: Palmetto Publishing Company, 1887.

Aptheker, Bettina. *Woman's Legacy: Essays on Race, Sex and Class*. Amherst: University of Massachusetts Press, 1982.

Ashbaugh, Carolyn. *Lucy Parsons: American Revolutionary*. Chicago: Charles H. Kerr Publishing Company, 1976.

Bailey, Thomas. *Race Orthodoxy in the South, and Other Aspects of the Negro Question*. New York: Neale Publishing Company, 1914.

Baker, Ray Stannard. *Following the Color Line: American Negro Citizenship in the Progressive Era*. New York: Doubleday, Page and Company, 1908.

Baker, Thomas Nelson. "The Negro Woman." *Alexander's Magazine* 2 (December 15, 1906), 71-85.

Baldwin, Maria L. "Votes for Teachers." *Crisis* 10 (August 1915), 189.

Barrows, Isabel, ed. *The First Mohonk Conference on the Negro Question*. Boston: George Ellis, 1890.

Bartlett, Irving, and C. Glenn Cambor. "The History and Psycho-dynamics of Southern Womanhood." *Women's Studies* 2 (1974), 9-24

Beard, Mary. *Woman as Force In History*. New York: Collier Books, 1971. [1946]

Berry, R. M. F. "Southern Training School for Colored Women." *Good Housekeeping* 53 (October 1911), 562-63.

Bethune, Mary McLeod. "Faith That Moved a Dump Heap." *Who: The Magazine About People* 1 (1941), 31-35.

Blackwell, Mrs. A. W. *The Responsibility and Opportunity of the Twentieth Century Woman*. n.p. n.d.

Blair, Lewis. *A Southern Prophecy: The Prosperity of the South Dependent Upon the Elevation of the Negro.* Richmond, Va.: Everett Waddey, 1889.

Blauvelt, Mary Taylor. "The Race Problem: As Discussed by Negro Women." *American Journal of Sociology* 6 (March 1901), 662-72.

Bloch, Ruth. "American Feminine Ideals in Transition: The Rise of the Moral Mother, 1785-1815." *Feminist Studies* 4 (June 1978), 101-26.

Bowen, J.W.E. "Spelman Seminary, Our Virgin Queen." *Spelman Messenger* 22 (May 1906), 5.

Brawley, Benjamin G. "Politics and Womanliness." *Crisis* 10 (August 1915), 179.

———. *Women of Achievement.* Chicago: Woman's American Baptist Home Mission Society, 1919.

Brown, John M. "The Ordination of Women." *A.M.E. Church Review* 2 (April 1886), 354-61.

Brown, Sterling. *The Negro in American Fiction.* Washington: Association in Negro Folk Education, 1917.

Bruce, Josephine B. "What Has Education Done for Colored Women." *Voice of the Negro* 1 (July 1904), 294-98.

Bruce, Philip. *The Plantation Negro as a Freeman: Observations on His Character, Condition, and Prospects in Virginia.* New York and London: G. P. Putnam's Sons, 1889.

Bullough, Verne and Bonnie Bullough. *The Subordinate Sex: A History of Attitudes Toward Women.* Urbana, Ill.: University of Illinois Press, 1973.

Burroughs, Nannie H. "Black Women and Reform." *Crisis* 10 (August 1915), 187.

———."Not Color But Character." *Voice of the Negro* 1 (July 1904), 294-98.

Butcher, Philip. "Mark Twain Sells Roxy Down the River." *College Language Assocation Journal* 8 (1965), 225-33.

Cazenave, Noel A. " 'A Woman's Place': The Attitudes of Middle Class Black Men." *Phylon* XLIV (March 1983), 12-32.

Chesnutt, Charles W. "Women's Rights." *Crisis* 10 (August 1915), 182-83.

Cooper, Anna J. *A Voice From the South by a Black Woman of the South.* Xenia, Ohio: Aldine Printing House, 1892.

———. "The Higher Education of Women." *Southland* 2 (1891), 190-94.

Carroll, Berenice A., ed. *Liberating Women's History: Theoretical and Critical Essays.* Urbana: University of Illinois Press, 1976.

Chafe, William. *Women and Equality.* New York: Oxford University Press, 1977.

Chafetz, Janet Saltzman. *Masculine/Feminine or Human? An Overview of the Sociology of Sex Roles.* Itasca, Ill.: F. E. Peacock Publishers, 1974.

Christian, Barbara. *Black Women Novelists: The Development of a Tradition, 1892-1976*. Westport, Conn.: Greenwood Press, 1980.

Clifford, Carrie W. "Votes for Children." *Crisis* 10 (August 1915), 185.

Cook, Coralie Franklin. "Votes for Mothers." *Crisis* 10 (August 1915), 184-85.

Cooper, Anna Julia. *A Voice from the South by a Black Woman of the South*. Xenia, Ohio: Aldine Publishing, 1892.

Cott, Nancy F., ed. *Root of Bitterness: Documents of the Social History of American Women*. New York: E. P. Dutton and Company, 1972.

Cox, James M. "*Pudd'nhead Wilson*: The End of Mark Twain's American Dream." *South Atlantic Quarterly* 58 (Summer 1959), 351-63.

Crummell, Alexander. *Africa and America: Addresses and Discourses*. Springfield, Mass.: Wiley and Company, 1891.

Culp, Daniel W., ed. *Twentieth Century Negro Literature*. Naperville, Ill.: Nichols and Company, 1902.

Davenport, Marguerite. *Azalia: The Life of Madame E. Azalia Hackley*. Boston: Chapman and Grimes Publishers, 1947.

Davis, Daniel Webster. "The Black Woman's Burden." *Voice of the Negro* 1 (July 1904), 308.

Day, Beth. *Sexual Life Between Blacks and Whites*. New York: World Publishing Company, 1972.

Delamont, Sara, and Lorna Duffin, eds. *The Nineteenth Century Woman: Her Cultural and Physical World*. New York: Barnes and Noble Books, 1978.

Dellinger, J. Elmer. "Hospital Work for Negro Women." *Spelman Messenger* 18 (March 1902), 1-7.

Denslow, Cornelia. "Spelman Seminary." *The Baptist Home Mission Monthly* 24 (January 1902), 9.

De Priest, Oscar. "Chicago and Woman's Suffrage." *Crisis* 10 (August 1915), 179.

Dickerson, C. Hatfield. "Woman Suffrage." *A.M.E. Church Review* 4 (October 1887), 196-99.

Dill, Bonnie Thornton. "The Dialectics of Black Womanhood." *Signs* 4 (Spring 1979), 543-55.

Dittmer, John. *Black Georgia in the Progressive Era, 1900-1920*. Urbana: University of Illinois Press, 1977.

Douglass, Frederick. *Life and Times of Frederick Douglass*. New York: Crowell-Collier Publishing Company, 1962.

Du Bois, William E. B. "The Black Mother." *Crisis* 5 (December 1912), 78.

———. "The Burden of Black Women." *Crisis* 6 (November 1914), 31.

———. *Darkwater: Voices From Within the Veil*. New York: Harcourt, Brace and Howe, 1920.

——. *The Negro American Family*. Atlanta: Atlanta University Publications, 1908.

——. *Social and Physical Condition of Negroes in Cities*. Atlanta: Atlanta University Publications, 1897.

——. *The Souls of Black Folk: Essays and Sketches*. Chicago: A. C. McClurg and Company, 1903.

——. "Votes for Women." *Crisis* 4 (November 1912), 234.

——. "The Woman Voter." *Crisis* 21 (March 1921), 200.

——. "The Work of Negro Women in Society." *Spelman Messenger* 18 (February 1902), 1-3.

——. "Suffrage." *Crisis* 21 (November 1917), 7-8.

Dunbar, Mrs. Paul Lawrence. "Votes and Literature." *Crisis* 10 (August 1915), 184.

Duster, Alfreda, ed. *Crusade for Justice: The Autobiography of Ida B. Wells*. Chicago: University of Chicago Press, 1970.

Elder, Arlene. *"The Hindered Hand": Cultural Implications of Early African-American Fiction*. Westport, Conn.: Greenwood Press, 1978.

"Experiences of the Race Problem." *The Independent* LVI (March 17, 1904), 590-94.

Fiedler, Leslie. *Love and Death in the American Novel*. New York: Stein and Day, 1960.

Fleming, Robert E. "Sutton E. Griggs: Militant Black Novelist." *Phylon* 34 (March 1973), 73-77.

Flexner, Eleanor. *A Century of Struggle: The Woman's Rights Movement in the United States*. Cambridge: Harvard University Press, 1959.

Foner, Philip, ed. *Frederick Douglass on Women's Rights*. Westport, Conn.: Greenwood Press, 1976.

——. *Major Speeches by Negroes in the United States, 1797-1971*. New York: Simon and Schuster, 1972.

——. *W. E. B. Du Bois Speaks: Speeches and Addresses, 1890-1919*. New York: Pathfinder Press, 1970.

Ford, Thomas. "Howells and the American Negro." *Texas Studies in Literature and Language* 5 (Winter 1964), 530-37.

Forrey, Carolyn. "The New Woman Revisited." *Women's Studies* 2 (1974), 37-56.

Frances, Nellie F. "Woman's Influence." *National Association Notes*, January 1903, 7-8.

Frederickson, George M. *The Black Image in the White Mind: The Debate on Afro-American Character and Destiny, 1877-1914*. New York: Harper and Row, 1971.

Friedman, Lawrence. *The White Savage: Racial Fantasies in the Post-Bellum South*. Englewood Cliffs, N.J.: Prentice-Hall, 1970.

Gaines, Bishop W. J. *The Negro and the White Man*. Philadelphia: A.M.E. Publishing House, 1897.

Gayle, Addison. *The Way of the New World: The Black Novel in America*. Garden City, N.Y.: Doubleday, 1976.

Grant, John Wesley. *Out of the Darkness*. Freeport, N.Y.: Books for Libraries Press, 1971. [1909]

Griggs, Sutton. *The Hindered Hand: or the Region of the Repressionist*. Nashville: Orion Publishing Company, 1905.

————. *Imperium in Imperio*. Cincinnati: The Editor Publishing Company, 1899.

————. *The Race Question in a New Light*. Nashville: Orion Publishing Company, 1890.

————. *Unfettered*. Nashville: Orion Publishing Company, 1902.

————. *Wisdom's Call*. Nashville: Orion Publishing Company, 1911.

Grimke, Archibald H. "The Sex Question and Race Segregation." *American Negro Academy Occasional Paper*, Nos. 18 and 19. Washington, D.C., 1916.

Grimke, Francis J. "The Logic of Woman Suffrage." *Crisis* 10 (August 1915), 178-79.

Gross, Seymour and John Edward Hardy, eds. *Images of the Negro in American Literature*. Chicago: University of Chicago Press, 1966.

Hacker, Helen. "Women as a Minority Group." *Social Forces* 30 (October 1951), 60-69.

Hackley, Enma Azalia. *The Colored Girl Beautiful*. Kansas City: Burton Publishing Company, 1916.

Haley, James T., ed. *Afro-American Encyclopedia*. Nashville: Haley and Florida, 1895.

Hall, Jacquelyn Dowd. *Revolt Against Chivalry: Jessie Daniel Ames and the Women's Campaign Against Lynching*. New York: Columbia University Press, 1979.

Hammond, Lily Hardy. *In Black and White: An Interpretation of Southern Life*. New York: Fleming H. Revell Company, 1914.

————. *Southern Women and Racial Adjustment*. Lynchburg, Va.: J. P. Bell Company, 1917. John Slater Fund Occasional Paper.

Harley, Sharon, and Rosalyn Terborg-Penn, eds. *The Afro-American Woman: Struggles and Images*. Port Washington, N.Y.: Kennikat Press, 1978.

Harlan, Louis R., ed. *The Booker T. Washington Papers*, Vol. 9. Urbana: University of Illinois Press, 1976.

Harper, Frances E. W. "Enlightened Motherhood: An Address Before the Brooklyn Literary Society." November 1892. n.p.

———. "National Woman's Christian Temperance Union." *A.M.E. Church Review* 5 (July 1888), 242-45.

Harris, Barbara J. *Beyond Her Sphere: Women and the Professions in American History*. Westport, Conn.: Greenwood Press, 1978.

Harris, Mrs. L. H. "A Southern Woman's View." *The Independent* LI (May 18, 1899), 1354-55.

Hartman, Mary, and Lois W. Banner, editors. *Clio's Consciousness Raised: New Perspectives on the History of Women*. New York: Harper and Row, 1974.

Haynes, Elizabeth Ross. "Negroes in Domestic Service in the United States," *Journal of Negro History* 8 (October 1923), 384-442.

Hobhouse, Jane. *Everybody Who Was Anybody: A Biography of Gertrude Stein*. New York: G. P. Putnam's Sons, 1975.

Hoggan, Frances. *American Negro Women During Their First Fifty Years of Freedom*. n.p.

Holm, John James. *Holm's Race Assimilation or the Fading Leopard's Spots*. Atlanta: J. L. Nichols and Company, 1910.

Hooks, Bell. *Ain't I A Woman: Black Women and Feminism*. Boston: South End Press, 1981.

Howells, William D. *The Shadow of a Dream and An Imperative Duty*. New Haven: College and University Press, 1962.

Hull, Gloria, et. al., eds. *. . . But Some of Us Are Brave*. New York: Feminist Press, 1982.

Hunton, Mrs. Addie. "Negro Womanhood Defended." *Voice of the Negro* 1(July 1904), 280-81.

Hurston, Zora Neale. *Their Eyes Were Watching God*. Philadelphia: J. B. Lippincott, 1937.

Hutchinson, Louise Daniel. *Anna J. Cooper: A Voice From the South*. Washington: Smithsonian Institution Press, 1981.

Jackson, Giles B., and D. Webster Davis. *The Industrial History of the Negro Race in the United States*. Richmond, Va.: The Virginia Press, 1908.

Jackson, M. E. "The Self-Supporting Woman and the Ballot." *Crisis* 10 (August 1915), 187-88.

James, Edward T., and Janet W. James, eds. *Notable American Women, 1607-1950: A Biographical Dictionary*, 3 vols. Cambridge: Harvard University Press, 1971.

Jefferson, Olive Ruth. "The Southern Negro Woman." *The Chautauquan* 8 (1893), 91.

Johnson, Abby Arthur, and Ronald M. Johnson. "Away From Accommodation: Radical Editors and Protest Journalism, 1900-1910." *Journal of Negro History* LXII (October 1977), **325-39**.

———. *Propaganda and Aesthetics: The Literary Politics of Afro-American Magazines in the Twentieth Century.* Amherst: The University of Massachusetts Press, 1979.

Johnson, James. "Female Preachers." *A.M.E. Church Review* 1(1884), 102-05.

———. "Woman's Exalted Station." *A.M.E. Church Review* 3 (1892), 402-06.

Johnson, James Weldon. "The Black Mammy." *Crisis* 10 (August 1915), 171.

———."About Aunties." *Crisis* 10 (August 1915), 180-81.

Johnson, William Noel. *Common Sense in the Home.* Cincinnati: Jennings and Pey Press, 1902.

Jones, Anna H. "A Century's Progress for the American Colored Woman." *Voice of the Negro* 2 (September 1905), 631-33.

———. "The American Colored Woman." *Voice of the Negro* 2 (October 1905), 692-94.

———. "Woman Suffrage and Social Reform" *Crisis* 10 (August 1915), 189-90.

Jones, J. McHenry. *Hearts of Gold.* West Va.: Wheeling Daily Intelligencer Steam Job Press, 1896.

Jones, Jacqueline. *A Bridge of "Bent Backs and Laboring Muscles": Black Working Women in the Rural South, 1880-1915.* Wellesley: Center for Research on Women, 1981. Working Paper No. 67.

———. *Soldiers of Light and Love: Northern Teachers and Georgia Blacks, 1865-1873.* Chapel Hill: University of North Carolina Press, 1980.

Katzman, David. *Seven Days A Week: Women and Domestic Service in Industrializing America.* New York: Oxford University Press, 1978.

Kellor, Frances A. "Opportunities for Southern Negro Women in Northern Cities." *Voice of the Negro* 2 (July 1905), 470-73.

King, Mae. "Oppression and Power: The Unique Status of the Black Women in the American Political System." *Social Science Quarterly* 56 (1975), 116-28.

King, Willie Mae. "Suffrage and Our Women." *Competitor* (June 1920), 60-61.

Kletzing, H. F., and W. H. Crogman. *Progress of a Race or the Remarkable Advancement of the Afro-American.* Atlanta: J. L. Nichols and Company, 1897.

Kraditor, Aileen. *The Ideas of the Woman Suffrage Movement, 1890-1920.* Garden City, N.Y.: Doubleday and Company, 1971.

Laney, Lucy. "The Burden of the Educated Colored Woman." Paper read at the Hampton Negro Conference, Report III, July 1899.

Leavell, Ullin Whitney. *Philanthropy in Negro Education.* Nashville: George Peabody College for Teachers, 1930.

Lerner, Gerda, ed. *Black Women in White America: A Documentary History.* New York: Vintage Books, 1973.

———. "Early Community Work of Black Club Women." *Journal of Negro History* 59 (April 1974), 158-67.

———. *The Majority Finds Its Past.* New York: Oxford University Press, 1979.

Logan, Adella Hunt. "Colored Women as Voters." *Crisis* 4 (September 1912), 242-43.

———. "Woman Suffrage" *Colored American Magazine* IX (September 1905), 487-89.

Logan, Rayford W. *The Negro in American Life and Thought: The Nadir, 1877-1901.* New York: Dial Press, 1954.

———, and Michael Winston, eds. *Dictionary of American Negro Biography.* New York: W. W. Norton and Company, 1982.

MacBrady, John E., ed. *A New Negro for a New Century.* Chicago: American Publishing House, 1900.

McPherson, James M. *The Abolitionist Legacy: From Reconstruction to the NAACP.* Princeton: Princeton University Press, 1975.

Majors, Monroe. *Noted Negro Women: Their Triumphs and Activities.* Chicago: Donahue and Hennesbery, 1893.

Marshall, Paule. "The Negro Woman in American Literature." *Freedomways* 6 (Winter 1966), 8-25.

Massa, Ann. "Black Women in the White City." *Journal of American Studies* 8 (December 1974), 310-37.

Meier, August. *Negro Thought in America, 1880-1915: Racial Ideologies in the Age of Booker T. Washington.* Ann Arbor: University of Michigan Press, 1963.

Miller, Kelly. *Race Adjustment: Essays on the Negro in America.* New York: Neale Publishing Company, 1908.

———. *Radicals and Conservatives.* New York: Schocken Books, 1970.

———. "The Risk of Woman Suffrage." *Crisis* 11 (November 1915), 37-38.

Mills, Joseph A. "Motives and Behaviors of Northern Teachers in the South During Reconstruction." *Negro History Bulletin* 42 (January-March 1979), 7-17.

Moore, Fred. "How to Keep Women at Home." *Colored American Magazine* 14 (January 1908), 7-8.

"More Slavery at the South, By a Negro Nurse." *Independent* LXXII (January 25, 1912), 196-200.

Moses, Wilson Jeremiah. "Domestic Feminism, Conservatism, Sex Roles, and Black Women's Clubs, 1893-1896." *Journal of Social and Behavioral Sciences* 24 (Fall 1978), 166-77.

Moss, Alfred A. *The American Negro Academy: Voice of the Talented Tenth.* Baton Rouge: Louisiana State University Press, 1981.

Mossell, N. F. *The Work of the Afro-American Woman.* Philadelphia: C. S. Ferguson Company, 1894.

Murray, Anna E. "The Negro Woman." *Southern Workman* 33 (April 1904], 232-34.

Nash, Gary B., and Richard Weiss, eds. *The Great Fear: Race in the Mind of America.* New York: Holt, Rinehart, and Winston, 1970.

"The Negro Problem, How It Appears to a Southern White Woman." *Independent* LIX (September 18, 1902), 2221-28.

Nichols, J. L., and W. H. Crogman, eds. *Progress of a Race.* Naperville, Ill.: J. L. Nichols and Co., 1920.

Noble, Jeanne L. *The Negro Woman's College Education.* New York: Columbia University Press, 1956.

"Observations of the Southern Race Feeling." *Independent* LVI (March 17, 1904), 594-599.

Odum, Howard W. *Social and Mental Traits of the Negro: Research into the Conditions of the Negro Race in Southern Towns.* New York: Columbia University Press, 1910.

Ovingon, Mary White. *Half a Man: The Status of the Negro in New York.* New York: Longmans, Green and Company, 1911.

———. *The Walls Came Tumbling Down.* New York: Harcourt Brace and World, 1947.

Page, Thomas N. *The Negro: The Southerner's Problem.* New York: Scribner's, 1904.

Patton, June O. "Moonlight and Magnolias in Southern Education: The Black Mammy Institute." *Journal of Negro History* LXV (Spring 1980), 149-55.

Penn, I. Garland. *The Afro-American Press and Its Editors.* Springfield, Mass.: Willey and Company, 1891.

———. and J. W. E. Bowen, eds. *The United Negro: His Problems and His Progress.* Atlanta: D. E. Luther Publishing Company, 1902.

Perkins, Linda. "The Black Female Missionary Educator During and After the Civil War." *Black Women's Educational Policy and Research Network Newsletter* 1 (March/April 1982), 6-9.

——. "The Impact of the Cult of True Womanhood on the Education of Black Women," *Journal of Social Issues* 29 (November 1983), 16-26.

Pickett, William P. *The Negro Problem: Abraham Lincoln's Solution.* New York: G. P. Putnam's Sons, 1909.

Quarles, Benjamin. "Frederick Douglass and the Woman's Rights Movement." *Journal of Negro History* 25 (January 1940), 35-45.

"The Race Problem: An Autobiography . . ." *Independent* LVI (March 17, 1904) 586-89.

Range, Willard. *The Rise and Progress of Negro Colleges in Georgia, 1865-1949.* Athens: University of Georgia Press, 1951.

Richings, G. F. *Evidences of Progress Among Colored People.* Philadelphia: George S. Ferguson Company, 1903.

Riegel, Robert E. *American Women: A Story of Social Change.* Teaneck, N.J.: Fairleigh-Dickinson University Press, 1970.

Riley, Benjamin F. *The White Man's Burden.* Birmingham: B. J. Riley, 1910.

Rosaldo, Michelle, and Louise Lamphere, eds. *Woman, Culture, and Society.* Stanford: Stanford University Press, 1974.

Rothman, Sheila. *Woman's Proper Place: A History of Changing Ideas and Practices, 1870 to the Present.* New York: Basic Books, 1978.

Ruffin, Josephine St. Pierre. "Trust the Women." *Crisis* 10 (August 1915), 188.

Ryan, Mary P. *Womanhood in America: From Colonial Times to the Present.* New York: New Viewpoints, 1975.

——, ed. Special Issue of *Women and History.* Number 2/3 (Summer/Fall 1982).

Scruggs, Lawson. *Women of Distinction.* Raleigh: L. A. Scruggs, 1893.

Spear, Allan H. *Black Chicago: The Making of a Negro Ghetto, 1890- 1920.* Chicago: University of Chicago Press, 1967.

Shannon, A. H. *Racial Integrity and Other Features of the Negro Problem.* Nashville: M. E. Church Publishing House, 1907.

Sterling, Dorothy. *Black Foremothers.* Old Westbury, N.Y.: Feminist Press, 1979.

——, ed. *We Are Your Sisters: Black Women in the Nineteenth Century.* New York: Norton, 1973.

Smith, Lillian. *Killers of the Dream.* New York: Norton, 1961.

Smith, William Benjamin. *The Color Line: A Brief in Behalf of the Unborn.* New York: McClure, Phillips and Company, 1905.

Spelman Messenger, 1885-1920. Atlanta, Georgia.

"Spelman Seminary." *Baptist Home Mission Monthly* 24 (January 1902), 9.

Stein, Gertrude. *Three Lives*. New York: Random House, 1909.

"Studies in the South." *Atlantic* XLIV (January 1882), 81-4.

Tayleur, Eleanor. "The Negro Woman: Social and Moral Decadence." *Outlook* 76 (January 30, 1904), 266-71.

Terrell, Mary Church. *A Colored Woman in a White World*. Washington, D.C.: Ransdell Publishing Company, 1940.

———. "A Plea for the White South by a Coloured Woman." *The Nineteenth Century* 60 (July 1906), 70-84.

———. "Frederick Douglass," in Appendix to *Frederick Douglass on Women's Rights*, ed. Philip Foner. Westport, Conn.: Greenwood Press, 1976.

———. "The Justice of Woman Suffrage." *Crisis* 4 (September 1912), 243-45.

———. "The Progress of Colored Women." *Voice of the Negro* 1 (July 1904), 291-94.

———. "Woman Suffrage and the 15th Amendment." *Crisis* 10 (August 1915), 191.

Terrell, Robert H. "Our Debt to Suffragists." *Crisis* 10 (August 1915), 181.

Thomas, William Hannibal. *The American Negro, What He Was, What He Is, and What He May Become*. New York: The Macmillan Company, 1901.

Thorne, Jack. *A Plea for Social Justice for the Negro Woman*. Yonkers, N.Y.: Lincoln Press Association, 1912.

Thompson, Mary Lou, ed. *Voice of the New Feminism*. Boston: Beacon Press, 1970.

Tillman, Katherine Davis. "Afro-American Women and Their Work." *A.M.E. Church Review* 2 (1895), 477-99.

———. "Paying Professions for Colored Girls." *Voice of the Negro* 4 (January/February 1907), 54-56.

Toll, William, "Free Men, Freedmen, and Race: Black Social Theory in the Gilded Age." *Journal of Southern History* 44 (November 1978), 571-96.

Twain, Mark. *Pudd'nhead Wilson and Those Extraordinary Twins*. New York: Penguin Books, 1969.

Villard, Oswald. "The Negro and the Domestic Problem." *Alexander's Magazine* 1 (November 15, 1905), 5-11.

"A Washerwoman." *Independent* LVII (November 10, 1904), 1073-76.

Walker, S. Jay. "Frederick Douglass and Woman Suffrage." *Black Scholar* 4 (March/April 1973), 24-31.

Wall, Rev. R. E. "Shall Our Girls Be Educated." *A.M.E. Church Review* 6 (July 1889), 45-8.

Washington, Booker T. *Industrial Training for Southern Women*. n.p. n.d.

———. "The New Negro Woman." *Lend A Hand* 15 (October 1895), 254.

———. *The Story of the Negro*. New York: Doubleday, Page and Company, 1909.

———, ed. *Tuskegee and Its People*. New York: D. Appleton and Company, 1905.

Washington, Mrs. Booker T. "The Gain in the Life of the Negro Women." *Outlook* LXXCI (January 30, 1904), 271-74.

———. "The Negro Home and the Future of the Race." In *Democracy in Earnest*, ed. James McCulloch. Washington, D.C.: Southern Sociological Congress, 1918.

———. "Social Improvement of the Plantation Woman." *Voice of the Negro* 1 (July 1904), 288-90.

Washington, E. Davidson, ed. *Selected Speeches of Booker T. Washington*. New York: Doubleday, Doran and Co., 1932.

Weatherford, W. D. *Negro Life in the South*. New York: Association Press, 1915.

———. *Present Forces in Negro Progress: Present Conditions and Needs*. New York: Association Press, 1912.

Welter, Barbara. "The Cult of True Womanhood, 1920-1860." *American Quarterly* 18 (Summer 1966), 151-74.

———. *Dimity Convictions: The American Woman in the 19th Century*. Athens: Ohio University Press, 1976.

Wertz, Richard W., and Dorothy C. Wertz. *Lying-In: A History of Childbirth in America*. New York: The Free Press, 1977.

Wiggins, Robert A. "*Pudd'nhead Wilson*: A Literary Caesarian Operation." *College English* 25 (December 1963), 182-86.

Williams, Fannie Barrier. "The Club Movement Among Colored Women of America." In *A New Negro for a New Century*, ed. John E. MacBrady. Chicago: American Publishing House, 1900.

———. "The Club Movement Among the Colored Women." *Voice of the Negro* 1 (March 1904), 99-102.

———. "The Colored Girl." *Voice of the Negro* 2 (June 1905), 400-03.

———. "The Intellectual Progress of the Colored Women of the United States Since the Emancipation Proclamation." In *The World Congress of Representative Women*, ed. May Wright Sewall. Chicago: Rand, McNally and Company, 1898.

———. "The Woman's Part in a Man's Business." *Voice of the Negro* 1 (July 1904), 209-300.

Williams, George W. *History of the Negro Race in America*, New York and London: G. P. Putnam's Sons, 1883.

Williams, Sylvania F. "The Social Status of the Negro Woman." *Voice of the Negro* 1 (July 1904), 298-300.

Woman's Era. Volumes 1-3, 1894-1895.

"Woman Suffrage and the Negro." *Messenger* 1 (November 1917), 6.

"Woman Suffrage and the *Messenger*." *Messenger* 2 (January 1918), 9.

Wood, Forrest G. *Black Scare: The Racist Response to Emancipation and Reconstruction*. Berkeley: University of California Press, 1968.

Yates-Silone, Josephine. "The National Association of Colored Women." *Voice of the Negro* 1 (July 1904), 283-87.

Yellin, Jean. "Du Bois' *Crisis* and Woman's Suffrage." *Massachusetts Review* 14 (Spring 1973), 365-75.

MANUSCRIPT COLLECTIONS

Anna Julia Cooper Papers, Moorland-Spingarn Research Center, Howard University, Washington, D.C.

Mary Church Terrell Papers, Library of Congress, Washington, D.C.

Tuskegee Institute Archives, Tuskegee, Alabama, NACW Files.

Spelman College Archives, Atlanta, Georgia.

UNPUBLISHED MATERIAL

Perkins, Linda Marie, "Fanny Jackson Coppin and the Institute for Colored Youth: A Model of Nineteenth-Century Black Female Educational and Community Leadership," Ph.D. dissertation, University of Illinois at Urbana-Champaign, 1978.

Terborg-Penn, Rosalyn, "Afro-Americans in the Struggle for Woman Suffrage," Ph.D. dissertation, Howard University, 1977.

Index

Black Women in
United States History:
A Guide to the Series

PUBLISHER'S NOTE

The sixteen volumes in this set contain 248 articles, in addition to five monographs. This *Guide to the Series* is designed to help the reader find *every* substantive discussion of a topic of interest in the articles. Included in the subject index are general topics such as education and family life, as well as individuals to whom articles are devoted. Geographical locations are included when they are an important part of the article. Professions are also included. Thus, one can look up Fannie Lou Hamer (three articles), Kansas (two articles), or nursing (four articles). The more than 200 authors represented in the index to authors are a who's who of contemporary scholarship.

For topics in the five monographs and for specific discussions in the articles, please see the comprehensive indexes for every title. The more than 10,000 entries in these indexes make this series a virtual encyclopedia of black women's history.

Contents of the Series

Vols. 1-4. **BLACK WOMEN IN AMERICAN HISTORY: FROM COLONIAL TIMES THROUGH THE NINETEENTH CENTURY,** Edited with a Preface by Darlene Clark Hine

Volumes 1-4, continued

24. Foster, Frances Smith. *Adding Color and Contour to Early American Self-Portraitures: Autobiographical Writings of Afro-American Women.*
25. Fox-Genovese, Elizabeth. *Strategies and Forms of Resistance: Focus on Slave Women in the United States.*
26. Fry, Gladys-Marie. *Harriet Powers: Portrait of a Black Quilter.*
27. Goldin, Claudia *Female Labor Force Participation: The Origins of Black and White Differences, 1870 and 1880.*
28. Goodson, Martia G. *Medical-Botanical Contributions of African Slave Women to American Medicine.*
29. Goodson, Martia G. *The Slave Narrative Collection: A Tool for Reconstructing Afro-American Women's History.*
30. Gregory, Chester W. *Black Women in Pre-Federal America.*
31. Griggs, A. C. *Lucy Craft Laney.*
32. Gundersen, Joan R. *The Double Bonds of Race and Sex: Black and White Women in a Colonial Virginia Parish.*
33. Gutman, Herbert G. *Marital and Sexual Norms among Slave Women.*
34. Gwin, Minrose C. *Green-eyed Monsters of the Slavocracy: Jealous Mistresses in Two Slave Narratives.*
35. Hanchett, Catherine M. *'What Sort of People and Families . . .' The Edmondson Sisters.*
36. Harris, William. *Work and the Family in Black Atlanta, 1880.*
37. Hartgrove, W. B. *The Story of Maria Louise Moore and Fannie M. Richards.*
38. Hartigan, Lynda R. *Edmonia Lewis.*
39. Hine, Darlene Clark. *Co-Laborers in the Work of the Lord: Nineteenth-Century Black Women Physicians.*
40. Hine, Darlene Clark. *Female Slave Resistance: The Economics of Sex.*
41. Horton, James Oliver. *Freedom's Yoke: Gender Conventions Among Antebellum Free Blacks.*
42. Jacobs, Sylvia M. *Three Afro-American Women Missionaries in Africa, 1882-1904.*
43. Johnson, Michael P. *Smothered Slave Infants: Were Slave Mothers at Fault?*
44. Jones, Jacqueline. *'My Mother Was Much of a Woman': Black Women, Work, and the Family Under Slavery.*
45. Kennan, Clara B. *The First Negro Teacher in Little Rock.*
46. Kulikoff, Alan. *Beginnings of the Afro-American Family.*
47. Lawson, Ellen N. *Sarah Woodson Early: 19th Century Black Nationalist 'Sister'.*
48. Lawson, Ellen N. and Merrell, Marlene. *Antebellum Black Coeds at Oberlin College.*
49. Leashore, Bogart R. *Black Female Workers: Live-in Domestics in Detroit, Michigan, 1860-1880.*
50. Lebsock, Suzanne. *Free Black Women and the Question of Matriarchy: Petersburg, Virginia, 1784-1820.*
51. Mabee, Carleton. *Sojourner Truth, Bold Prophet: Why Did She Never Learn to Read?*
52. Massa, Ann. *Black Women in the 'White City'.*
53. Matson, R. Lynn. *Phillis Wheatley—Soul Sister?*
54. Matthews, Jean. *Race, Sex and the Dimensions of Liberty in Antebellum America.*
55. Mills, Gary B. *Coincoin: An Eighteeenth Century 'Liberated' Woman.*
56. Moses, Wilson Jeremiah. *Domestic Feminism Conservatism, Sex Roles, and Black Women's Clubs, 1893-1896.*
57. Newman, Debra L. *Black Women in the Era of the American Revolution in Pennsylvania.*
58. Obitko, Mary Ellen. *'Custodians of a House of Resistance': Black Women Respond to Slavery.*

Volumes 1-4, continued

59. Oden, Gloria C. *The Journal of Charlotte L. Forten: The Salem-Philadelphia Years (1854-1862) Reexamined.*
60. Parkhurst, Jessie W. *The Role of the Black Mammy in the Plantation Household.*
61. Perkins, Linda M. *Heed Life's Demands: The Educational Philosophy of Fanny Jackson Coppin.*
62. Perkins, Linda M. *The Black Female American Missionary Association Teacher in the South, 1861-1870.*
63. Perkins, Linda M. *The Impact of the 'Cult of True Womanhood' on the Education of Black Women.*
64. Perkins, Linda M. *Black Women and Racial 'Uplift' Prior to Emancipation.*
65. Pleck, Elizabeth H. *The Two-Parent Household: Black Family Structure in Late Nineteenth Century Boston.*
66. Porter, Dorothy B. *Sarah Parker Remond, Abolitionist and Physician.*
67. Quarles, Benjamin. *Harriet Tubman's Unlikely Leadership.*
68. Riley, Glenda. *American Daughters: Black Women in the West.*
69. Reiff, Janice L., Michael R. Dahlin, and Daniel Scott Smith. *Rural Push and Urban Pull: Work and Family Experiences of Older Black Women in Southern Cities, 1880-1900.*
70. Schafer, Judith K. *'Open and Notorious Concubinage': The Emancipation of Slave Mistresses by Will and the Supreme Court in Antebellum Louisiana.*
71. Sealander, Judith. *Antebellum Black Press Images of Women.*
72. Seraile, William. *Susan McKinney Steward: New York State's First African-American Woman Physician.*
73. Shammas, Carole. *Black Women's Work and the Evolution of Plantation Society in Virginia.*
74. Silverman, Jason H. *Mary Ann Shadd and the Search for Equality.*
75. Sloan, Patricia E. *Early Black Nursing Schools and Responses of Black Nurses to their Educational Programs.*
76. Soderlund, Jean R. *Black Women in Colonial Pennsylvania.*
77. Sterling, Dorothy. *To Build A Free Society: Nineteenth-Century Black Women.*
78. Sumler-Lewis, Janice. *The Forten-Purvis Women of Philadelphia and the American Anti-Slavery Crusade.*
79. Tate, Claudia. *Pauline Hopkins: Our Literary Foremother.*
80. Terborg-Penn, Rosalyn. *Black Women Freedom Fighters in Early 19th Century Maryland.*
81. Thompson, Priscilla. *Harriet Tubman, Thomas Garrett, and the Underground Railroad.*
82. Tucker, David M. *Miss Ida B. Wells and Memphis Lynching.*
83. Vacha, John E. *The Case of Sara Lucy Bagby: A Late Gesture.*
84. Wade-Gayles, Gloria. *Black Women Journalists in the South, 1880-1905: An Approach to the Study of Black Women's History.*
85. White, Deborah G. *The Lives of Slave Women.*

Vols. 5-8. BLACK WOMEN IN AMERICAN HISTORY: THE TWENTIETH CENTURY, Edited with a Preface by Darlene Clark Hine

1. *Votes for Women: A Symposium by Leading Thinkers of Colored America.*
2. Anderson, Karen T. *Last Hired, First Fired: Black Women Workers During World War II.*
3. Anderson, Kathie R. *Era Bell Thompson: A North Dakota Daughter.*
4. Blackwelder, Julia Kirk. *Quiet Suffering: Atlanta Women in the 1930s.*

Volumes 5-8, continued

5. Blackwelder, Julia Kirk. *Women in the Work Force: Atlanta, New Orleans, and San Antonio, 1930 to 1940.*
6. Brady, Marilyn Dell. *Kansas Federation of Colored Women's Clubs, 1900-1930.*
7. Brady, Marilyn Dell. *Organizing Afro-American Girls' Clubs in Kansas in the 1920's.*
8. Breen, William J. *Black Women and the Great War: Mobilization and Reform in the South.*
9. Brooks, Evelyn. *Religion, Politics, and Gender: The Leadership of Nannie Helen Burroughs.*
10. Brown, Elsa Barkley. *Womanist Consciousness: Maggie Lena Walker and the Independent Order of Saint Luke.*
11. Bryan, Violet H. *Frances Joseph-Gaudet: Black Philanthropist.*
12. Cantarow, Ellen and Susan Gushee O'Malley. *Ella Baker: Organizing for Civil Rights.*
13. Carby, Hazel V. *It Jus Be's Dat Way Sometime: The Sexual Politics of Women's Blues.*
14. Chateauvert, Melinda. *The Third Step: Anna Julia Cooper and Black Education in the District of Columbia, 1910-1960.*
15. Clark-Lewis, Elizabeth. *'This Work Had a End:' African-American Domestic Workers in Washington, D.C., 1910-1940.*
16. Coleman, Willi. *Black Women and Segregated Public Transportation: Ninety Years of Resistance.*
17. Ergood, Bruce. *The Female Protection and the Sun Light: Two Contemporary Negro Mutual Aid Societies.*
18. Farley, Ena L. *Caring and Sharing Since World War I: The League of Women for Community Service—A Black Volunteer Organization in Boston.*
19. Feinman, Clarice. *An Afro-American Experience: The Women in New York City's Jail.*
20. Ferguson, Earline Rae. *The Women's Improvement Club of Indianapolis: Black Women Pioneers in Tuberculosis Work, 1903-1938.*
21. Ford, Beverly O. *Case Studies of Black Female Heads of Households in the Welfare System: Socialization and Survival.*
22. Gilkes, Cheryl Townsend. *'Together and in Harness': Women's Traditions in the Sanctified Church.*
23. Gilkes, Cheryl Townsend. *Going Up for the Oppressed: The Career Mobility of Black Women Community Workers.*
24. Gilkes, Cheryl Townsend. *Successful Rebellious Professionals: The Black Woman's Professional Identity and Community Commitment.*
25. Gunn, Arthur C. *The Struggle of Virginia Proctor Powell Florence.*
26. Guzman, Jessie P. *The Social Contributions of the Negro Woman Since 1940.*
27. Harley, Sharon. *Beyond the Classroom: Organizational Lives of Black Female Educators in the District of Columbia, 1890-1930.*
28. Harley, Sharon. *Black Women in a Southern City: Washington, D.C., 1890-1920.*
29. Haynes, Elizabeth Ross. *Negroes in Domestic Service in the United States.*
30. Helmbold, Lois Rita. *Beyond the Family Economy: Black and White Working-Class Women during the Great Depression.*
31. Hine, Darlene Clark. *The Ethel Johns Report: Black Women in the Nursing Profession, 1925.*
32. Hine, Darlene Clark. *From Hospital to College: Black Nurse Leaders and the Rise of Collegiate Nursing Schools.*
33. Hine, Darlene Clark. *Mabel K. Staupers and the Integration of Black Nurses into the Armed Forces.*
34. Hine, Darlene Clark. *The Call That Never Came: Black Women Nurses and World War I, An Historical Note.*

Volumes 5-8, continued

35. Hine, Darlene Clark. *'They Shall Mount Up with Wings as Eagles': Historical Images of Black Nurses, 1890-1950.*
36. Hull, Gloria T. *Alice Dunbar-Nelson: Delaware Writer and Woman of Affairs.*
37. Hunter, Tera. *The Correct Thing: Charlotte Hawkins Brown and the Palmer Institute.*
38. Jacobs, Sylvia M. *'Say Africa When You Pray': The Activities of Early Black Baptist Women Missionaries Among Liberian Women and Children.*
39. Jacobs, Sylvia M. *Afro-American Women Missionaries Confront the African Way of Life.*
40. Jacobs, Sylvia M. *Their 'Special Mission': Afro-American Women as Missionaries to the Congo, 1894-1937.*
41. Janiewski, Dolores. *Seeking 'a New Day and a New Way': Black Women and Unions in the Southern Tobacco Industry.*
42. Janiewski, Dolores. *Sisters Under Their Skins: Southern Working Women, 1880-1950.*
43. Jones, Beverly W. *Race, Sex and Class:Black Female Tobacco Workers in Durham, North Carolina, 1920-1940, and the Development of Female Consciousness.*
44. Kendrick, Ruby M. *'They Also Serve': The National Association of Colored Women, Inc., 1895-1954.*
45. Lee, Don L. *The Achievement of Gwendolyn Brooks.*
46. Leffall, Dolores C. and Janet L. Sims. *Mary McLeod Bethune—The Educator; Also Including a Selected Annotated Bibliography.*
47. Lerner, Gerda. *Early Community Work of Black Club Women.*
48. Matthews, Mark D. *'Our Women and What They Think,' Amy Jacques Garvey and the Negro World.*
49. McDowell, Deborah E. *The Neglected Dimension of Jessie Redmon Fauset.*
50. McDowell, Margaret B. *The Black Woman As Artist and Critic: Four Versions.*
51. Nerverdon-Morton, Cynthia. *Self-Help Programs as Educative Activities of Black Women in the South, 1895-1925: Focus on Four Key Areas.*
52. Newman, Debra L. *Black Women Workers in the Twentieth Century.*
53. O'Dell, J. H. *Life in Mississippi: An Interview With Fannie Lou Hamer.*
54. Parks, Rosa. *Interview.*
55. Peebles-Wilkins, Wilma. *Black Women and American Social Welfare: The Life of Fredericka Douglass Sprague Perry.*
56. Pleck, Elizabeth H. *A Mother's Wages: Income Earning Among Married Italian and Black Women, 1896-1911.*
57. Porter, Dorothy B. *Maria Louise Baldwin, 1856-1922.*
58. Ross, B. Joyce. *Mary McLeod Bethune and the National Youth Adminstration: A Case Study of Power Relationships in the Black Cabinet of Franklin D. Roosevelt.*
59. Saunders, Deloris M. *Changes in the Status of Women During The Quarter Century (1955-1980).*
60. Seraile, William. *Henrietta Vinton Davis and the Garvey Movement.*
61. Smith, Elaine M. *Mary McLeod Bethune and the National Youth Administration.*
62. Smith, Sandra N. and Earle H. West. *Charlotte Hawkins Brown.*
63. Stetson, Erlene. *Black Feminism in Indiana, 1893-1933.*
64. Still, Judith Anne. *Carrie Still Shepperson: The Hollows of Her Footsteps.*
65. Terborg-Penn, Rosalyn. *Discontented Black Feminists: Prelude and Postscript to the Passage of the Nineteenth Amendment.*
66. Trigg, Eula S. *Washington, D.C. Chapter—Links, Incorporated: Friendship and Service.*
67. Tucker, Susan. *A Complex Bond: Southern Black Domestic Workers and Their White Employers.*

Volumes 5-8, continued

68. Woods, Sylvia. *You Have to Fight for Freedom.*
69. Woodson, Carter G. *The Negro Washerwoman: A Vanishing Figure.*
70. Yancy, Dorothy C. *Dorothy Bolden, Organizer of Domestic Workers: She Was Born Poor But She Would Not Bow Down.*

Vols. 9-10. BLACK WOMEN'S HISTORY: THEORY AND PRACTICE, Edited with a Preface by Darlene Clark Hine

1. Aldridge, Delores. *Black Women in the Economic Marketplace: A Battle Unfinished.*
2. Allen, Walter R. *Family Roles, Occupational Statuses, and Achievement Orientations Among Black Women in the United States.*
3. Allen, Walter R. *The Social and Economic Statuses of Black Women in the United States.*
4. Armitage, Susan, Theresa Banfield, and Sarah Jacobus. *Black Women and Their Communities in Colorado.*
5. Biola, Heather. *The Black Washerwoman in Southern Tradition.*
6. Bracey, John H., Jr. *Afro-American Women: A Brief Guide to Writings from Historical and Feminist Perspectives.*
7. Brown, Minnie Miller. *Black Women in American Agriculture.*
8. Collier-Thomas, Bettye. *The Impact of Black Women in Education: An Historical Overview.*
9. Dickson, Lynda F. *Toward a Broader Angle of Vision in Uncovering Women's History: Black Women's Clubs Revisited.*
10. Dill, Bonnie Thornton. *Race, Class, and Gender: Prospects for an All-Inclusive Sisterhood.*
11. Dill, Bonnie Thornton. *The Dialectics of Black Womanhood.*
12. Fox-Genovese, Elizabeth. *To Write My Self: The Autobiographies of Afro-American Women.*
13. Higginbotham, Evelyn Brooks. *Beyond the Sound of Silence: Afro-American Women in History.*
14. Hine, Darlene Clark. *An Angle of Vision: Black Women and the United States Constitution, 1787-1987.*
15. Hine, Darlene Clark. *To Be Gifted, Female, and Black.*
16. Hine, Darlene Clark. *Opportunity and Fulfillment: Sex, Race, and Class in Health Care Education.*
17. Hine, Darlene Clark. *Lifting the Veil, Shattering the Silence: Black Women's History in Slavery and Freedom.*
18. Jackson, Jacquelyne Johnson. *A Partial Bibliography on or Related to Black Women.*
19. Katz, Maude White. *The Negro Woman and the Law.*
20. Katz, Maude White. *She Who Would Be Free—Resistance.*
21. King, Deborah K. *Multiple Jeopardy, Multiple Consciousness: The Context of a Black Feminist Ideology.*
22. Ladner, Joyce A. *Racism and Tradition: Black Womanhood in Historical Perspective.*
23. Lewis, Diane K. *A Response to Inequality: Black Women, Racism, and Sexism.*
24. Marable, Manning. *Groundings with my Sisters: Patriarchy and the Exploitation of Black Women.*
25. Palmer, Phyllis Marynick. *White Women/Black Women: The Dualism of Female Identity and Experience in the United States.*
26. Patterson, Tiffany R. *Toward a Black Feminist Analysis: Recent Works by Black Women Scholars.*

Volumes 9-10, continued

27. Reagon, Bernice Johnson. *My Black Mothers and Sisters, or On Beginning A Cultural Autobiography.*
28. Reagon, Bernice Johnson. *African Diaspora Women: The Making of Cultural Workers.*
29. Rector, Theresa A. *Black Nuns as Educators.*
30. Render, Sylvia Lyons. *Afro-American Women: The Outstanding and the Obscure.*
31. Scales-Trent, Judy. *Black Women and the Constitution: Finding Our Place, Asserting Our Rights.*
32. Shockley, Ann Allen. *The Negro Woman in Retrospect: Blueprint for the Future.*
33. Smith, Eleanor. *Historical Relationships between Black and White Women.*
34. Snorgrass, J. William. *Pioneer Black Women Journalists from 1850s to the 1950s.*
35. Strong, Augusta. *Negro Women in Freedom's Battles.*
36. Terborg-Penn, Rosalyn. *Historical Treatment of Afro-Americans in the Woman's Movement, 1900-1920: A Bibliographical Essay.*
37. Terborg-Penn, Rosalyn. *Teaching the History of Black Women: A Bibliographical Essay.*
38. Thornbrough, Emma Lou. *The History of Black Women in Indiana.*
39. Walker, Juliet E. K. *The Afro-American Woman: Who Was She?*
40. Yellin, Jean Fagan. *Afro-American Women 1800-1910: A Selected Bibliography.*

Vol. 11. Daughters of Sorrow: Attitudes Toward Black Women, 1880-1920, by Beverly Guy-Sheftall

Vol. 12. Jane Edna Hunter: A Case Study of Black Leadership, 1910-1950, by Adrienne Lash Jones; Preface by Darlene Clark Hine

Vol. 13. Quest for Equality: The Life and Writings of Mary Eliza Church Terrell, 1863-1954, by Beverly Washington Jones
including Mary Church Terrell's selected essays:

1. *Announcement* [of NACW].
2. *First Presidential Address to the National Association of Colored Women.*
3. *The Duty of the National Association of Colored Women to the Race.*
4. *What Role is the Educated Negro Woman to Play in the Uplifting of Her Race?*
5. *Graduates and Former Students of Washington Colored High School.*
6. *Lynching from a Negro's Point of View.*
7. *The Progress of Colored Women.*
8. *The International Congress of Women.*
9. *Samuel Coleridge-Taylor.*
10. *Service Which Should be Rendered the South.*
11. *The Mission of Meddlers.*
12. *Paul Laurence Dunbar.*
13. *Susan B. Anthony, the Abolitionist.*
14. *A Plea for the White South by A Coloured Woman.*
15. *Peonage in the United States: The Convict Lease System and Chain Gangs.*
16. *The Disbanding of the Colored Soldiers.*
17. *What It Means to Be Colored in the Capital of the United States.*
18. *A Sketch of Mingo Saunders.*
19. *An Interview with W.T. Stead on the Race Problem.*
20. *The Justice of Woman Suffrage.*
21. *Phyllis Wheatley—An African Genius.*
22. *The History of the Club Women's Movement.*
23. *Needed: Women Lawyers.*
24. *Dr. Sara W. Brown.*
25. *I Remember Frederick Douglass.*

Vol. 14. **To Better Our World: Black Women in Organized Reform, 1890-1920**, by Dorothy Salem

Vol. 15. **Ida B. Wells-Barnett: An Exploratory Study of an American Black Woman, 1893-1930**, by Mildred Thompson

including Ida B. Wells-Barnett's Selected Essays

1. *Afro-Americans and Africa.*
2. *Lynch Law in All Its Phases.*
3. *The Reason Why the Colored American is not in the World's Columbian Exposition.* Chapter IV. *Lynch Law*, by Ida B. Wells Chapter VI. *The Reason Why*, by F.L. Barnett
4. *Two Christmas Days: A Holiday Story.*
5. *Lynch Law in America.*
6. *The Negro's Case in Equity.*
7. *Lynching and the Excuse for It.*
8. *Booker T. Washington and His Critics.*
9. *Lynching, Our National Crime.*
10. *How Enfranchisement Stops Lynchings.*
11. *Our Country's Lynching Record.*

Vol. 16. **Women in the Civil Rights Movement: Trailblazers and Torchbearers, 1941-1965**

Edited by Vicki Crawford, Jacqueline A. Rouse, Barbara Woods; Associate Editors: Broadus Butler, Marymal Dryden, and Melissa Walker

1. Black, Allida. *A Reluctant but Persistent Warrior: Eleanor Roosevelt and the Early Civil Rights Movement*
2. Brock, Annette K. *Gloria Richardson and the Cambridge Movement*
3. Burks, Mary Fair. *Trailblazers: Women in the Montgomery Bus Boycott.*
4. Cochrane, Sharlene Voogd. *'And the Pressure Never Let Up': Black Women, White Women, and the Boston YWCA, 1918-1948.*
5. Crawford, Vicki. *Beyond the Human Self: Grassroots Activists in the Mississippi Civil Rights Movement.*
6. Grant, Jacquelyn. *Civil Rights Women: A Source for Doing Womanist Theology.*
7. Knotts, Alice G. *Methodist Women Integrate Schools and Housing, 1952-1959.*
8. Langston, Donna. *The Women of Highlander.*
9. Locke, Mamie E. *Is This America: Fannie Lou Hamer and the Mississippi Freedom Democratic Party.*
10. McFadden, Grace Jordan. *Septima Clark.*
11. Mueller, Carol. *Ella Baker and the Origins of 'Participatory Democracy.'*
12. Myrick-Harris, Clarissa. *Behind the Scenes: Doris Derby, Denise Nicholas, and the Free Southern Theater.*
13. Oldendorf, Sandra. *The South Carolina Sea Island Citizenship Schools.*
14. Payne, Charles. *Men Led, But Women Organized: Movement Participation of Women in the Mississippi Delta.*
15. Reagon, Bernice Johnson. *Women as Culture Carriers in the Civil Rights Movement: Fannie Lou Hamer.*
16. Standley, Anne. *The Role of Black Women in the Civil Rights Movement.*
17. Woods, Barbara. Modjeska Simkins and the South Carolina Conference of the NAACP.

Author Index

Boldface indicates volume numbers and roman indicates article numbers within volumes.

Akers, Charles W., **1-4**:1
Aldridge, Delores, **9-10**:1
Alexander, Adele L., **1-4**:2
Allen, Walter R., **9-10**:2, 3
Anderson, Karen T., **5-8**:2
Anderson, Kathie R., **5-8**:3
Aptheker, Bettina, **1-4**:3
Armitage, Susan, **9-10**:4
Axelson, Diana E., **1-4**:4

Banfield, Theresa, **9-10**:4
Berkeley, Kathleen C., **1-4**:5
Berlin,Ira, **1-4**:6
Biola, Heather, **9-10**:5
Black, Allida, **16**:1
Blackburn, George, **1-4**:7
Blackwelder, Julia Kirk, **5-8**:4, 5
Bogin, Ruth, **1-4**:8
Bracey, John H., Jr., **9-10**:6
Brady, Marilyn Dell, **5-8**:6, 7
Breen, William J., **5-8**:8
Brock, Annette K., **16**:2
Brooks, Evelyn, **1-4**:9, **5-8**:9
Brown, Elsa Barkley, **5-8**:10
Brown, Minnie Miller, **9-10**:7
Bryan, Violet H., **5-8**:11
Burks, Mary Fair, **16**:3
Burnham, Dorothy, **1-4**:10
Butler, Broadus (ed.), **16**
Bynum, Victoria, **1-4**:11

Cantarow, Ellen, **5-8**:12
Carby, Hazel V., **5-8**:13
Chateauvert, Melinda, **5-8**:14
Clark-Lewis, Elizabeth, **5-8**:15
Clinton, Catherine, **1-4**:12
Cochrane, Sharlene Voogd, **16**:4
Cody, Cheryll Ann, **1-4**:13
Cole, Johnnetta, **1-4**:14
Coleman, Willi, **5-8**:16

Collier-Thomas, Bettye, **9-10**:8
Conrad, Earl, **1-4**:15
Crawford, Vicki, **16**:5
Crawford, Vicki (ed.), **16**
Cunningham, Constance A., **1-4**:16

Dahlin, Michael R., **1-4**:69
Davis, Angela, **1-4**:17
de Graaf, Lawrence B., **1-4**:18
Dickson, Lynda F., **9-10**:9
Dill, Bonnie Thornton, **9-10**:10, 11
Dodson, Jualynne, **1-4**:19
Dorsey, Carolyn A., **1-4**:20, 21
Dryden, Marymal (ed.), **16**

Ergood, Bruce, **5-8**:17

Farley, Ena L., **5-8**:18
Farnham, Christie, **1-4**:22
Feinman, Clarice, **5-8**:19
Ferguson, Earline Rae, **5-8**:20
Fish, Beverly, **1-4**:23
Ford, Beverly O., **5-8**:21
Foster, Frances Smith, **1-4**:24
Fox-Genovese, Elizabeth, **1-4**:25, **9-10**:12
Fry, Gladys-Marie, **1-4**:26

Gilkes, Cheryl Townsend, **5-8**:22, 23, 24
Goldin, Claudia, **1-4**:27
Goodson, Martia G., **1-4**:28, 29
Grant, Jacquelyn, **16**:6
Gregory, Chester W., **1-4**:30
Griggs, A. C., **1-4**:31
Gundersen, Joan R., **1-4**:32
Gunn, Arthur C., **5-8**:25
Gutman, Herbert G., **1-4**:33
Guzman, Jessie P., **5-8**:26
Gwin, Minrose C., **1-4**:34

Hanchett, Catherine M., **1-4**:35

Subject Index

Boldface indicates volume numbers and roman indicates article numbers within volumes.